PRAISE F

Cashvertising Online

"Fasten your seatbelt! This book is like attending an intense, live seminar packed with the latest tips, tricks, and techniques—all based on sound scientific research—about what persuades online consumers to buy. Best of all, it's 100 percent practical. You can start using it tonight and see dramatic changes in your response."

> —DR. JOE VITALE, author of *Hypnotic Writing* and *Buying Trances*

"Dr. Direct hits it out of the park again! *Cashvertising Online* is so good—so full of powerful, quantifiable tips based on actual research—that I found myself taking notes like a diligent college student. At the same time, Whitman's easy, conversational style makes for a delightful read. If you really want to smash the competition in the age of social media, this book is an absolute must."

> —RICHARD BAYAN, author of *Words That Sell*

"*Cashvertising Online* is a fascinating read. What I love most about this book is the continuation of up-to-date research and the psychology behind the results. The practical steps make it invaluable. For me, the twenty-nine ways to make ads more effective and fifty powerful opt-in headlines reinforce that this is a manual for success. This is a book to keep close to hand when working on your ads and campaigns."

> —PATRICIA FRIPP, past president of the National Speakers Association, author of *Deliver Unforgettable Presentations*

"This book unlocks a treasure-trove of practical, 'real-world' marketing strategies designed to maximize your online potential."

—THOMAS A. FREESE, bestselling author of *Secrets of Question Based Selling*

"If you want to make money online today, you need this book. With simple and powerful insights that you can use to up your ads game, *Cashvertising Online* is the book you must implement—or be left in the dust by your competition."

—PHIL GERBYSHAK, social selling pioneer, author of *Zero Dollar Consultancy*

"Insightful and accessible. Drew Eric Whitman has distilled advertising dos and don'ts into simple changes that will help you create more effective ads."

—JONAH BERGER, Wharton professor, bestselling author of *Contagious, The Catalyst,* and *Magic Words*

Ca$hvertising

ONLINE

How to Use the
Latest Findings in
Buyer Psychology to
Explode Your Online Ad Response

DREW ERIC WHITMAN
Author of *Cashvertising*

CAREER
PRESS

This edition first published in 2023 by Career Press, an imprint of
Red Wheel/Weiser, LLC
With offices at:
65 Parker Street, Suite 7
Newburyport, MA 01950
www.careerpress.com
www.redwheelweiser.com

ISBN: 978-1-63265-205-8

Library of Congress Cataloging-in-Publication Data

Names: Whitman, Drew Eric, author.
Title: Cashvertising online : how to use the latest findings in buyer
  psychology to explode your online ad response / Drew Eric Whitman.
Description: Newburyport, MA : Career Press, 2023. | Includes
  bibliographical references and index. | Summary: "This book examines the
  hidden principles specific to successful online ads and email promotions
  and the numerous and potent psychological techniques they employ to make
  them so persuasive"-- Provided by publisher.
Identifiers: LCCN 2023016083 | ISBN 9781632652058 (trade paperback) | ISBN
  9781633412910 (ebook)
Subjects: LCSH: Internet advertising. | Internet marketing. |
  Advertising--Psychological aspects. | Marketing--Psychological aspects.
  | BISAC: BUSINESS & ECONOMICS / Advertising & Promotion | BUSINESS &
  ECONOMICS / Marketing / Research
Classification: LCC HF6146.I58 .W49 2023 | DDC 659.14/4--dc23/eng/20230427
LC record available at https://lccn.loc.gov/2023016083

Cover design by Sky Peck Design
Interior photos/images
  Page 20: photo by Freepik, *freepik.com*
  Page 21: photo by Freepik, *freepik.com*
  Page 22: photo by Magnus D'Great M, *pexels.com*
  Page 23: photo by Ksenia Balandina, *unsplash.com*
  Page 25: photo by Freepik, *freepik.com*
  Page 26: photo by Freepik, *freepik.com*
  Page 27: photo by Marcelo Moreira, *pexels.com*
  Page 28: photo by Vecteezy, *vecteezy.com*
  Pages 29–30: photo by Freepik, *freepik.com*
Interior by Happenstance Type-O-Rama
Typeset in Helvetica LT Std, RBNo2.1a, and Warnock Pro

Printed in the United States of America
IBI
10 9 8 7 6 5 4 3 2 1

In memory of my late, great father, Robert,
whose limitless love, profound creativity,
and invaluable business instruction comprise
an enduring constellation that guides me daily.

Contents

Drew's Welcome Message

Ready to blast your advertising to the next level? This book will help you do it.

When I wrote the first *Cashvertising* back in 2008, I didn't know it would take the advertising world by storm. That little book has been translated into eleven languages and is currently the highest-rated advertising book of its kind on Amazon, with well over a thousand reviews and an average five-star rating.

The reason for its popularity? Not because it's entertainingly written, although that certainly contributed to its success. Boring books suck. (Actually, boring *anything* sucks.) But *boring* is especially bad when you're trying to *learn*. It's like attending a seminar. You go for the information—the data—but unless it's also *entertaining*, it's just a snoozefest. While the speaker drones on and on, you start thinking about pizza . . . island vacations . . . or a nice fluffy bed you can fall onto.

Cashvertising is popular primarily because of its *practicality*. People buy it because they want to learn how to put more money in their pockets.

Good news: I wrote *this* book in exactly the same way. I begin by giving you the foundational basis for what's to follow, and then we dive right into the how-tos. And, just like the original *Cashvertising*, this book is not intended to be a scholarly tome. I've written it like a friendly and personal one-on-one consultation. Like it's just you and me sitting together, discussing how to improve what you're currently doing.

That being said, this book is not for everyone. (Maybe it's not for *you*.) Maybe you already know everything in the following pages. Maybe, after reading it, you'll say, *"I know this . . . I know that."* Or *"This doesn't apply . . . that doesn't apply."*

That's like going into a restaurant and looking to find fault. Believe me, *you will.* The food will come out wrong. It will be cold . . . the table will be sticky . . . the server will have an attitude . . . the air-conditioning vents will be blowing on the back of your neck . . . you'll smell the cleaning fluid in the bathroom toilets, and so on. *Ugh.* So much for a pleasant dining experience.

Instead—just as I suggest to participants in my seminars—try to have an open mind. Look for what *will* work, rather than simply trying to find that which will not.

> *Let yourself be open and life will be easier.*
> *A spoon of salt in a glass of water makes the water*
> *undrinkable. A spoon of salt in a lake is almost unnoticed.*
>
> —BUDDHA SIDDHARTHA GUATAMA SHAKYAMUNI

The good news is that everything in the following pages doesn't need to apply *exactly* to you for you to benefit enormously. Just *one* single idea, properly applied, could make a huge difference for you. Apply more than one—as many as you see fit—and you could literally revolutionize your business and—*KA-CHING!*—your bank account.

Introduction

Welcome to *Cashvertising Online!*

Okay, that's enough small talk; let's jump right in and get practical.

True or false? "If you build a better mousetrap, the world will beat a path to your door."

When I ask that question in my seminars, the "true" answers I get are often surprising. Some say, "It's *true*, Drew, because . . .

- *"People are always looking for ways to improve their lives.* If you create such a product, they will buy it.

- *"People love new things* and the mere fact that it's new will excite them enough to want to check it out, and . . .

- *"Good news spreads fast.* If it's a quality product of value, people will find out about it one way or another."

While these answers all sound reasonable, as a professional direct-response guy, I know they all belong to a mindset of failure. The mindset of "Why am I broke?"

That's because . . .

It doesn't matter how great your product is if you don't effectively communicate its value to the right audience.

Sure, you could act on the assumption that people might eventually learn about it. But that's not a great business success plan, is it? *Hope* is not a strategy. Hope is what you employ when you think you're out of options.

Book of Secrets

Imagine being handed a highly guarded book of secrets. A book so valuable that it's protected by a lock and key. And in this book are the distillation of dozens and dozens of well-funded advertising experiments. Test after test.

Control versus control. The insider notes of smart, well-financed advertisers who constantly asked questions like

- ▸ "What works better, A or B . . . C or D?"

- ▸ "How about if we changed the timing?"

- ▸ "What if we tried a more personal approach?"

- ▸ "What happens if we intentionally misspell words?"

- ▸ "How about if we use red instead of blue?"

- ▸ "What's the best time to post for maximum readership?

- ▸ "Would it matter if we changed *Order Now* to *Buy Now*?"

- ▸ "Would a green button make any difference?"

- ▸ "Should we offer more than one product option?"

- ▸ "What's the best way to show discounts?"

- ▸ "Will long copy work better?"

- ▸ "What happens if we put the word *You* in headlines?"

- ▸ "Should we do a two-step or try to snag the sale right now?"

. . . and scores of similar questions.

Imagine if the answers to these questions actually existed in one handy book . . . and that you could use the results of all their testing and money spent in your own advertising and reap the rewards? (And save yourself years of annoying and frustrating trial-and-error experimentation.)

You're reading that very book right now. And the reason I call these things "secrets" isn't because they're locked away in a dusty old, padlocked chest somewhere, but simply because so few advertisers know anything about them. To the uninformed, they are, in fact, the *exact dictionary definition* of the word *secrets*: *"things not known or seen by others."* Oh sure, they might know a few of the things we'll discuss, but the vast majority haven't a clue. They're still busy conducting trial-and-error experiments. (Which is fine as long as you're testing elements exclusive to your own product and offer, rather than reinventing the wheel of a principle that's already known.)

Like the original *Cashvertising*—widely acknowledged as today's number-one book on advertising persuasion and now published in eleven languages worldwide—this is not a story book. It's a *how-to* guide. And every page is packed with information you can start using right now . . . today. Because, to me, there's nothing worse than buying a book, spending your time reading it, and when you finish the last page, you say, *"Okay, that was interesting. Now, uh, what do I do?"* This book will tell you exactly what to do. It's simply up to *you* to actually do it.

Fact is, no book—no matter how good—is of benefit to everyone. Some people expect magic. They want good results, but they're not willing to do what's necessary to make them happen. It's human inertia, plain and simple. Much easier to watch TV and eat chips and salsa than actually do the work.

You know what I mean. You see a book that promises to teach you how to improve your life. You excitedly buy it and start reading. Suddenly, the green dollar signs in your eyeballs begin to fade, *"Oh, damn . . . you gotta set goals! Argh . . . you gotta make lists! Ugh . . . you gotta spend time every day doing positive visualizations! Oh, crap . . . you gotta actually DO STUFF!"* You kinda wanted the success to happen without that whole annoying "do-this, do-that" process.

> *Dreams don't work unless you take action. The surest way to make your dreams come true is to live them.*
>
> —ROY T. BENNETT

Hey, that's life. Dreaming about it is easy. When you're awake, you gotta do stuff to make stuff happen. My goal is to make that "doing stuff" as easy as possible and give you the greatest chances for success. And that's exactly what this book has the power to do. You simply need to put its teachings in your brain and then take actions that correspond to what you learned. You'll feel the result as monetary weight in your pockets. (That's a fancy way of saying, *"KA-CHING!"*)

Oh, one more thing before we jump in. This book is distributed around the world in many languages. And since my goal is to be valuable to people in all stages of learning, I have to cover a lot of ground. And I can't always assume you know X or Y. You might know one . . . or both. (But I can't assume.)

For example, some people who read this book have many years of advertising experience. Let's call them the "pros." Maybe that's *you*. If so,

I'm sure you could teach *me* a few things and I'd benefit greatly. But even as a pro, you still want to do better, right? You still want to augment your knowledge and hone your present skills. In this case, this book is for you.

Others, however, have more limited experience. Let's call them the "seekers." They're looking to springboard their education by learning from someone who has been doing it for decades. That way they can save time . . . make massive strides . . . get faster results . . . and save years' worth of trial-and-error hassles. If you happen to be a seeker, this book is definitely for you, too.

My job? To deliver useful information. *Your job?* To decide what parts are valuable to you and start using them. But no matter which of these two categories of learners you might happen to belong to, you might come across things you *already* know. When that happens, just say to yourself, *"Okay, this bit must be for the other guy,"* and just move forward to the next point.

Okay, enough warmup. Ready? Then as I say in my seminars, "Fasten your seat belt . . . open your mind . . . and let's get started!"

CHAPTER 1

Social Media and the Human Brain: Understand the Connection and Learn to Tap Its Tremendous Addictive Power

FACT: Browsing social media is fun, isn't it? But there's a lot more going on than meets the eye. And while it's both informative and entertaining, it's nothing like reading a newspaper, magazine, or book. That's because while you're reading, scrolling, and clicking away on social media, those sites and apps are actually *doing something to you.*

This chapter explains how these services are intentionally created to *lure you in,* keep you reading, and encourage you to repeatedly engage by literally *altering your brain chemistry.*

"But, Drew! Why do I need to know this stuff? Can't you just teach me what to do right now?"

That's the beauty of a book as opposed to a short seminar. In my seminars I spend a few minutes laying down the foundation, and then we jump right in with the how-tos. As an audience member, you'd get a quick overview and some useful tidbits, but only as much as I could pack into an hour or two.

However, you're a book reader. The 200+ pages of info you're holding right now allow you and me to dive deeper. The more impatient types won't buy this book. Instead, they'll spend weeks Googling or YouTubing in the hopes to get bits and pieces of what I've compressed into the pages of this one handy guide. (Not to mention taking the time required to analyze and extract the practical lessons from some of the most abstrusely written research papers you could imagine. Some seem to be purposely written to thwart even the most minimal degree of comprehension.)

Plus, this book isn't just about throwing you a captain's hat, a $900 Crowder Bluewater fishing rod, a $3,000 Daiwa Dendoh reel (yes, really), and the keys to a mega-luxury yacht. (But wouldn't it be nice?!)

No. My job is to also teach you about properly operating your craft (your copywriting), navigating the waters (the media you choose to use), and hauling in the beautiful shiny fish (your prospects) that swim in it. Believe me, that deeper understanding will change your whole advertising operation. If you want a more superficial learning experience, then stop reading this book, grab your phone, and see if Google can help.

Okay, so how does social media "do" things to you while you're innocently reading, scrolling, and clicking? Simple. By providing countless opportunities to send your body's feel-good chemical—dopamine—surging through your bloodstream to literally *addict* you into participating. Yes, I said "addict." *Ouch.*

Conspiracy theory? Nope. In fact, during a Congressional hearing, former Facebook executive Tim Kendall said that the company *"intentionally made its product as addictive as cigarettes."*[1] This is the cerebral fuel that keeps them going, growing, and attracting their advertisers to spend a projected $47.9 billion this year.

> *We took a page from Big Tobacco's playbook,*
> *working to make our offering addictive at the outset.*
>
> —TIM KENDALL, FACEBOOK'S FORMER
> DIRECTOR OF MONETIZATION

Truth is, social media has the power to change—and is changing—the way our brains function. Evil? I'm not judging. I'm simply saying how it affects us . . . and how it uniquely captures, holds, and delivers an audience unlike traditional media—TV, radio, magazines, and newspapers.

You see, those traditional media—newspapers, magazines, radio, and TV—kinda just . . . uh . . . sit there. The extent of your interaction with them is looking—often actually just staring—or listening . . . or both. That's about it. Sure, the words and images might stimulate you in one way or another, but you don't *actively engage* with them. Your role—and, likewise, their effect—is more passive. And, as a result, they occupy you mentally and physically on a far more superficial level than does social media.

Did you catch the word I just used? *Engage.*

QUESTION: What's your number-one goal as an advertiser? And please don't say, "to sell." That's a given. Instead, your number-one goal is to first *capture your prospects' attention.* And until you do that, you can't engage them in your sales presentation. And ultimately, without that, you're not selling much of anything.

"But, Drew! That's not quite true! If my product rocks . . . and there's a good market for it . . . and it's priced right, the market will find me."

Really? Let's test that.

You're in the Mojave Desert. You sell ice-cold lemonade. Perfectly sweetened. Nice tall glasses, too. Heck, you even slip a juicy lemon wheel on the edge of every glass and toss in a cute paper umbrella.

Your market? It's huge . . . and tailor-made for your product. That's because you chose the perfect August weekend. Thousands of people are in the desert making a grueling fifty-mile trek as part of some crazy annual "Survive Death Valley Without Actually Dying" competition. Unfortunately, the participants are indeed dying . . . of *thirst.* Price? It's fair . . . just $3.00 a glass. Quality? It's fresh-squeezed, perfectly sweetened, and delicious!

But WTH?! *Nobody is buying!*

Could it be because your lemonade stand is positioned behind a thirty-seven-foot saguaro cactus and you're positioned across from a place of great distraction—a scorpion pit—where every contestant looks down to avoid the poisonous-tailed beasts?

"Aww, c'mon Drew . . . "

Yeah, yeah, I get it. It's not quite the same as *your* situation. But the *essence* of the elements *is* the same. Because it doesn't matter how great your product or service is if your audience is *distracted* (by other ads, posts, emails, websites, and videos) and you don't *grab their attention* (with your headline, subject line, graphics, and thumbnails) and you don't *engage* them with your content. Online—or "on sand"—the *end result* is the same: *No Sale.* No matter where you are or what you sell, you need to grab people's attention *first* or absolutely nothing happens.

Social media apps were specifically designed to engage and influence our brains and how they work. (Read that again.) Developers worked hard to make sure these sophisticated pieces of technology keep their users (consumers) clicking and swiping away for hours. Talk about a captive audience.

How many users? 4.62 billion! That's over half of the world's population: 58.4 percent of it to be exact. Overall, 93.4 percent of internet users are on social media of some kind. The average person spends two hours and twenty-seven minutes daily and uses seven and a half different social media platforms every month. It's not surprising, really. While some people are more introverted and solitary, most humans have an innate desire to bond with each other en masse.

What the heck did we do before social media? We either picked up a phone or headed someplace where other humans gathered—a mall, movie theater, museum, amusement park—or just walked down a busy store-lined street.

Today it's a breeze. From the comfort of your couch—without needing to dress up and by barely lifting a finger—you can interact with thousands, express your opinions, share your creativity, get answers to your most pressing questions, and get a river of social validation right in the palm of your hand. It's perfect, really. You can be totally lazy in wrinkled sweatpants and still get your fill of human interaction. Is it any wonder it's so popular?

According to *Hootsuite's 2002 Digital Report*, every month, on average, people spend 23.7 hours streaming YouTube videos.[2] That's nearly an entire day. The topic? It doesn't matter—although comedy, music, entertainment, pop culture, and how-to are the top five most-watched.

Fact is, YouTube doesn't exist to show you videos. Facebook doesn't exist to help you connect with friends and family. Instagram and TikTok don't exist to entertain you with fascinating posts and short-form videos.

Surprised? You shouldn't be. *These apps and media all exist to sell ad space.* Same holds true for TV, radio, magazines, and other traditional media.

Truth is, the entertainment you derive from these addictive platforms is just a clever *vehicle* to get you (and *keep* you) watching so that commercial messages can be delivered. All that fun stuff is simply *bait*. It's bait that lures you in front of various electronic devices that have the ability to display ads. Don't kid yourself. Without the ads, all that fun entertainment would stop dead.

Think about it. What TV shows get the biggest ad dollars? The ones with the biggest audiences, of course. Take Super Bowl LVI, for example. According to NBC Sports, the Los Angeles Rams' 23–20 win over the Cincinnati Bengals had 112.3 million fans superglued to their screens.[3] To reach them, a cool $6.5 million was spent for a quick thirty-second spot.[4]

What does that mean to the average football fan? Nothing. What does it mean to businesses trying to reach consumers? $$$. Big $$$. The bigger and more attentive the audience, the greater the possibility for sales. That's a fact that even a kid running a lemonade stand understands.

But why is so much time spent on social media? Ready? (It's "red pill" time.) Keep reading, and you'll never be the same.

Have you ever heard of the *Fogg Behavior Model*, or *FBM*? It's a standard blueprint among app developers today. You should know about it because, for you as a social media advertiser, it helps persuade prospects to respond to your offers.

Referred to as "the three-pronged approach" by *Business Insider*, the FBM guides the design of social media apps to drive humans to take action.[5] This magical triad consists of 1) Motivation, 2) Ability, and 3) Prompt. Let me explain.

To get humans to take action:

1. **They must be MOTIVATED to take action.**

2. **They must also have the ABILITY to take action.** (Ability, in the context of behavioral design, refers solely to the *simplicity* of the action required.) And finally . . .

3. **They must then be PROMPTED to do more than just think about it.** They must also be *moved* to take the next step, whether that's clicking a link, completing a form, or clicking a PayPal button.

Let's make things easy, okay? Let's call the three elements (*Motivation, Ability,* and *Prompt*) *MAP* for short. Now, let's get practical.

Let's say I'm a landscaper. You're a homeowner. I want you to hire me to cut your grass. For my sales pitch to be successful (regardless of how it's delivered—online, in print, or in person), you first have to *want* to have your lawn cut by a professional. Simple enough, right? If you're already satisfied with your lawn and the way it's being cut (whether by you or someone else), you're not going to call me. In other words, you'll have no *Motivation*. However, if I can convince you of the joy of having someone else sweat and toil to keep your grass beautifully fluffy and green, then I can likely motivate you to hire me. But that's just step one.

Next, I have to make it easy to hire me. That's the *Ability* prong. If you saw my landscaping ad on Facebook and were motivated to contact me (either because you were already searching for a landscaper, or my ad convinced you to move ahead), I wouldn't want to send you to a website with multiple pages talking about all the different services I offer: hardscaping, snow removal, fence installation, and the like. Nor would I make you complete a long form asking for your square footage and any peculiarities about your property.

Nope. I'd make it as easy as possible for you to simply sign up, therefore making your *Ability* to take action as effortless as possible. In fact, to capitalize on a possible impulse sale and catching you at what might be your peak moment of interest—*"Damn! I hate mowing this blasted lawn. It's too hot . . . my mower sucks . . . adding gas and oil is a drag . . . starting it's a pain . . . and getting rid of all the clippings is a hassle!"*—I'd try to make the sale *immediately*, meaning getting you to book without even first scheduling a "come see" appointment. Read on.

I'd drive you to *one simple page* that speaks only about my lawn-mowing services and tells why I'm your best choice. That's the *Prompt* prong. I'd feature a few select testimonials and beautiful photos of gorgeous lawns, along with an inset photo of me and a short "personal letter" to make a warm connection with you. I'd have a bold coupon good for a mowing of up to 10,000 square feet—about the average in the area I'd be targeting—with a big discount offer as an irresistible get-acquainted price. If I were supersmart, I'd have a short, punchy, well-edited video of me working (and the great results), and me on camera saying a few brief words about why I'm your best choice.

By the way, one of the primary purposes of this book is to help you think like an advertising professional. That's because when you adopt this mindset, your decisions will be guided by more than just the techniques you learn. You'll have the overall philosophy of someone who understands the reasons why we'd choose A over B. Why we instantly get turned off by headlines without offers and deadly specific benefits. You might not always have an exact formula for your exact situation, but you'll have a foundational understanding that will guide your decisions far more effectively than someone who just works from a "If A, then do B" checklist. Of course, having both is ideal, and you'll get both in this one book.

Now, back to me as the landscaper trying to land you as a new client.

Fact is, I'd be happy to break even on the first "get-acquainted job." That's because it costs me five times as much to *acquire* you than to keep you. The faster I can snag you as a client, the less your acquisition will ultimately cost me. Plus, my long-term client stats tell me that once I book you, I'll keep you on board for an average of four and a half years—and that's above average.

One customer, well taken care of, could be more valuable than $10,000 worth of advertising.

– JIM ROHN

Your lifetime value to me is worth a breakeven on your first cutting. By offering a killer introductory price, I can undercut the competition and substantially raise my chances of you trying my services. My $29 cut versus their $49 cut. Who would you try first, everything else being the same? That's a rhetorical question, of course. Most people would go with the less expensive option. Less risk, less to lose, right?

Lastly, my website would also feature the simplest of contact forms and a chat option. I'd test this against a page with a *Schedule-Your-Own-Service* form that allows you to both pick the date of your first mowing and conveniently pay for it online. (This is how you make things easy for your prospects and push them past the second prong—Ability—in the "take action" process.) The saddest thought is busting your butt to get eyeballs on your ad, but once they arrive, they're entirely lost (or bored) because 1) you're not guiding them exactly where you want, or 2) it's just too much trouble to make the next contact with you, or 3) you're not outright selling them on why they need to choose you over the slew of competitors.

I might feature the simplest of price-quote calculators and a clean, easy-to-complete form that gets my services started immediately. I'd have another form to simply request more info, plus a Chat Now option—including a smiling rep's face—to add a personal touch and satisfy the impulse to get questions answered on the spot, along with my phone number prominently displayed. So, in other words, I'd want to make you jump as few hurdles as possible for you to satisfy the desire that you've come to my site to satisfy.

Now, this is where the "trickery" of social media app design gets interesting. According to the National Center for Biotechnology Information, seven addictive mechanisms capturing and holding our brains' attention are built into every app:[6]

1. **Endless Scrolling and Intermittent Conditioning.** This is what I call the "Bottomless Fries" principle. As long as the server keeps filling up your basket, chances are you'll keep munching. (Far more than if you had to *ask* for refills.) Likewise, if you've ever tried to scroll to the "end" of YouTube, for example, you know that the end

never comes. It's no accident. Developers purposely try to keep you from arriving at an end point. That's because reaching "the end" would cause you to become aware of your involvement . . . think about what else you *should* be doing . . . and possibly quit.

These developers know that the longer you keep scrolling, the more and deeper involved you'll become. Plus, occasionally stumbling across videos that are especially appealing gives you intermittent jolts of feel-good dopamine that further fuels your desire to keep scrolling. This *intermittent conditioning* keeps you hooked, craving your next "fix." Don't stop now; another great jolt, er, video, could be just around the corner.

> *Remember when people had diaries and got mad when*
> *someone read them? Now they put everything*
> *online and get mad when people don't.*
> —UNKNOWN

2. **Endowment Effect.** Simply put, the more you use the app, the harder it is to stop using it and/or delete it. With every use, you become both more familiar with it, more invested, more "skilled" at navigating around—often until it's second nature. It simply becomes "what you do" after or during lunch, at break time, or before bed. A digital habit.

3. **FOMO.** The *fear of missing out,* a phenomenon first identified in 1996 by marketing strategist Dr. Dan Herman. The term, popularized by author Patrick J. McGinnis in his op-ed appearing in Harvard Business School's publication, *Harbus,* identifies the unnerving feeling that you're missing out on information, events, or experiences that could somehow make your life better.[7] *"What will happen next?" "Will she get that expensive cosmetic surgery?" "Did his risky investment—similar to the one I'm considering—really pay off?" "Will her amazing shirt-folding technique save me hours on laundry day?" "What's his sixty-second trick for repairing drywall with a butter knife?"* Gee, think of everything you'll miss if you stop checking your social media feed.

4. **Social Pressure.** This one's really sneaky. You know how many apps show you when your message and post have been sent,

delivered, and read? Knowing that others know that you've received their message or read their post puts pressure on you to engage . . . reply. There's pressure to encourage your followers to respond to your posts. Pressure to post. Pressure to not miss out on what your friends are doing or seeing. And when someone posts something particularly important (to them, perhaps not especially to you), you feel pressure to acknowledge it. All this pressure encourages you to participate more fully. And this keeps you glued to your screen . . . right where advertisers want you.

5. **Displaying Confirmed-Liked Information.** While you're busy clicking away, you're being closely "watched." Not by creepy humans—hopefully—but by sophisticated technologies that track what you do, what you like, what you post (both text and photos), what sites you visit, what ads you already clicked on, how long you stay, and much more. But you knew this already, right? It's just one more way to keep you engaged. I call it "techno-targeting."

Old-school direct-mail marketers buy mailing lists of people whose personal data conforms to the profiles they're looking for: owners of VitaMix blenders who also subscribe to *Prevention* magazine who also purchased at least $100 worth of vitamins in the past ninety days and, prior to that, made similar purchases over the course of at least twelve months. Whoa! That's pretty specific, right?

Or Buick LaCrosse owners living in Phoenix, between the ages of twenty-five and fifty-five, who subscribe to *Car and Driver* magazine, own their own homes, earn at least $75,000 annually, have bought at least $100 in car accessories online within the past ninety days (called a "hotline" list), and repeatedly did so over the past twelve months. Micro-targeting is nothing new.

Social media isn't very different. But your ability to target is even more precise. Take Facebook, for example. It's currently offering more than thirty ways to target your prospects. These include location, gender, age, language, income, relationship status, education, work (employers, job titles, industries), parental status, life events (new job, birthday, recently moved, long-distance relationship [*yikes!*]), politics and many others.

Or, create a look-alike audience that matches the characteristics of your current customers, website visitors, mobile app data, or fans of your page. Upload your data and in six to forty-eight hours Facebook will create a list of its users with qualities that most closely match those people. Scary, but a marketer's dream. It's like dropping a broad-market audience into a funnel fitted with your own personal business filter and only the best prospects fall out the bottom.

Knowing so much about their audience gives social media platforms the ability to show users exactly what they think they'd most likely want to see. Result? Users keep clicking, scrolling, reading, and watching. *They stay engaged.* Just the kind of audience we want.

6. **Social Validation.** *"Be sure to smash that Like button and drop a comment below . . ."* Everybody wants to be liked, and—for many—the more "likes" and follows they get, the more validated they feel . . . to the extent that they'll check their post throughout the day to see just how popular and "liked" it was. Each "like" and "follow" provides a little shot of dopamine to their brain, chemically addicting them to posting more and seeking still more validation.

Initially proposed by social psychologist Leon Festinger in 1954, the psychological theory of *social validation* says that there's a strong need within each of us to gain accurate self-evaluations . . . to be confident that the way we view ourselves is accurate.[8]

We compare ourselves *up* by reading posts and watching videos of people whom we believe are superior to us for whatever the reason, i.e., status, income, beauty, and other personal characteristics. We also compare ourselves *down* to others to whom we feel superior.

> *Social media is addictive precisely because it gives us something which the real world lacks: it gives us immediacy, direction, a sense of clarity and value as an individual.*
>
> —DAVID AMERLAND

According to social psychologists, if your self-esteem has recently been threatened, for example, you might benefit from downward comparisons to help you feel better about yourself. Someone says you're ugly and you see photos of people who look like diseased farm animals, and you might not feel so bad looking in the mirror in the morning.

Is your self-esteem strong? An upward comparison could help you aspire to move closer to the social group in which such people belong. (That's why gyms often have photos of extremely fit people on their walls, and why people looking to get in shape often post photos of complete strangers whose physiques they admire.)

7. **The Ovsiankina Effect.** Named for psychologist Maria Ovsiankina, this phenomenon is the urge to return to a discontinued activity or action until you complete it. In social media, once you begin scrolling, it's tough to stop. You told yourself that you'd "just check the response to my last post real quick" and realize that twenty-five minutes have passed. There's the ever-present cliff-hanger. The "wait for it" moment. And the feeling that the *next* post . . . the *next* image or video . . . will be the one that really satisfies. It's the photo you share, the post you "like," the video that you forward. But until you find it, you'll keep looking. And, by the way, don't forget to finish writing your profile! There's that nagging progress bar or "percentage complete" to remind you to load it up with personal details, or you, my friend, are "incomplete." Ugh, such pressure.

But, hey, I'm not judging. And although many medical professionals proclaim that social media can be damaging to our mental health if used to excess, the purpose of this chapter wasn't to talk about its purported dangers. It was simply to tell you some of the ways that it's been shown and designed to be addictive. This sets the stage to discuss this advertising medium that has extraordinarily high engagement, which is ideal for any business that wants to sell more.

Okay, now that we've explored the primary psychological mechanisms that are built into social media to keep us hooked, let's explore a principle that, if fully understood, could help you and me—the advertisers—take advantage of its impact on users.

CHAPTER 2

The Social Media Slot Machine: You Can Make Money Like Crazy If You Understand This One Big Idea

In the first chapter, I explained the driving force behind social media's popularity. In this chapter, I'll reveal why people engage with it and what specific psychological rewards they obtain from its use, so you'll know better how to ride this psychological current all the way to the bank. It's all about understanding why people do what they do. How they keep returning to their apps for another "hit," another pull of the social media "slot machine lever" to get another jolt of behavior-reinforcing pleasure. When you know this, you'll know how to tap into the forces of Mother Nature itself. That also means you'll know how to construct ads that speak to people's true wants and needs.

Let's face it: people don't use social media to see our ads. In fact, many people consider them to be interruptions. It's no different from classic media, TV, and radio, though, is it? The annoying TV commercial about toilet cleaner (along with the happy woman singing about the pleasures of her "spring-fresh bowl") always comes at the worst time . . . like in the middle of the hard-core documentary about how WWII was won by the Allies. (Talk about a lousy segue.) Likewise, the blaring radio commercial for the local car dealer with screaming announcers shouting about their "Mammoth-Sized, Turbo-Charged, Epic Car-Blow-Out Sale" always interrupts your enjoyment of the easy-listening music when you're just trying to chill with fresh-ground coffee and a biscotti.

In *Cashvertising* I explained the *Life-Force 8* (*LF8* for short): the eight inborn needs that we are literally hardwired to satisfy. And since you can't write a book about skiing, for example, without ever mentioning *snow*, let's take a quick look at what these forces are and why they're important when it comes to writing advertising. But rather than simply listing and defining them like I did in *Cashvertising*, I'm also going to also give you concrete examples of ad copy that incorporates them.

THE LIFE-FORCE 8

FACT: We human beings are hardwired from birth to want the following eight things:

1. Survival . . . enjoyment of life . . . life extension

2. Enjoyment of food and beverages

3. Freedom from fear, pain, and danger

4. Sexual companionship

5. Comfortable living conditions

6. To be superior . . . winning . . . keeping up with the Joneses

7. Care and protection of loved ones

8. Social approval

And, while the primary eight have controlled us practically since birth, we've also learned *Nine Secondary Wants* (*SW9s*) that play an important part in how we make our buying decisions.

THE NINE SECONDARY WANTS

1. To be informed

2. Curiosity

3. Cleanliness of body and surroundings

4. Efficiency

5. Convenience

6. Dependability/Quality

7. Expression of beauty and style

8. Economy/Profit

9. Bargains

The preceding brief list is all you need to know about those things we cannot "refuse to want." They're programmed into our DNA. We have to have them. And throughout our lives, we continually strive to acquire them until we do.

Knowing these eight needs is a powerful shortcut when creating your advertising. Because rather than starting from square one and attempting to *create* desires, you can simply tap into those that Mother Nature herself installed into each of us.

For example, if on one lazy summer day you wanted to ride a raft while sipping iced tea, would you rather

1. Grab a shovel, dig a canal, and then build an extensive network of piping to supply water to fill the canal and then handcraft a raft using hand-cut logs and vine, or . . .

2. Simply buy a raft, throw it into an *existing* stream, and start sipping your tea?

The answer is obvious. This reminds me of a great line from Eugene Schwartz's classic book, *Breakthrough Advertising*. In it, Schwartz says that you can't create needs; you can only tap into those already existing.[1]

Okay, but how? Just look at which of the eight primary desires your product or service most satisfies and create your big appeal using *that* as your primary driver.

Want examples? Okay, here are some positioning lines showing the difference between using ordinary appeals based on features versus the Life-Force 8 drivers.

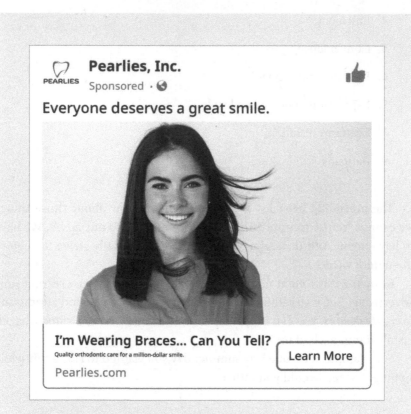

PRODUCT: Invisible Teeth Aligners

Current Copy: "Everyone deserves a great smile" and "I'm Wearing Braces . . . Can You Tell?"

Takeaway: Do you see how this appeal is based on a product feature rather than one of the LF8 appeals? The braces are transparent. And great smiles are for everyone. But now consider copy with a *Life-Force 8 ingredient inserted . . .*

Ad Revised with LF4 (Sexual Companionship) and **LF8** (Social Approval)

Revised Copy: "Psssst . . . She's Looking at Your Teeth. (But what's she thinking?)" and "Straighter Teeth: Faster, Easier, Cheaper with New Invisible Pearlies"

Takeaway: If you're like most people, you get more of a gut reaction to this one. It's a feeling of social pressure and acceptance. Of wanting to look good. Your smile can be likened to your recent social media post. You want that "like." And the possibility of a date? Who knows, but the tension is there. You then bring in stats from Invisalign's own study that says, *"When it comes to attracting a possible mate on a dating site, those with straight teeth are seen as 57% more likely than those with crooked teeth to get a date based on their picture alone."*[2] Ouch.

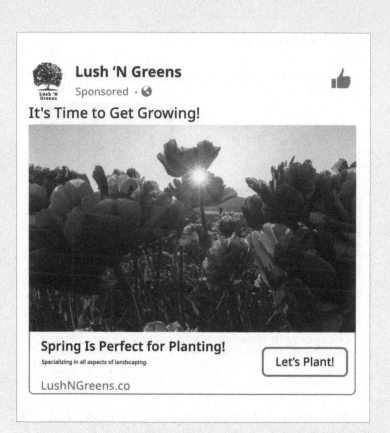

PRODUCT: Landscaping Services

Current Copy: "It's Time to Get Growing!" and "Spring Is Perfect for Planting!"

Takeaway: Your number-one job is not to tell what season it is, yet this was the headline, the most important part of the ad.

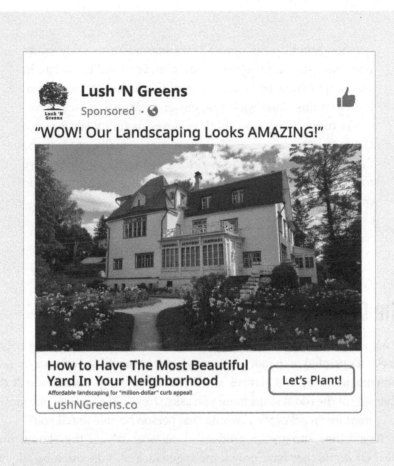

Revised Ad with LF6 (Be Superior/Winning/Keeping Up with the Joneses) and **LF8** (Social Approval)

Revised Copy: "WOW! Our Landscaping Looks AMAZING! and "How to Have The Most Beautiful Yard In Your Neighborhood"

Takeaway: Rather than simply telling people that plants will grow well in the spring (as if that does anything for your business), you're tapping into people's innate need to keep up with their neighbors, to not be the "ugly" house in the neighborhood, to be admired. It's important to understand that these positioning lines—sometimes headlines—might not come across to you as clever, unique, or all that great. For one thing, in advertising, clever is often a curse. Clever is like funny. What you think is clever or funny is often not clever to someone else. Plus, cleverness usually needs to be figured out, and that's the last thing you want people to have to do when they read your promotions. Your meaning should transmit instantly.

The Old Reliable Table Test

In my seminars, I say, "Pretend that your ad is on a table in a big room. Maybe it's printed on paper . . . or maybe it's being displayed on a screen. Someone walks by and glances at it without stopping. If someone at the other side of the room stops them and asks, *'Hey . . . that ad you just looked at . . . what was it selling?'* . . . would that person be able to tell you?"

Would they know your product or service? Would they know your offer? Or would they have only some vague idea? A stop-smoking ad with a headline about sickness might provide an interesting stat to consider, but would it stop someone looking to quit smoking as well as one promising to help you to *"Crush Your Nasty Smoking Habit in 30 Days Flat or Your Money Back"*? You know the answer.

PRODUCT: Wedding Photography Services

Current Copy: "Let OUR shotz tell YOUR love story." and "FIND. MEET. LOVE."

Takeaway: Trite. Means nothing. Says nothing about the business or its services. Doesn't inform. Doesn't persuade. Doesn't do much of anything at all except maybe make the person who wrote it feel really clever. At least they offer a coupon.

Ad Revised with LF8 (Social Approval) and **SW6** (Dependability/Quality)

Revised Copy: "UGH! Don't let this happen to you!" and "GETTING MARRIED? 8 Horrible Mistakes to Avoid EMBARRASSING Wedding Photography Disasters!"

Takeaway: Here the ad starts off with the emotional *"UGH!"* (expressions of strong emotions are always good on social media) and then offers solid information that could help prospects save thousands on lousy photography services for one of the most important days of their lives.

All I did was take one *Life-Force* and one *Secondary Want* and write a headline for it. By doing this, I automatically tapped into two powerful human desires. I didn't have to make people want anything. I also didn't have to create any new desires. I jumped into an *existing* boat and floated down an *existing* canal. Plus, I didn't have to do any guesswork, either. I didn't have to say, *"Hmmmm, do people want to be approved of by others? Do people want quality and dependability?"* If it's on those two Life-Force lists, you can be assured that they want those things.

PRODUCT: Home Fire Extinguisher

Current Ad: Photo of fire extinguishers

Current Copy: "Fire Can Strike When You Least Expect It!" and "Fire Extinguisher Twin Pack—UP TO $40 VALUE!"

Takeaway: This ad needs a blood transfusion. It's dull, weak, lifeless . . . and the headline is true but—*Yawn!*—trite.

Ad Revised with LF7 (Care and Protection of Loved Ones)

Revised Copy: "SCARY FACT: The temperature inside your home reaches 1,100 degrees just 3-½ minutes after fire breaks out!" and "This Top-Rated $29 Extinguisher Can Save You & Your Family from Dying in a House Fire"

Takeaway: People don't want fire extinguishers. They want to save their families' lives and homes should a fire break out. The first ad focuses on the thing. The second ad focuses on *what people actually want*. When you think of it this way, it just seems obvious, doesn't it? Even better, hire a local firefighter to pose with your product decked out in official bunker gear, and you add both personality and credibility, plus a human face . . . all important ingredients for capturing attention and encouraging engagement and sales. Note how the emojis add a little emotion and personality even without featuring any human faces.

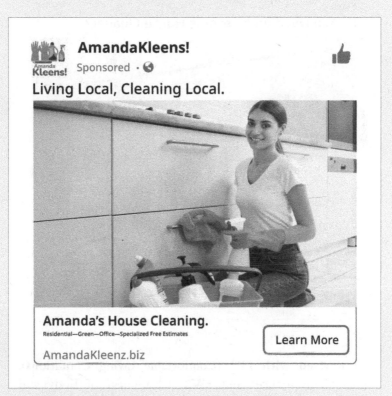

PRODUCT: House Cleaning Services

Current Ad: Photo of a woman kneeling and smiling, holding a spray bottle and cloth

Current Copy: "Living Local, Cleaning Local." and "Amanda's House Cleaning. Residential—Green—Office—Specialized Free Estimates"

Takeaway: This is what I call a *business card ad*. It simply tells you that Amanda is in business. It doesn't *sell*. It doesn't set her apart from her competition. It doesn't make you want to choose her to clean your house. *It gives you no reason to prefer her.*

AmandaKleens!
Sponsored · 🌐

Do You Need an Awesome House Cleaner?

Dozens of your neighbors say I'm the best house cleaner in the Westboro area. Try me once and you'll agree! Click here >>>

Get Free Quote!

I professionally scrub your house from top to bottom. I bring all my own pro equipment. You sit back and relax. Friendly. Reliable. Efficient. Hardworking. I won't stop until your house sparkles... or I'll give you all your money back—GUARANTEED!

AmandaKleenz.biz

Ad Revised with LF5 (Comfortable Living Conditions), **SW5** (Convenience) and **SW3** (Cleanliness of Body and Surroundings)

Revised Copy: "DO YOU NEED AN AWESOME HOUSE CLEANER?" and "Dozens of your neighbors say I'm the best house cleaner in the Westboro area. Try me once and you'll agree! Click here>>>"

But Amanda doesn't stop there. Nope. She sells her heart out and adds: "I professionally scrub your house from top to bottom. I bring all my own pro equipment. You sit back and relax. Friendly. Reliable. Efficient. Hardworking. I won't stop until your house sparkles . . . or I'll give you all your money back—GUARANTEED!"

Takeaway: Wow, what an *incredible* difference! Do you feel it? In the first ad, Amanda was only *telling*. In the second ad, she was *selling like a direct-response pro*. She didn't just say a bunch of stuff. She said things that land with a money-bag thud. She said things that people *want* to hear. She tapped into the LF8 and SW9. She didn't just mention features of her service. She said what she'll do *and how it will benefit you*. And did you see what else she did? (It's something *you* should do, too.) She expressed confidence in herself and her services. She said she's the best house cleaner in her area according to dozens of reviews. (She suggested social proof . . . very effective . . . even though the actual reviews aren't shown.) I'd plaster one of her best quotes right next to that awesome "#1-Rated" seal.

To me, this short and simple ad conveys that 1) she's confident, 2) she's professional, 3) she has lots of happy and satisfied clients, 4) my house will be very clean when she's done, 5) lots of other people think she's the best, and 6) I take little risk trying her services because she's offering me a guarantee. Now that's selling, my friend.

QUESTION: What feelings do you get when you read this ad? Yes, *feelings! Please don't consider ads to be simply information-distribution tools. That's only part of their job. The most effective ads are also emotion generators.* (Read that sentence again.) They shouldn't just make you think. They should also make you *feel*.

Do you remember what I wrote in *Cashvertising*? I said:

People buy with emotions and then use reasoning to justify the expenditure of money.

According to Harvard professor Gerald Zaltman, 95 percent of human purchase decisions are subconscious, affected by emotions rather than conscious reasoning, comparisons, reviews, and facts.[3]

Neurosurgeons aren't surprised. They've discovered that people whose brains are damaged in the area that produces emotions—the limbic system—are actually *incapable* of making decisions.

Fascinating, right? But what does this mean for you and me as advertisers?

Simple. It means if you focus only on pumping your ads full of *data* rather than words that stimulate strong *emotions*, you're leaving your prospects dramatically less likely to make a buying decision because their emotions are hardly being affected, if at all.

That's why when you write your next ad, you need to do more than simply tell them stuff. You need to stir their emotions somehow. Make them excited, happy, hopeful, scared, angry—or any number of other emotions—to move your prospects to the *"I'm spending my money on this right now"* stage.

> *When dealing with people, let us remember we are not*
> *dealing with creatures of logic. We are dealing*
> *with creatures of emotion. . . .*
> —DALE CARNEGIE

Bottom line: "Sell the sizzle, not the steak." State the features, but play up the romance, the benefits. Remember that people need to know the features to justify the purchase, but you have to slather on the benefits in a colorful and visual way to create the desire that causes them to make the purchase in the first place.

CHAPTER 3

The Power of Psychological Inoculation Remarketing:

How to Automatically Chip Away at Your Competition's Sales Copy and Destroy the Effectiveness of Their Claims without Lifting a Finger

Now I want to share with you a very important concept that—if you apply it—will do the following three things for you:

> **IT'LL BOOST** *your company's credibility, which means more prospects will trust you and feel more comfortable buying from you, and . . .*

> **IT'LL BUILD** *tremendous goodwill and an overall feeling that you're looking out for your customers' best interests, and . . .*

> **IT'LL TURN** *more of your lookers into buyers, convert far more of your traffic, and start filling up your pockets with more of that green stuff.*

NOTE: This chapter is an entire seminar in itself. Stick with it, and you'll learn one of the most powerful ways to cause consumers to "aggressively prefer" your products and services over those of your competition. It's devilishly sneaky, and not 1-in-100 online marketers are using it. Start now . . . before *they too* read this book and start using it *against* you.

Let's talk about the awesome power of *Psychological Inoculation Remarketing*, or *PIR* for short. It's based on the *Inoculation Theory*, the consumer psychology principle that I discuss in my other book, *Cashvertising*, and here's how it works.

First, understand that nowadays it takes little effort for consumers—your prospects—to check out your competition. Years ago, before Google, Amazon, and the internet . . . before you bought something . . . to make sure you were making a good decision, you either asked people what they thought about the product (if they owned it or knew about it), or you read *Consumer Reports*, or you just took the chance and bought it. (And you kept the receipt just in case it was junk and you needed to return it.)

But nowadays, it's very different, isn't it? Because before buying—unless it's an impulse sale and you *have* to have it *right now*—no matter what anyone else thinks about it, you do at least a little research before spending money, right?

Many people do a *lot* of research. I sure do. Fact is, I want to make a good purchase decision. Not because I want to own the best-quality products to gratify my ego in some way, but because I simply don't want the hassles associated with crappy products and having to go through the whole annoying return process.

So, let me give you a real-life example. Let's say that you love coffee. Every day, or a few times a week, you stop into Starbucks, Costa Coffee, Coffee Bean & Tea Leaf, or your other favorite coffee shop. You drop a ridiculous amount of money for coffee while you're there. (Hey, it's coffee. It's easy to rationalize.)

But eventually—after you unload your mailbox that's stuffed with credit card and utility bills—you one day realize that you're spending too much for something that costs them pennies to make. So you begin thinking, *"Hey, maybe I should just make my own coffee."*

Notice the seed of the idea that gets planted. Next, notice how the mind naturally starts to "water" this seed to bring its idea to fruition.

You think, *"I won't have to go out of my way, find parking, stand in line, explain what I want, wait for it to be made, pay ridiculous prices, and hope to find a seat among all the people who finished their coffee two hours ago and are now posting photos of their overweight cats on Facebook."*

So, just like what your prospects are doing—when they have a desire for whatever it is that your product or service satisfies—you, too, begin thinking about how that desire can be satisfied better or differently.

So let's say I'm that guy going to the coffee shop. I start thinking, *"How can I make my own coffee? What options are available to me?"*

Assuming I had some knowledge about it, I immediately know some of my options:

- I could buy instant coffee. (This is essentially "coffee in name only.")

- I could buy a traditional drip coffee like a classic Mr. Coffee.

- I could buy an old-fashioned 1800s-style percolator. (Yes, people still use these things.)

- I could buy a Keurig machine and a slew of those little pods.

- Or, maybe a simple French press.

- Or an AeroPress, Chemex, or Kalita Wave.

- Or maybe a Moka pot that forces steam through the coffee.

- Or—if I were really a coffee aficionado—I could buy a bean grinder and an espresso machine with a milk steamer.

Whew, that's a lot of choices for "just a cup of coffee." This is why many people let someone else make it for them. They simply order . . . pay . . . drink. Easy.

Now this is where it gets interesting. And where you, as the business-person looking to outflank your competition, can control that psychological "trim tab"—that little element that makes all the difference in the direction your prospect goes to satisfy their desire for that thing you're selling.

Faced with all these decisions—just like *your* prospects—I start Googling: *"What's the best way to make the best cup of coffee at home?"*

Let's stop for a second. I need to make a point. It's the same point I make in my live seminars, whether I'm speaking to a chamber of commerce group in the beautiful state of Virginia or in a massive conference hall in Berlin, Germany. Because this is about the time you might be thinking, *"But, Drew, I don't sell coffee, so this example doesn't apply to me."*

Oh, but it really does. Ignore the product I'm discussing. In fact, ignore the products and services I mention throughout this entire book. They're simply convenient vehicles to demo the *principles* that apply to *any* product or service being advertised. Don't let the *type* of product distract you. Look past them to the underlying psychological principle being employed. Back to our scenario . . .

Okay, I'm Googling for the answer to the "how to make the best cup of coffee" question. What I'm doing now is exploring my options for satisfying my desire. (This is what your prospects are doing before they make contact with your company.)

And, as you recall, Life-Force 2 is the *enjoyment of food and beverages.* In this particular instance we have to add one of the Nine Secondary Wants: *Economy*, or the desire to save money.

Remember, to most consumers, most products are a *necessary evil*, as bad as that sounds. Fact is, if your prospects could receive the satisfaction of the desire that your product or service provides without having to actually buy your product or service, they would gladly do it. Egads, that sounds so bad. (But it's true.)

In other words, if your prospects could satisfy their desires without having to

- Do the research . . .

- Spend the money . . .

- Hassle with the product . . .

- Deal with warranties . . .

- Mess with breakdowns . . .

- Recharge batteries or buy and add fuel . . .

- Spend even more money on associated expenses . . .

- Buy replacement parts . . .

- Deal with a limited life span and need to ultimately start the whole annoying process over again . . .

. . . and anything else that a physical product unfortunately brings with it, they would very quickly opt to satisfy their desire without having to buy your product.

In other words, if I could simply snap my fingers and have the freshest, most delicious cup of coffee in my hand every morning, I wouldn't hassle with boiling the water, grinding the beans, waiting for the brew, cleaning the equipment, etcetera.

I'd simply wake up every day, take a shower, get dressed, snap my fingers, and—Poof!—in my hand is a freshly brewed cup of coffee. But that's magic, right? We can't do that. So we *need* the products and services to act as the vehicles that deliver the benefits that ultimately satisfy our desires.

In my seminars, I say,

- **We don't want** drills; we want holes!

- **We don't want** ovens; we want hot cooked food!

- **We don't want** ads, emails, websites, and other marketing materials!

- **We just want people to send us their money!**

Okay, back to our coffee example.

Let's say I'm the guy who loves coffee, and I'm looking for ways to stop spending a fortune on it and getting ripped off at coffee shops. So I've done my research, and I've determined that a French press is probably the best way to get a great cup of coffee at home. It's simple, fast, cheap, and reliable.

I also learn that grinding my own beans is the best way to get the most flavorful cup of coffee. I also learn that not any old grinder will do, but a burr grinder—one that actually crushes the beans rather than cuts them (like a blender or nut grinder)—is the choice of "true coffee connoisseurs."

Do you see what's happening here? I'm starting to do research. This is exactly what *your* prospects are doing.

Remember the *Life-Force 8*? Remember the mental path that people's brains take? It's . . .

TENSION→DESIRE→ACTION

Step #1: *They have a Tension (which could be for food, comfort, protection of loved ones, social approval, or others that I described earlier).*

Step #2: *That Tension leads to the Desire to ease that tension.*

Step #3: *The Desire leads to them taking an Action to fulfill that desire.*

See what's happening? To successfully progress through and complete the cycle, they begin by searching for ways to satisfy the desire. To do this, they begin researching and learning about the product category (unless they're already fully familiar with it). Only then do they begin paring down the choices.

Okay, after all this research, I decide I want a French press and burr grinder. Remember, all this is new information that I didn't know before.

Next, I start looking at specific products that fall into those two categories. *This is exactly what your prospects are doing* unless your product is unique—there's nothing else out there like what you sell. And it doesn't matter if you sell an e-book that helps guys get more weekend dates, an online service, or a physical product or service of any type. Fact is, whatever you're asking people to send money for, if you have *any* competition, most people are going to compare you to your competition before they click your order button.

So here I am, ready to begin looking at specific products. And let's say, for example, that Amazon is the best way for me to do this, especially because I'm a *Prime* member and I want to satisfy my desire fast. (Remember that *speed* and *ease* are two things most every human being wants when it comes to satisfaction of desires.)

So now, I'm on my phone . . . on Amazon's home page . . . and I begin by typing *French press coffee makers* in the search bar.

What comes up? Dozens and dozens and dozens of different manufacturers' French press coffee makers. What do I see? I see the photographs and the copy written by different individuals. Now let's break this down to the fundamentals.

It's a Battle of Copywriters!

I want you to imagine there are twenty-four different French press coffee makers and twenty-four different copywriters sitting at their desks somewhere in the world, and each of them is creating an army of words about their version of their French press.

Their words are charged with doing battle with all those other copywriters' words. The strongest words usually win the battle. Winning, in this case, of course, means to get the sale.

It's a battle of copywriters! Sure, in a lot of cases the copywriters have a whole team behind them, but ultimately it's the words that are going to cause the prospect to buy or not to buy.

As soon as you upload your words to that server, you've officially entered the battle against every other copywriter in your product category.

That's how professional copywriters are thinking about it . . . *and so should you!*

Now, let's get into the crux of this discussion. It rarely happens nowadays, when somebody reads your copy, when there are competitive products to be considered, that they'll read your copy and buy instantly without first researching what other options are available to them.

That means that they'll read your copy, and it'll make some kind of mental impression on them. Rarely will they buy on the spot unless they've already done what they believe is sufficient research.

Next, they'll look at other copywriters' copy. Meaning, they'll look at advertising written by other writers for other people's products. They'll then compare the impressions—both logical and emotional—that your copy provided with the logical and emotional impressions that those other writers' copy created in their brains.

Searching . . . Researching . . . More Searching

Then they'll look at still *another* copywriter's copy selling yet *another* company's product. They'll then compare the logical and emotional impressions they get from the copy written for both product number two and product number one with *your* product.

Now, after looking at several different products, they're more informed, but they're also likely to start getting confused! Whether or not they recall anything you wrote in your ad or web page before they began their research, nobody knows. Human memory being what it is, your copy and photos—no matter how much you slaved over them—could be completely forgotten by now.

"I looked at so many products, I'm getting tired, frustrated, and overwhelmed!" says the poor prospect who just wants to satisfy some nagging desire.

Your number-one goal is to make sure they return to your offer so they can be reminded about what you said and, hopefully, then sufficiently informed about the competition, click your add-to-cart button and buy from *you.*

But how do you get them back? Remarketing.

"Oh, I know about remarketing, Drew."

Nope, not the traditional remarketing that simply has your ads pop up while people are exploring other sites. Of course, you know about that. Instead, I'm talking about a form of remarketing that affects consumers far more powerfully, on a deep neurological level.

I'm talking about *Psychological Inoculation Remarketing*—a different beast altogether. Truth is, it's devastatingly powerful . . . almost to the point of making you feel guilty for using it. But it's 100 percent legal, honest, and ethical. Let me explain.

The *PIR* strategy consists of teaching your prospects exactly how to be dissatisfied with your competitors' offerings.

Huh? Let me repeat and explain: You actually teach your prospects exactly *how* to be dissatisfied with the products and services your competitors are selling. You literally psychologically "inoculate" them against your competitor's claims (or lack of them). You install in their heads information that causes them to critically review and process any information regarding your type of product that they read after they see your copy. You interrupt the natural buying process and insert a "self-talk critic" that follows them no matter where else they go online to research competitive products.

"Okay, Drew, what the hell are you talking about?"

Let me give you some concrete examples. In your copy for your French press coffee maker, not only do you describe the wonderful benefits and features that your product provides, but you also tell readers to *beware* of the many pitfalls that they are now facing just by being a consumer searching for a similar product.

You transform yourself from just another seller of stuff into a hard-core *consumer advocate* who wants to help guide people into making a good purchase decision . . . no matter whose products they ultimately buy. (You want them to buy yours, of course.)

You're showing them *first* that you're more than just another seller, someone committed to helping people make the best decisions . . . not just trying to grab their money.

See the difference? The strength of this positioning is tremendous. And here's how to easily do this.

First, you jump onto Amazon, Yelp, or Google and look at your competitors' reviews. Let's assume for this example that a competitor's product is being sold on Amazon. What you do is you look at the one-, two-, and three-star reviews and find out what people don't like about your competitors' products. Then, in your product copy (whether you use it on your website, in emails, Facebook, Twitter, or other social media platforms, or Amazon itself), you teach people to beware of these things! As a seller of quality French press coffee makers, for example,

▸ **YOU TEACH THEM** how some manufacturers use an inferior type of glass that's far more prone to cracking. (You learned this fact from the crummy reviews, so it's not only 100 percent true, but it's the same negative information your prospects will see when they do their comparative shopping research! *BOOM*— instant credibility, which causes them to more readily accept your other claims.)

▸ **YOU TEACH THEM** that your glass is tempered in a different way to resist chipping and cracking.

▸ **YOU TEACH THEM** that your French press is made from borosilicate glass that's also heat-resistant. You tell them that borosilicate glass is a type of glass with silica and boron trioxide. (Now they'll start looking for the previously unknown word *borosilicate* in your competitors' sales copy. If it's not there, it'll be suspect. Do you see where this is going?)

▸ **YOU TEACH THEM** that this special glass—*your glass*—has a very low coefficient of thermal expansion, making it resistant to thermal shock, more so than any other common glass. (Scientific explanations increase credibility.)

This kind of superior glass is less subject to thermal stress and is commonly used for the construction of reagent bottles—thick and strong bottles made for the rigors of containing strong chemicals in professional laboratory use.

Do you see how you're teaching them?

They likely have no idea about any of this stuff unless they've already done their research. **TIP:** Consumers look favorably upon those who educate them in a sometimes confusing marketplace where 99 percent of sellers are only out for their money.

You're also preparing them for their shopping research trip and informing them of what they'll find should they leave your offer and look at others to compare with what you're selling. What happens when they see on other sites exactly the things you already told and warned them about? *BOOM!* Instant greater credibility and added trust.

But we don't just tell them what to beware of. Nope. We don't stop there.

We also install legitimate doubt and cautious mistrust in their minds with questions like:

"Why do many other French press manufacturers use inferior glass that's more likely to split, crack, or chip? Who needs the hassle? Why don't they tell you this? Why do they use inferior materials? Why don't they include the things we do?"

The most effective construction of the question is, *"Why don't they_____?"* *"Why doesn't theirs_____?"* and *"Why do they_____?"*

Then you really expose and pile up the factual negatives and immediately question the competition for having such negatives and not being open and honest and telling people about them. It's devastating.

> *"Our French press also features a special BPA-free plastic liner attached to prevent the lid from overheating and burning your hands.*
>
> *"And while most other companies use plastic and rubber components, we use only stainless steel.*
>
> *"Is this important? YES! Because some plastic and rubber parts can give your coffee an odd chemical taste. One hundred percent stainless steel and glass French presses like ours guarantee you the ultimate in coffee flavor.*
>
> *"Why do so many other presses have only one mediocre filter screen? Ours has three to filter out grounds and deliver the richest, cleanest, purest coffee flavor."*

Do you see the power of this? It's remarkable.

> *"Why don't they all use stainless steel filters? Why don't they tell you that their cheap filters can rust and need to be replaced every few months at an average cost of $XX each?*
>
> *"Why don't they say that you can't just throw the parts in your dishwasher, but instead, you need to wash and dry them by hand? What a hassle!"*

Boom . . . boom . . . boom . . . you're chopping down the competition with a big old copywriter's ax. *Get the picture?* You see, the most effective form of selling is more than just saying good things about what *you* sell. It's also about steering your prospects *away* from those competitors who would love to see you go out of business! See what we're doing?

We're installing a mind frame in your prospects so they take with them (when they visit your competition's copy) information that carries greater significance than just typical product claims. That's because it's framed as "consumer help."

You're giving them information that they use to process all the other information that they'll read from that point forward!

You've actually given them a new context for judging. *You* gave it to them! You're installing a mental context by which they will—from that point on—process other copywriters' claims. Incredibly smart, and 100 percent ethical, as long as you're 100 percent honest and use only factual information, which you certainly should.

Now, it's important to note that you don't want to simply state these superior features and benefits. (I hope you *always* state what's better about what you're selling.)

But you're also purposely *selling against your competition.*

You don't just say what's great about yours. You also intentionally say that *many others do not* have these same features and benefits. Do you get the difference? You're not just saying that you're great, but you're acting like a consumer advocate and teaching them what to watch out for. In fact,

- ▸ You're actually providing a valuable buying service.

- ▸ You're inoculating them against what they'll see on your competitors' sites so that they're better equipped to counter those claims and argue in favor of your product.

- ▸ You're giving them "inside industry" information that nobody else is telling them.

- ▸ You're framing this information in such a way as to make it something other than just more sellers' claims about their own products.

- ▸ And once they buy, you're helping to reduce the possibility of buyer's remorse because you've framed the product in such a way as to literally change the filters they were using to make their decision from "I don't know what's good or bad about these things" to "This one is superior because of A, B, and C. Others don't have that, so I made a good decision."

The ultimate result is that they feel you are on their side. You're the one helping them decide.

While your competition does little more than tell them to buy, you're saying, *"Our product is superior.* Here's why . . . and here's what you need to look out for because there are so many inferior products on the market today that can cause you nothing but aggravation and dissatisfaction. We think ours is the best, but no matter whose French press you buy, please keep these critical things in mind so you make the best choice. . . . "

So instead of just hoping that they'll remember your claims, you're giving them ammunition for a method of critical inquiry, actually training your prospects' brains to be critical when reading your competition's claims. The idea, of course, is to cause them to become dissatisfied with what they see when they read your competitors' sales copy. Which serves as the inoculation, or protection, against those claims.

Essentially, what you're doing is providing all the negative information that your competition is sure to not give them on their own sales pages. Now, armed with this new information, they can more critically compare what you're offering to what the other guys are selling, with the goal being, of course, that they see your product or service more favorably. You're looking out for them, protecting them, teaching them how to be better consumers. And what effect do you think this has on their impression of you?

A *very* positive one. You're opening their eyes to things they never even considered. Things that, if unknown, could cause them to make an unwise buying decision that could result in disappointment and the possible loss of money. The end result? *Greater trust!*

And when people trust you, they trust your claims, your sales copy. And this is the ideal way to do it. Of course, your product does need to offer advantages over what your competitors are selling. And if it does, you simply need to tease out those advantages and clearly explain those advantages.

Want another example? Okay, let's say you're a web designer. You create landing pages and websites for businesses of all types. Now, the way most designers work is they sell only their own services. That's all they talk about. Them, them, them, them. Oh sure, they might say they're fast, professional, and guarantee satisfaction, but not even one in one hundred ever sells *against* their competition.

Why not? It's ridiculous! The people you're trying to convince are going to be exposed to your competitors' sales copy. It's downright crazy not to inoculate them before they see it!

Put yourself in their shoes. If *you* were a web designer, what should you say?

You not only should talk about how aesthetically pleasing and effective your designs are, but you should also *inoculate*! Tell them how many *other* designers use worn-out and dated templates that give you a web page that looks like zillions of others out there. No wonder they can turn around a job in forty-eight hours. They're just pasting in text and images and doing no original design work at all!

And since so many people are buying design work from people living in countries where English is not the native language, you mention how you're 100 percent English-fluent (or whatever your native tongue), unlike so many non-English-fluent designers, who make dozens of mistakes and are very difficult to communicate with.

You also talk about your experience. You have ten, twenty . . . years, while many others recently bought their design software and some are using their first few dozen customers as guinea pigs for their own practice.

What about their depth of knowledge about the psychology of web design? What do they know about how colors can affect buyers? Do they know which typefaces are easiest to read? Did they ever hear about the many typeface studies, or do they just use the font they (or their baby daughter) happen to like best? Or the ones chosen by the template designer, who might not know any more than they do.

Do you see what we're doing here? (I'm inoculating right before your eyes as you read these words.)

We're doing what most business people never do. *We are selling against the competition.* We are teaching people what to look out for. *We are teaching them to be dissatisfied with our competitors' sales copy before they even see it!*

Let's look at yet another example. Let's say you run an online and offline self-defense school. Do you simply say what you teach, declare how great your instructors are, state your monthly membership fee, and say how new members get free live testing via Zoom?

Not if you're a smart advertiser. And not if you're reading this book! Because here's what you'd also do:

You'd *inoculate!* And you'd do this by educating your prospects (your potential new members) how you

1. **TEACH** only the most *practical* self-defense methods . . .

2. **TEACH** dozens of techniques that can help them escape dangerous situations . . .

3. **TEACH** proven tricks that help their kids avoid being bullied . . .

4. **TEACH** tactics that give them the upper hand on the street, unlike the crazy and flashy Hollywood nonsense with the ridiculous high kicks and complicated multistep moves that could get them seriously injured . . . or worse!

Do you stop there? No. You also talk about how your instructors have all undergone in-depth background checks and have an average of twenty-two years' experience. (Unlike many other local schools that do *zero* background checks and often use other *students* [yes, really] to help teach . . . just to save a buck and boost their profits.)

Do you see how we're now differentiating? Do you see how we're actually doing *multiple inoculations,* each helping to protect our business from our competitors' claims?

We're spelling out our USP (Unique Selling Proposition)—what makes us different—and giving people things to be critical about when they look at other schools before signing up for ours.

Do you stop there? Oh no! We're just getting started.

Next, when you discuss your in-person training at your neighborhood dojo, you also talk about how often your school is cleaned and how you insist on it being immaculate—floors, equipment, bathroom—everywhere! Why don't other schools even mention cleanliness? (Probably because most of them are filthy.)

And unlike many other schools, you don't ask your paying *students* (!) to clean the school "as part of their discipline." (Yeah, some really do.) It's ridiculous, and you actually *say* that it is:

"We'll never ask you or your child to mop our floors like they do in many other karate schools. You're here to learn, not to do our janitorial work. It's a ridiculous—and common industry practice—and we never do it!"

Instead, you respect your students and have a professional cleaning crew come in on a regular basis to dust, sweep, dry and wet mop, power-scrub, and disinfect the bathroom and studio floors with antibacterial cleaning products to prevent athlete's foot and the spread of illness. Unlike many other schools that clean so infrequently that you see a buildup of hair and dust on their floors that gets stuck between your toes. After class, you have filthy feet, covered with who knows what?!

I'm not trying to be funny here to get you to laugh at this example. *You actually say this in your ads!*

Okay, are we done now? Not until you also tell them to watch out for schools that charge for every single belt test as a way to keep the cash coming in. (That's how they lure you in with their cheap monthly rates.) And don't forget about their annoying testing fees! And their *legally binding contracts* that lock you in for at least *one full year*, no matter what you or your child think about the classes!

By the time you're through with them, they'll be armed to the teeth should they choose to check out your competition! (And your competitors will hate you for it because everything you've said is 100 percent true.)

Some will buy on the spot because they love what they hear. You've put their minds at ease. You've *sold them away* from your competitors! Not only do you simply *say* these things, but you also really ramp up the power of this tactic by showing comparison charts that quickly show how you're better, what you offer, and what those other guys don't. This approach takes advantage of something we discuss in the original *Cashvertising*: *Principle 17–Heuristics* and "peripheral-route" (versus "central-route") processing.

As a reminder, *heuristics* give cues and shortcuts to consumers so they don't need to exert as much mental effort to decide. And since we humans like to typically take the easy route—the shortcut—we readily accept the assistance that comparison charts provide. We also select testimonials that reflect the product differences that we want prospects to become aware of when looking at their options.

For example, we don't use just generic quotes like this:

> "It's a great school with great teachers and I learned so much it's amazing! My kids love it, too. Join today . . . you won't regret it!"

Quotes like that do not inoculate!

That quote *seems* okay, doesn't it? Yes, but quotes like that don't serve our purpose of teaching prospects to be *dissatisfied* with our competition, and along with selling the benefits of our own product, that's our primary goal.

Instead, we run powerful, more extensive quotes like this:

> "*Wow . . . what a difference!* The teachers are patient . . . they're more interested in training you than selling you stuff . . . the lessons are easy to learn and practical for real-life situations . . . and the school itself is immaculate. I love that they have no annoying contracts and rip-off belt tests. Highly recommended."

Ask and Ye Shall Receive Quotes

Simply ask your most satisfied customers for a review and their comments on specific issues you'd like them to address.

In this case, you'd ask: *"What do you think about our school? Our teachers? Our cleanliness? The fact that we don't rope you into contracts and have ridiculous charges for belt tests?"*

They'll give you exactly what you're looking for . . . in their own words! You'll then have excellent ammunition to use in the marketplace to suppress your competition. Don't stop there! Go all out and create and advertise a *free report* that teaches would-be students how to choose a great school.

Title it with consumer-advocate appeal, like this:

"Free Report Reveals 12 Shocking Things Parents MUST Watch Out for When Signing Up Their Kids for Any Karate School"

In it, you tell them exactly what to watch out for. You're putting into their hands a *"How to Be Dissatisfied with the Competition"* guide. You can do this for your business, too. The competition will hate you for it, but you'll be smiling all the way to the bank.

Because talking only about your products and services is like driving a car with half its horsepower switched off. Your job isn't to make it easier for your competition to sell against you! Not only do you want to talk about what you do, but you also want to make it as difficult as possible for everyone else to grab what could be *your* customers!

And you have one chance to do it. When? When they're reading your sales copy! In other words, don't write the copy and simply hope that prospects come back after they leave your ad or site. Help ensure that they do by quashing the appeal of the copy on your competitors' sites *while prospects are still on your site.*

CHAPTER 4

Success Leaves Clues: What Makes Some Social Media Ads So Successful and How You Can Copy Their Winning Formulas

In this chapter, we'll look at six of Facebook's biggest advertising winners and dissect and uncover the elements that made them go viral. From the offbeat Squatty Potty ad with its famous rainbow-pooping unicorn to ads for irresistible tech gadgets, each is packed with thousands of dollars' worth of success lessons that you can "install" into your own promotions to dramatically boost your chances of running a massively profitable campaign.

First, let's agree on how we define success in the context of advertising. For me, that definition has always been:

> **A successful ad is a promoted message that persuades the greatest number of well-targeted prospects to take a specific desired action, within a specific timeframe, which either elicits an outright sale or moves them progressively toward purchasing.**

For the purpose of this particular study, we're simply going to look at what made these ads go *viral*. Because one way to help boost the success of your ad on any social media platform—if it already contains the essential elements to sell the product or service—is to have it spread far and wide, organically reaching an exponentially larger audience than the advertiser paid for. More eyeballs = more potential sales.

Now, those shared views are not going to be targeted like your original ad. Because when you set up your campaigns, you targeted your ad—you chose the demographics of your desired audience. When people share, they share with *everyone*. Meaning, their shares are not specifically targeted to your market. Some will care about what you're selling; others not at all. Still, a viral ad will geometrically expand your reach, your mass-market penetration, and a percentage of that mass reach *will* be your market.

Can you learn how to create successful ads by looking at other successful ads? The first answer is: *"YES, you can learn from successful ads because all the elements that help these ads to be successful are there right in front of your eyes!"*

But the second part of the answer is, *"NO, you can't learn if you don't know the distinctions . . . if you don't recognize the elements contained in those ads that make them successful . . . if you don't know what to look for."*

I'm going to help you see exactly what is being done to these ads that push them to go viral. I want you to see the psychological elements that went into these ads and what helped them achieve success.

Now, some of these ads are crazy. Some are shocking. Some are totally off the wall. Some of them are right on the money. So let's jump in and see what we can learn.

AD #1: SQUATTY POTTY
Stats: 135 Million Views • 1.5 Million Shares
463,000 Comments • 683,000 Likes
(See it at: *DrewEricWhitman.com/Cashvertising2/Ads*)

With a whopping $175+ million in sales since first appearing on *Shark Tank* and funded with $350,000 in assistance from shark Lori Greiner, the company now has expanded to over twenty products and has taken the colonic world by storm. Could your ad benefit from the kind of engagement this ad enjoyed . . . even if a good percentage of viewers were not within your defined target market? No doubt.

What's so great about this promotion? And can you apply its principles to your own ads? Well, in this case, its sales power isn't in the ad itself—it's in the video—which is masterfully done. The video, itself, *is* the ad. Fact is, many social media ads go viral simply because they're so outrageous. People pass them along partly because they're entertaining. Which doesn't mean they don't also sell. But the unique aspect of social media is that it makes sharing easy: you simply click.

But why do we share? According to a study by the *New York Times*, there are five primary motivations:[1]

1. **94 percent share** to help improve the lives of others.

2. **84 percent share** to spread the word about something we believe in.

3. **81 percent share** because we like the feeling of having others comment on it and engage.

4. **80 percent share** to grow and nourish our relationships, and . . .

5. **68 percent share** because we identify with the content (or we wish to) and use it to promote (or help establish) this identity.

What kinds of articles get the most views and shares? Authors Jonah Berger and Katherine Milkman decided to find out. They pored over 7,000 articles published by the *New York Times* and crunched the numbers.[2] According to their research, the more that the content evoked high-arousal emotions such as anger, fear, anxiety, awe, wonder, humor, or sadness, the better its chances of being shared and going viral.

The major takeaway? *Emotions!* Interestingly enough, emotions are also what compel us to buy. (And then we justify the purchase with "adult reasoning," so we feel as if we made a good decision.) So, we *buy* with emotions, and we *share* because of emotions.

Back to the freaky unicorn. The likes, shares, and clicks on this ad were driven by a veritable smorgasbord of *high-arousal emotions*. It's outrageous, funny, embarrassing, and intriguing all at the same time. This is the engine driving its popularity and sharing. The engine propelling its healthy sales is a solid foundation of clear benefits supported by "scientific" facts, all addressed by the video script and graphics.

QUESTION: Which of these elements does your current ad contain? Does it evoke high-arousal emotions that encourage interaction? Start with your headline. How do the words you've written make you *feel*? Not *think*, but *feel!* If you've written a good ad and you want it to go viral, you need to get your readers to *feel* something. So, does your current ad elicit a bland, *"Er, okay, another sales message"* response, or an *"OMG! That's amazing/crazy/fantastic/scary/happy/sad/horrifying!"* response? There's a massive difference. The first ad might interest prospects to read more if it's well constructed. The second ad might cause the same response . . . and *also* compel them to *share* this emotion-generating ad with others so that their friends, family, and coworkers can also enjoy the dopamine-producing jolt of emotions that they experienced themselves.

"But, Drew! My product isn't as dramatic as the Squatty Potty! What could I possibly do?" You need to get a little creative to stir up emotions. Here are four examples:

Do you design websites?

✖ **DON'T SAY:** *"We Design Custom Websites for Startups & Enterprises"*

✔ **DO SAY:** *"I'll Turn Your Dog-Ugly Website into a Powerful Sales Magnet in Just 24 Hours for Just $495!"*

Do you sell homemade chocolate biscotti?

✖ **DON'T SAY:** *"To Dunk or Not to Dunk, Our Fresh Biscotti Make Coffee Great!"*

✔ **DO SAY:** *"DUNK . . . CRUNCH . . . MMMM! Watch Us Pour Melted Chocolate over Our Homemade Biscotti & Ship to You Overnight!"*

Do you run a mobile dog-grooming service in your city?

✖ **DON'T SAY:** *"Vet Valley Mobile Pet Grooming Offers a Full Array of Services"*

✔ **DO SAY:** *"STOP! Don't Let Your Dog Groomer Use the Deadly Groomer's Noose on Your Beloved Pet! Here's Why . . . "*

Do you sell plants and seeds for gardeners?

✖ **DON'T SAY:** *"Get Ready for Spring Planting . . . We Have It All!"*

✓ **DO SAY:** *"WOW! My Wife & I Were Blown Away by How Many Giant Tomatoes & Cucumbers We Picked Using These Crazy New Seeds . . . "*

To be clear, a powerfully effective ad doesn't have to contain high-arousal emotions to make the cash register ring. You could follow the old tried-and-true AIDPA (Attention, Interest, Desire, Persuasion, Action) formula and rake in the profits. But when you're advertising on social media, it only makes sense to take advantage of the massive additional free exposure from all the interaction you can stir up. Heck, I'd be telling you the same thing if this could be done with print ads. But few people share newspaper and magazine ads. Few people pass around the direct-response paper letters that arrive in their mailboxes. There's no Click-to-Share option there.

So, while you're always looking to create using the classic ad-copy formulas and principles I teach in the original *Cashvertising* (*because that's how you create good ads for any medium*), you want to go *heavy on emotion* on social media. You want to make your ads more human and personal. Use more pronouns, exclamations, and emotion-generating words and phrases. Instead of writing your ads from your company's perspective, try using a spokesperson (or put yourself in the ad if you're a solo entrepreneur) and writing the ad as if it's that person speaking it . . . and show that person in your ad. Here are three more examples:

✖ **DON'T SAY:** *"We Need People to Feed Our Horses"*

✓ **DO SAY:** *"HELP! My Horse Farm Needs Helpers! Will You Help Feed Our Sweet (and Hungry) Little Ponies?"*

✖ **DON'T SAY:** *"These Attorneys Will Help Protect Your Rights"*

✓ **DO SAY:** *"My Team of Tough-as-Nails Lawyers Will Fight for You in Court"*

✖ **DON'T SAY:** *"Visit the Best Little Cozy Café in San Diego"*

✓ **DO SAY:** *"CRUNCH . . . SIP . . . CHILL! Enjoy Fresh-Baked Biscotti . . . Artisan-Roasted Coffees and B-I-G Fluffy Chairs at JavaFlow Café . . . "*

Speaking of "making it look more personal," I've seen advertisers make their ads look less commercial by intentionally using poor grammar or the wrong word choice. Seems counterintuitive, right? Why would a company want to define itself as being one that corrupts the English language? Could the trade-off somehow be worth it? The Squatty Potty people surely knew it wasn't entirely correct to say, *"This Unicorn Change the Way I Poop,"* yet they let the ad run on and on. *Why?* Because it worked. Did they test a grammatically correct version? Who knows. But the video production and copywriting are so slick it's inconceivable that they accidentally used poor English in the ad itself. Believe me, it was proofed multiple times and they let it ride.

We're getting into minor details that, like a single brick in a giant wall, are just one part of a larger construction project. My hypothesis is that such intentional errors convey less polish than would be expected from a big successful company. And before you say, *"But, Drew, it's not the silly grammar mistake that made that ad so successful; it's everything else: the concept, the product, the video, etc.!"* Of course. An ad's success is usually an amalgam of many factors: prospect targeting, headline, offer, body copy, overall positioning, credibility/proof, call to action, price, and other factors. Everything we discuss in this book is just one part of the recipe. You wouldn't put birthday candles into a pile of baking soda. Not any one element is the entire cake.

Back to making it sound more human . . . like it was created by a person versus a boilerplate-generating AI copywriting app. As a quick test right here, which of the following sounds more personal versus corporate?

BEFORE:

"Our Highly Trained Cleaners Make Your House Sparkle for Less"

AFTER:

"Look How I Clean Your Nice House Until It Sparkle Like Sunshine . . . Cheeep!"

———————

BEFORE:

"Our Dog Trainers Are Ready to Give Your Dog the Discipline It Needs"

AFTER:

"HELLO! I'm Joe . . . a Local Dog Expert. I Train Even CRAZY Dogs 5 Days or Less"

———————

BEFORE:

"Need Slick, Smooth Hair? Our Keratin Treatments Work Like Magic"

AFTER:

"YEAH, BABY! Look How SMOOOTHY My Keratin Treatments Make Your Frizzy Hair Look Like Shiny Glass!"

Social media is all about relationships—friends, family, coworkers— and creating new connections with people yet unknown. That's why it's effective to use down-to-earth language, like the "you and me" approach, like a "real person," not a cold faceless corporation. The effect is a closer personal connection. A greater sense of credibility. Of course, you wouldn't use the misspelling/casual language ploy if you're a financial services company, business consultant, or other category that needs to maintain a more distinguished, refined persona.

AD #2: PERFECT SALAD & FRUIT CUTTER
Stats: 80 Million Views • 754,000 Shares • 151,000 Comments
(See it at: *DrewEricWhitman.com/Cashvertising2/Ads*)

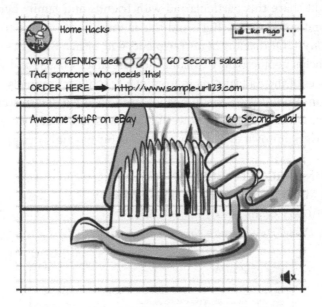

You wouldn't think people would go so crazy about a plastic device that holds vegetables while you cut them, would you? The copy is simple: *"What a GENIUS Idea.* [VEGGIE & FRUIT EMOJIS]. *60 Second salad. Tag someone who needs this! ORDER HERE ➡ URL."*

Simple copy, right? So why was it so popular? **Answer:** Because it was new, unique, and unusual—three big ingredients for social media ad success. And the *video demonstration* brought those elements together beautifully.

It follows the typical late-night infomercial problem-solution formula. A harried-looking, grimacing woman (produced in black and white, of course) struggling to make a salad. Tense music. She's annoyed by having to peel, chop, and slice. Suddenly, the music changes to happy, the video goes full-color, and the product (solution) is introduced. (Did you catch the before and after?) It's a formula that has worked since the advent of advertising. The woman puts all those previously annoying veggies into the contraption, slides the knife through the multiple plastic dividers, and, hallelujah, her salad is magically ready for eating. (How did Edison possibly overlook such a life-changing wonder?)

The positioning is simple but smart: it's not simply a plastic thing that helps with salad prep. It's *"The 60-Second Salad Maker."* (Note how my use of Initial **C**aps somehow makes the term look more official and substantive.) In just one quick tagline, it gives a context in which to mentally hold the product. It's also *specific*.

I might share this particular ad with friends and family because it's unique and entertaining. But—and this is important—it doesn't mean I want to *buy* it. Or that any of my recipients will, either. But that's okay. My sharing helps geometrically expand the advertiser's reach and increases the chances of their ad landing in front of a *real* buyer's eyeballs.

Bottom line: If your product lends itself to video demonstration, do it. It's your number-one most powerful sales weapon. When we see things working with our own eyes, many of our doubts instantly disappear.

AD #3: UNDERCOVER BED FAN
Stats: 61 Million Views • One Million+ Shares
        200,000 Comments • 152,000 Likes
(See it at: *DrewEricWhitman.com/Cashvertising2/Ads*)

Here's another unusual product: a fan that blows air under your bed sheets to keep you cool. Secondary benefit: it helps lower your air conditioning bills. Copy: "*Tag someone who won't let you turn on the A/C during summer.* [CRYING EMOJIS]" Copy under the video: "*I MUST HAVE THIS BED FAN FOR HOT SUMMER NIGHTS.*"

With 61 million views and over 1 million shares, it was a viral superpower. Like the salad chopper, it's a new and unusual product—a big part of its appeal. We humans are neophiliacs—we like new things. *But why?* Studies have shown that the brain's reaction to novelty results in an increase of dopamine, the feel-good chemical that affects mood and feelings of reward and motivation. This drives us to seek similar experiences to get another dopamine shot. That *"Ooooo, so cool!"* is a response produced by *chemistry*. It feels good. And we want more. We advertisers are literally playing with people's brain chemistry. If your product isn't new and doesn't have a novelty appeal, then you need to get creative . . . develop a hook, a "fascination" that captures people's attention.

This bed fan ad is powered by demonstration. You see someone put it next to the bed and then point the fan's thin curved opening under the sheets. She switches it on, and you see the sheets rise up and get puffy. You witness the air flowing with your own eyes. You can imagine the cooling effect!

A professional salesperson knows the power of demonstration. It's **V-A-K-O-G** proof: *Visual* (you SEE it working), *Auditory* (you HEAR it), *Kinesthetic* (You FEEL it), *Olfactory* (You SMELL it), and *Gustatory* (you TASTE it).

Go to Costco (weekends are best) and you'll often see professional demonstrators showing off products of all kinds. Cooking demonstrations, food and drink sampling, vacuum testing, and more. They'll be demonstrating Vitamix blenders and handing out smoothies. They'll be demonstrating nonstick cookware. Companies hire people specifically to put on demos. Still other companies train people to hire out to companies to demo their products. *Why?* Because it works! Take infomercials, for example. What are they loaded with? *Demonstrations.* Demonstrations sell because they're real life. They plainly say to anyone watching, "*This really works. And I'm going to show it to you in front of your own eyes.*"

Can *your* product be demonstrated? You don't need an incredible, expensive production. It can be very simple. Just show the product in use. Show it doing the thing(s) you claim it does. Show others using it, too. And show their reactions. This meta-perspective is a powerful form of both social proof and the *Bandwagon Effect* rolled into one.

Even with its success, the text could still be improved. *"Tag someone who won't let you turn on the AC in summer"* requires me to figure out what they're talking about. It doesn't instantly communicate. What's the product? Sure, we see a bed and some unknown contraption in the video still, but the question remains: *what is this thing?* If it's a bed-cooling fan, then why not *say it? There's no risk in telling people what you're selling . . .* there's only an *upside.* The upside? That people will know what you're selling. <INSERT EYEROLL>

Remember, the vast majority of readers—83 percent according to the great David Ogilvy—read headlines and no more.[3] Therefore, a big chunk of people will read this text, not understand it, and move on. (Even if they were ideal prospects.)

AD #4: ZUNGLE SPEAKER-SUNGLASSES
Stats: 135 Million Views • 491,000 Shares
389,000 Likes • 241 Million Comments
(See it at: *DrewEricWhitman.com/Cashvertising2/Ads*)

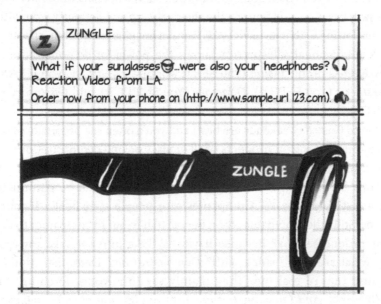

Want to really capitalize on the power of social proof? Create a reaction video like the one featured in this *Zungle* ad that asks in its copy, *"What if your sunglasses* [SUNGLASSES EMOJI] *were also your headphones?*

[HEADPHONE EMOJI] *Reaction video from LA. Order now from your phone on [URL].* [FISTBUMP EMOJI]"

Because the sunglasses deliver sound via bone conduction, which transmits sound waves through the bones in the wearer's skull rather than their ear canals, reactions among young random users on the street range from *"Wow, I need these"* to *"Oh my God, these are so cool"* to asking others standing right next to them, *"You can't hear it? No way!"* with bleeped-out expletives from the enthused.

The reaction portion of the fast-paced 2:50-minute-long video ends with multiple users asking, *"What's the brand? What's it called?"* when the video neatly segues into a beauty shot of the glasses at 0:34, with a male voice talent confidently answering, *"This is Zungle."* The video continues with tightly edited slice-of-life scenes following a young man bicycling to his girlfriend's house, wearing the glasses, and listening to "Just Want to Love You" by Analog Champion as he wends his way through traffic and graffiti-adorned city streets.

A reaction video is essentially a testimonial that features *multiple examples of first usage.* Very clever. Because just prior to pulling out their credit card, buyers conduct a little self-talk. *"Is this any good? Will I like it? Does it really work?"* Reactions captured at the first use of a product give *your* prospects examples of how *they too* might respond when *they* try it for the first time. See the power? And the essential element—aside from using real people on the street versus actors—is strong emotion. These people are enthralled with the product, and their surprise/excitement shows. It's contagious.

Now back to *you.* Have you ever thought about creating a reaction video for your product? Can you have people interacting with your product or service for the first time? But not just two or three, but seven, ten, or more quick clips—each mere seconds—compressed into a very small, tightly edited video like this one for Zungle. Then pour on the benefits and features and show them in use. How would you improve the ad itself? Instead of the minimalistic side-view photo of the glasses, I'd show an image that gives more story. Perhaps an attractive male or female face, perhaps both, each wearing the glasses and looking as happily surprised as were the people in the reaction videos. Perhaps one covering his or her mouth in shock and excitement. That conveys far more and also gets a human face in the ad—the most eye-catching image of all.

AD #5: KABOOST

Stats: 44 Million Views • 752,000 Shares
32,000 Comments • 232,000 Likes
(See it at: *DrewEricWhitman.com/Cashvertising2/Ads*)

Here's another interesting product that easily lends itself to demonstration. KABOOST is a portable chair booster that raises the height of a chair; you use it by spreading open its arms and snapping it under the chair's four legs.

The ad copy is clean, simple, and direct to the point. It immediately says what it is. There's no question, nothing to figure out, unlike the Undercover Bed Fan that said only, *"Tag to someone who won't let you turn down the air conditioner."* Instead, this KABOOST ad says the product's name, it tells what it does, and it also expresses its benefit in only nine words: *"so little kids can sit just like big kids."* No doubt the product's eye-appealing design helped the ad become a viral success. The video script, too, is clean and direct. When the product is good, there's no need for overkill hype. A straightforward expression of what it is and what it does usually suffices. On social media, ads with products that generate *"Wow, cool!"* responses have one of the most important catalysts for virality.

AD #6: PANCAKE FLIPPER

Stats: 40 Million Views • 309,000 Shares
127,000 Comments • 827,000 Likes
(See it at: *DrewEricWhitman.com/Cashvertising2/Ads*)

"Do you like pancake?" [sic] Look how this emoji-sprinkled text immediately selects its target audience with *Life-Force 2: Enjoyment of Food and Beverages.* Visually, the strange red object being held above a frying pan grabs your eyeballs. **QUESTION:** Who do you think is most likely to click and watch the video? Obviously, someone who likes pancakes or has a general interest in eating and kitchen tools, right? Likewise, how about the headline *"Love Chocolate?"* Who's most likely to read that? Or *"Attention Dog Lovers!"* Or *"Attention Soccer Fans!"* Or *"Do You Hate Spiders?"* It's called *instantly selecting your target market.* Not clever. Not difficult. But extremely effective.

The ad continues with *"Never been easier to make it!!"* Anytime you can work the idea of simplicity and ease into your advertising, *do it.* Everybody wants to simplify their life. (Don't you?) Recall that *Convenience* is number five on the *Nine Secondary Wants.* We hate waiting. We want results fast. Example:

> ✖ **WRONG WAY:** *"Teach Your Kids Not to Fight—100% Guaranteed to Work."*

> ✔ **RIGHT WAY:** *"Presenting the Fastest & Easiest Way to Teach Your Kids to Stop Fighting—100% Guaranteed to Work in 23 Days or Less or Your Money Back."*

Same product, same guarantee, but which is more appealing? It's obvious.

This pancake flipper ad also features a 50 percent discount and, like many other successful Facebook ads, instructs readers to *"Tag & Share with your Friends & Family."* Click the video, and in two seconds you see exactly how it works. Showing multiple uses builds value. The ad is shared because the video is interesting, fascinating, and intriguing, not necessarily because the person thinks, *"This is the world's greatest way to make pancakes."*

To maximize your shares—after making sure your copy contains a strong selling message—inject your video with entertainment and/or informational value. Your product doesn't need to be an exciting new invention to do this. Let's say you happen to sell a self-defense course. Those have been around forever, right? So what can you do differently? How about a video that shows ten techniques to teach your child to escape from kidnappers? *BOOM!* That's going to be shared like crazy. How about seven proven techniques for escaping an assailant with a dramatic video still of a man or a woman escaping from the clutches of a big, ugly thug? High drama = high emotion, which—as you recall—is one key to social media post effectiveness. Drama gets engagement: views, clicks, shares, likes, comments. People love drama . . . and conflict. Think hard on this one. Just one powerfully dramatic video could skyrocket your ad circulation and, therefore, your product sales.

There are many more examples of fantastically successful Facebook ads, but alas, I have limited space in which to describe them here in this book. Please visit *DrewEricWhitman.com/Cashvertising2/Ads*, where I show live links to the ads I've described in this chapter. There you can watch the videos and see how truly successful ads are constructed. Plus, I'll continue to add content to that page to keep this chapter going in perpetuity!

CHAPTER 5

Online Ad-Agency Secrets:
Twenty-Seven Proven Techniques for Creating Psychologically Powerful Online Ads, Emails, and Web Pages That Sell Like Crazy

ONLINE AD-AGENCY SECRET #1:

The Psychology of Peer Recommendation

FACT: Buying is scary. You're asking people to trade the result of hours of their sweat for your stuff. Not just that, but chances are your stuff isn't as important as much of the other stuff they need to buy . . . like shelter, food, clothing, and medicine. Where does your stuff fall on that scale of importance? For most of us, it's nowhere close.

Now consider that according to the Federal Reserve's 2019 Survey of Consumer Finances, the average U.S. consumer has a median account balance of only $5,300.[1]

And—*Ouch!*—according to *Bankrate*, fewer than half of U.S. households could readily handle an unexpected cost of just $1,000 for a medical expense, car breakdown, or house repair.[2]

Then there are everyday living expenses: the mortgage; car loan; gas, auto repairs, and maintenance; groceries; upkeep on the house; clothing; health insurance; and a multitude of other financial stressors. And, oh, the average credit card debt in the United States is $5,221, with its associated interest gnawing away at what little money they have left over to spend—none of it tax deductible anymore—thanks to Congress passing the Tax Reform Act in 1986.[3]

Then there's you and me asking consumers for their money to buy our stuff. And, oh, don't forget the many times they've been ripped off before. (Many "thanks" to those previous scammers who are making our job more difficult.)

Sigh. No wonder people don't just throw their money at every ad they see. You've got to be *very* convincing, tap into what they consider to be a real need (or desire), and make them comfortable enough to pull out their credit card or click your *BUY NOW* button.

Assuming you've piqued their interest with a good offer for a product that's priced right (and they can afford it), and you've made ordering it easy, the biggest hurdle you face is convincing them that 1) your claims are factual, and 2) your company will fulfill their order and stand behind the sale with customer service should your product flop.

What to do? You convince in the best way possible: *using positive reviews from others who have "taken the risk and gone first."* It's like the line of cars at the red light that never changes. Everyone is afraid to be the first to drive, but everybody knows the light is obviously broken and isn't going to turn green. Their minds are like your prospects' minds. Their brains are jammed full of scary *what if* thoughts.

Fact is, *those drivers—like your prospects—simply want someone to go first.* (Anyone but themselves.) And what happens when one brave soul drives ahead? All the rest of them follow! *Why?* Because they saw that Mr. Brave did so and was okay. He didn't get into an accident, get arrested, or die. His action furnished social proof that it was actually okay to drive ahead. And so, with reduced stress and new confidence, they *all* follow, happily relieved.

I'm Not Jumping First . . . YOU Jump First!

Years ago—participating in a "face your fears" ropes course—I stood on the top of a sheer cliff in Santa Rosa, California. Affixed to the edge of the cliff was a wooden board. Nailed to the far end of that board—even closer to what looked like an endless drop over a canyon filled with tall pines—was an even narrower wooden board. At the end of that skinny little board was a sloppily painted red letter X. I would soon be instructed to "walk the plank" and stand on that red X after being hooked up to the longest zipline

I'd ever seen in my life. So long, in fact, that the assistant on the ground on the other end of the line was literally not visible to the naked eye.

Fortunately, I watched about a dozen other participants go before me, all screaming at the top of their lungs as they flew across the canyon at ridiculous speeds—hundreds of feet above the treeline—each disappearing into a vanishing point somewhere on the ground on the other side.

Long story short: I did it. But—and here's the question for you—if *you* were in my shoes and you didn't see anyone go before you, assuming you were 1) either the only one there doing it or 2) the first person in line, how much less likely would you be to grab that T-bar and leap off that skinny board?

Do you think these two scenarios are much different from what produces the maelstrom of thoughts and fears that go through your prospects' heads before clicking your *BUY NOW* button? It's not. Because the bottom line in both situations is *fear*. No matter what kind of fear, it paralyzes your prospects and makes them do one thing: not act. And not acting spells the death of even the most skillfully created promotions.

> *Fear defeats more people*
> *than any other one thing in the world.*
> —RALPH WALDO EMERSON

Researchers found that 92 percent of people will trust a recommendation from a peer, and 70 percent will trust a recommendation from a complete stranger.[4] And that's why reviews and testimonials work so well. And case studies. And user metrics. And comparison charts. All your ads should contain them. The big question is, *do they?*

My consulting clients tell me they understand the importance of social proof, yet they don't all use it. That's like asking your potential buyers to be the first to jump off the cliff. (What could go wrong?) Always include your strongest reviews and quotes to quell the fear and stimulate action. Include full names, their city, and state (and country when it's an international client). Video reviews are best, of course, and should be part of your full pitch on your website after they click your ad for more info.

Do you have a healthy following on social media? Drop some numbers! *"Over 145,000 Followers and Growing!"* Even if you haven't made your first sale, just boasting about your popularity lends credibility to your claims because it connotes acceptance. It suggests that *other people are okay with you.* It often takes less than you think to move lookers to buyers. It's like a big apothecary scale, with *Skepticism* on the left side and *Desire to Believe* on the right. You often need to press down on that right side just enough to overcome the skepticism. *How?* Do the following:

1. **Tell them what the experts think.** Because experts see your product through the eyes of knowledgeable discernment, buyers hold their opinions in high regard. They figure, *"Hey, the experts know what they're talking about. If they like it, it's gotta be good."*

2. **Tell them what your buyers think.** Buyers already took that "dangerous" step and actually experienced the buying, receiving, and using-the-product process.

3. **Tell them what influencers think.** Influencers, or people and celebrities with a massive following, are put on a pedestal for their opinions for reasons I'll never know. Many aren't any more insightful or intelligent than the average Joe or Jill, but, *"Oh, if the Kardashians love it, it must be great!"* Sigh. In any event, see **Online Ad-Agency Secret #4: How to Persuade Online Influencers to Respond** for samples of emails you can send to increase your chances of getting them to help promote your product.

4. **Tell them what the press thinks.** *"If the press reports it, it must be true."* (Not!) But this is what many people think. What's newsworthy about your product or service? You can usually tease out something that the press will bite on! They're constantly looking for things to report about. One great idea to create "news" is to take a survey—or look for existing research and stats—relevant to what you're selling.

   For example: Let's say you're dropshipping inexpensive digital cameras for parents to buy for their kids (because they don't want their kids smashing their expensive cell phones or using them as a hammer to open walnuts). Here's a great stat I found in about twenty seconds on Google: *"5.3 billion cellphones to become waste in 2022."*[5] Whoa, that's a lot of dead phones! How about broken screens? Fixing a broken iPhone screen costs between $130 and $300; for Androids, it's between $80 and $480. Shocking numbers like this would make a great headline for your press release, teamed with information about how parents of young kids are giving their budding photographers the low-cost *Kidd-Cam* (or whatever you name it) as a smart alternative for their creative toddlers.

After getting into all the stats and facts about breakage, you gently mention, *"One smart alternative parents are choosing is to give kids their own low-cost digital cameras, such as the virtually indestructible KiddCam from [Your Company Name]. For just $29.95, young shooters can take up to 1,000 beautiful color photos. . . ."* You get the idea. You can make news for just about any product or service.

Do you sell coffee beans online? How about a press release that "exposes" the crazy profits on a simple cup of coffee sold at fancy coffee shops—coffee that's often no better than what's available on supermarket shelves? In fact, that $4.00 coffee might cost you only 25 cents at home. According to workplace psychologist Bill Dyment, quoted in *Forbes,* *"A savings calculator will tell you that such a once-a-day habit adds up to $133,000 over thirty years if the same amount was invested instead at a modest interest rate. That's twenty-five safaris or nice trips to Europe, a very nice car, or addition to one's retirement."*[6] Think you could start a press release with shocking stats like those?

Do you sell premium cotton baby diapers? According to The American Academy of Pediatrics: *"Families spend close to $936 on disposable diapers in the first year alone . . . that's 6,000 diapers to buy over the first two years. 92% of them will get buried in landfills. Disposable diapers take over five hundred years to decompose. Cotton diapers can be reused around 50 to 200 times."*[7]

Do you think you could create an eye-grabbing press release from these stats? You bet you can, and you'd get lots of free advertising as a result.

The simple formula is: 1) Craft a powerful newsy headline, 2) write a strong introductory paragraph that plays off the headline, 3) develop the problem, 4) introduce a solution, and 5) mention your product in a (totally) non-salesy fashion as one possible solution that "some have found useful."

5. **Tell them how many shares and likes you have.** This approach capitalizes on the Bandwagon Effect, which takes advantage of the fact that we humans are social beings and we all want to belong. While we're talking about the Bandwagon Effect, let's quickly review the three types of groups you can leverage:

  ▷ **Aspirational**—groups to which you'd *like* to belong

  ▷ **Associative**—groups that *share* your ideals and values

  ▷ **Dissociative**—groups to which you *do not want* to belong

By linking products and services to any of these three reference groups, you can persuade buyers to make decisions based solely on the group they identify with or want to identify with by persuading them to forgo an active, deep analysis of what you're selling.

Here's the mindset: *"Hey, if all these other people like this company, there must be something good about it!"* This is why people are more likely to buy after seeing reviews by people they know nothing about. On the one hand, it's great to hear what others think, right? On the other hand, who knows if those people have the same standards? The 100 people who love Joe's SnakePit Pizza might have never had anything better than a frozen pie from Walmart. Still, the psychology works. Don't be studying the roots while your competitors are picking the fruit. Don't be shy. Brag about your popularity and take advantage of a time-tested principle.

What Social Proof Is Most Believed?

Okay, we know it works. But which *type* of social proof works best? Let's look at some stats, and there's a slew of them:

▸ **88 percent of consumers** trust user reviews as much as personal recommendations.

▸ **The average consumer reads** ten online reviews before deciding to buy.

▸ **57 percent of consumers** will buy only if the product or service has at least a four-star rating. (**TIP:** If you collect reviews on your site, even if you've received only ten reviews, if the average review is four stars, be sure to highlight that fact, e.g., *"100% Average 4-Star Reviews!"*)

- **Only 13 percent of consumers** said they would do business with a company rated two or fewer stars.

- **80 percent of consumers** say what they trust most are ratings that have four, four and a half, and five stars.[8]

> *Good advertising does not just circulate information.*
> *It penetrates the public mind with desires and belief.*
>
> – LEO BURNETT

According to the good folks at Brightlocal, consumers are more actively reading reviews than ever before to find local products and services. For example, in 2021, 77 percent said they "always" or "regularly" read reviews when browsing for local businesses. That's up from 60 percent just the year before. In addition:

- **67 percent will consider leaving a review** for a positive experience, while 40 percent will consider leaving a review for a negative experience. Make sure to placate your disgruntled buyers. Each could post multiple negative reviews and cost you thousands in lost sales—far more than you providing a cheerful refund. It's not worth letting an unhappy customer stay unhappy.

- **89 percent of consumers are "highly" or "fairly" likely** to use a business that responds to all of its online reviews. It's nice to know that the business actually cares enough to reply to both the positive and negative reviews. Most that I've seen don't. This behavior unconsciously communicates, *"Yeah, whatever. We don't value what you said enough to spend thirty seconds to reply."*

- **57 percent say they would be "not very" or "not at all" likely** to use a business that doesn't respond to reviews at all. Especially the negative ones. Nothing says, *"I don't give a damn what you think"* more than flat-out ignoring the people who 1) gave you their money and 2) could possibly give you their money again.

- **Make it your policy to reply to all reviews.** I often see complaints that are pretty disparaging, but after reading the owner's or manager's reply, I'm usually open to still giving them my business. Let's say you own a Mexican restaurant and someone writes, *"Ugh! Your*

*guacamole is nauseating! It tastes like it was made from mummi-
fied avocados pulled out of King Tutankhamun's tomb! If I wanted
a lesson in ancient history, I'd go to a museum. Never again!"* You'd
probably be left with negative feelings about the guac unless others
left comments praising it.[9]

✓ **DO THIS:** Always, always, always respond—even if you write only
one single sentence. In the preceding scenario, if the owner/man-
ager/kitchen manager took three minutes to craft a sincere reply like
the following, he'd probably see that same customer again within
a week or two (rather than, uh, *never*): *"Thanks so much for your
heartfelt comment about our guacamole. As the kitchen manager, I
extend my personal apologies to you! This is definitely not the quality
of food that we strive to serve to our valuable patrons, so I'm so glad
you brought it to my attention. I personally inspect every shipment
of avocados we receive (and we go through thousands of them every
month), but apparently some overly ripe ones were missed. Please
accept personal apologies and accept my invitation for you and a
guest to enjoy your next dinner with my compliments."*

Ahhh, now *that's* customer service. And it does a lot more than just
make this customer happy again. It serves to show potential new customers that this place really cares about customer satisfaction and
that its manager won't hesitate to make things right. Don't you see?
The response is actually an ad! Nobody else sees it this way, but that's
exactly what it is. It's goodwill at work. Now contrast that to the business owner or manager who either replies with a nasty comment like,
*"You're the first person who ever complained about our guac. We serve
dozens of orders of it every day, and nobody else ever does anything but
rave about it. Are you sure you visited this restaurant?"*

And before you say, *"Drew, that's not realistic!"* I assure you it's 100 percent true. And it's not the first time I saw a response by management
accusing the customer of not knowing where he or she was. Fact is,
it happened to *me* . . . in response to my own complaint. Many business owners and managers view negative feedback as an attack on their
egos. Instead, they should look at it as *free consumer research* that helps
them tweak their operation to help them become more profitable.

▶ **81 percent of consumers** use Google to check out a business
before buying. That's up from 63 percent in 2020. Long ago

buyers relied on word of mouth alone. Old-timers would say things like, *"If you're gonna stay in business in this town, son, you better do right by the public!"* Word of mouth traveled, but not as fast. Today we have computers and phones and internet connections. In seconds we see what others say, and we compare what other companies offer.

✓ **ALWAYS DO THIS:** Always provide enough social proof in your advertising so you don't unintentionally drive people elsewhere looking for it because you didn't provide it . . . or enough of it. When you show your reviews and quotes and videos and photos and charts and seals of approval, you're staying in control of what your prospects see. When they leave your site, email, or ad and go looking for it, who knows what they'll find? Actually, I'll tell you *exactly* what they'll find. They'll find the social proof that your competitors decided to post on *their* sites, emails, and ads . . . and possibly beat you to the sale. (And *you* gave them the impetus to do it.)

▸ **62 percent believe they've seen a fake review** for a local business in the past year. Consumers say the leading sources of fake reviews are 1) Amazon, 2) Google, and 3) Facebook. In fact, a whopping 93 percent of consumers say they're suspicious of the reviews they see on Facebook. *Meaning?* Make sure the reviews you post are credible. *"OMG! This changed my life—you gotta try it!"* isn't as credible as *"Yes, it's a really good product. I've used 4 others and this gave the best results by far."* It's not as flashy, but it's far more believable.

Hype doesn't work in social proof because people are already suspicious and on edge about spending their money. You don't want to aggressively *force* them over the edge of hesitation. You want to gently *guide* them. It's like pushing a scared kid to get on the roller coaster. The more you push him to get in line, the more he'll resist.

Unless they're the kind that subscribes to the "feel the fear, but act anyway" style of confronting challenges, you'll need to ease prospects through the process. In the roller coaster example, you might show your kid the heavy-duty safety bar and seat belt, say how long the ride has been running and explain its awesome safety record, say many people ride every year and rate it as one of the best coasters in the United States, and let him see scores of little kids—the same age—exiting the ride with giant smiles. These things might or might not get your kid to change his mind about riding, but it's far more likely than grabbing him by the arm and trying to throw him in the car.

Listen: When people don't buy something that they think would be beneficial, it's because of just one thing: **FEAR**. *Fear* of being ripped off. *Fear* of it not working as well as expected. *Fear* of it not working at all. *Fear* of it taking too long to arrive. *Fear* of it not arriving at all. *Fear* of spending money. *Fear* of overpaying. *Fear* of making a bad decision. *Fear* of looking stupid for buying it. *Fear* of not being able to get sufficient help from customer service. *Fear* of not being able to get any post-purchase support at all. *Fear* of not being able to exchange it. *Fear* of not being able to return it for a refund.

What we call "social proof" is nothing more than a way to tell people that others took the same risk and "it turned out well for them." *That's its sole function.* Consider it a "bandwagon of consumer security." So, if others have indeed "survived" after buying your product or service . . . and enjoyed the experience and end result . . . *play it up big!* It's the most powerful weapon in your advertising arsenal for weakening the defensive shell that buyers erect before spending money.

> ✖ **NEVER DO THIS:** Don't relegate your social proof to a separate page. That just decreases the chances that anyone will ever see them. Imagine having a slew of great reviews from thrilled customers that don't get read before most prospects click away.
>
> Don't say, *"Okay, I'll create a tab for just the testimonials and keep the site nice and clean. That way, if people want to read reviews, they can just click that tab."* [Insert eyeroll here.]
>
> It's fine to have a separate page, but be sure to also feature a few of your strongest reviews on your main selling page, too. You want them there to bolster your pitch, not just to give people something extra to read "if they want to."
>
> **Remember:** You can't ever have too much social proof. Load it on thick and take advantage of the *Length Equals Strength* heuristic, which conveys the message, *"If there's a lot of it, there must be something to it!"*

In fact, I recall a sales pitch for a tear gas personal-defense product years ago called "Paralyzer." This was not your typical red-pepper spray. No. This stuff was CS military tear gas—affectionately known as orthochlorobenzalmalononitrile—a wickedly potent chemical developed by the U.S. Army for riot control and combat training.

The dealer information package contained about thirty photocopied pages of letters from both satisfied customers (who used it to defend themselves against attackers) and happy dealers (who were selling it like hotcakes). Even graphic descriptions by those who "tested it" and described the resulting pain: *"It's like having hot acid thrown in your face and having the dead skin scraped off with dull razor blades."*

Most reviews were in the buyers' own handwriting or were typed on the dealer's stationery. (Extremely credible!) Page after page of complimentary comments and reviews of the product's efficacy.

Whew! By the time you were done reading, you were flat-out convinced. Such quantity starts you thinking, *"How could all of these credible-looking reviews be wrong?"* The end result? You unwittingly develop a chink in your *"I don't want to get ripped off"* armor, you think less about getting scammed, and you start enjoying more thoughts of the product actually delivering the benefits you're craving. It worked. And now the **DESIRE** for the benefits outweighs the **FEAR** of getting scammed. You're moments away from clicking that *BUY NOW* button.

> ✓ **DO THIS:** Begin an intentional campaign of relieving your buyers' fears when engaging with your company. Really think of it this way. *"My buyers are afraid. I'm going to reduce their fear and make them more comfortable with the process."* This mindset changes the typical, robotic, *"Gotta add some quotes"* ad-development process and makes you more aware of what your prospects are dealing with when considering spending money. And reinforce that social proof and resulting increased comfort with the longest, strongest guarantee you can muster. It's the final line of defense—the last perceived element of security—that helps push the still-timid prospect to take that leap that spells $$$ in your pocket.

The Psychology of Online Color

Would you be surprised to learn that about 3,800 colors are possible on any website you visit? *No?* Then how about 84,977? Still not impressed? Then I suppose I'll lay the *real* number on you: 16,777,216! Now *that's* impressive . . . in a crazy kind of way. Especially since the human eye is able to see "only" 7 million colors.[10]

Fact is, twenty-four bits are used to specify colors online, and that's the extent of the massive palette that you can choose from. Of course, this is insane, right? We simply don't need to get so nuanced when it comes to promotional color selection, especially since most people can't discern between a red hex #ed2b2b and e82323 or a yellow hex #f4fc05 and f3f70c. That's good because it makes our job much easier. All we have to do is focus on the colors with the most appeal:

RANKING	COLOR
1	Blue
2	Red
3	Green
4	Violet
5	Orange
6	Yellow

Color studies aren't new. Thousands of years ago, the ancient Egyptians studied the effects of different colors and how they affected people's mood and health. For example:

TO MAKE	THEY BLENDED	TO REPRESENT
Red	Oxidized iron and red ocher	Vitality, energy, fire, blood, and danger
Blue	Copper and iron oxide	Water, birth, life, and protection
Yellow	Ocher and oxides	Sun and eternity
Green	Malachite, a copper mineral	Growth
White	Gypsum with pulverized chalk	Purity and cleanliness
Black	Ground charcoal and carbon	Death and darkness and, contrastingly, also for life, birth, and resurrection

Amazingly, five thousand years later, we use these same colors to convey similar meanings. *Coincidence?* Or could it be that these colors *innately* convey these feelings and imagery? Who would argue that *red* suggests danger? *Blue*, coolness? *Yellow*, sunshine? *Green*, nature?

Fast-forward to today and you could spend years reading contemporary studies. Let's look at one in particular that explored the emotions produced by the primary colors used by today's web designers. The 2003 Hallock study asked people to choose the color they associated with high quality, high tech, reliability, trust, speed, cheapness, security, courage, fear, and fun.[11] Here are the results:

RESULTS OF THE HALLOCK COLOR STUDY

THE COLOR . . .	. . . PRODUCES EMOTIONS ASSOCIATED WITH
Blue	Trust, courage, security, and reliability
Yellow and Orange	Fun, cheapness
Red	Fear/terror, speed
Black	Fear/terror, high-tech, and quality

Choosing your promotional colors isn't just the fun part of the designing process (although it can also be painstaking and stressful), it's important in the whole string of psychologically influential decisions marketers make daily. We don't just say, *"Okay, the sales page is done. Hmmm, let's make it pretty with blue and some yellow. Splash in some green, and it's a wrap!"* Well, perhaps that's how some do it, but not those interested in tweaking every aspect of their promotions with influential appeal.

In 2006, Dr. Satyendra Singh, professor of marketing and international business at the University of Winnipeg, conducted research on the topic. His study, titled "Impact of Color on Marketing," explored consumers' relationships with certain colors.

The study noted that most people often *"make up their minds within 90 seconds of their initial interactions with either people or products."* Dr. Singh said that roughly 62–90 percent of this assessment is based solely on colors alone. Very interesting, considering all the time we spend crafting all the other aspects of our promotions. Singh's study also found that *"managers can use colors to increase or decrease appetite, enhance mood, calm down customers, and reduce perception of waiting time, among others."*

Great! All we need to do is pop in the "right" colors, and we'll get the response we want, right? Not so fast. Dr. Singh ultimately throws a big monkey wrench into the gears by dropping this technicolor bomb on our marketing heads: *"Color experiences vary from individual to individual . . . it is not possible to know how another person experiences color. One person's experience of a shade of red can be perceived differently from another person."*[12]

Yikes. Okay, maybe we need more research. If you have lots of time and patience, you might treat yourself to reading the study titled "The Interactive Effects of Colors and Products on Perceptions of Brand Logo Appropriateness" conducted by Bottomley and Doyle of the Cardiff Business School in the United Kingdom After we wade through its in-depth analysis, charts, and painstakingly detailed explanations specifically covering color research and its effects on consumer perception, it concludes with *"But, color is only one element of a brand's projection endowed with inherent meaning."*[13]

Even more studies? Okay. According to one, 84.7 percent of consumers state that color is the main reason that they buy specific products, whereas 80 percent think that color helps to increase overall brand recognition when contrasted to colorless images.[14]

In addition, 93 percent of consumers consider the visual appearance of the product and not just its potential capabilities or performance alone, while 6 percent consider the actual texture of the product. Just 1 percent will make their decision on the item's sound or smell.[15]

Let's clarify something here: *color is 100 percent personal.* You either like your new coworker's lime-green business suit, or you don't. It's not usually a case of being talked into liking a color. Your liking of it (or not) is innate. It's like food. You're not going to be talked into liking squid-ink pasta if you don't.

▸ It's not like making a claim for a product that could save your child's life in case of a fire. *Everyone* would want something to do this.

▸ It's also not like another product that claims to relieve you from the stabbing, above-the-eye headaches that are boring into your skull like an 8-amp Milwaukee hammer drill. *Everyone* with migraines would want to be free of this pain.

▸ It's also not like telling a pet owner that the competition's dog food contains melamine compounds and cyanuric acid that could start a bumper crop of cancer cells inside their beloved Fluffy.

Why are such things any different from color preferences? Because these are Life-Force 8 claims. We can't escape their influence. *But color?* Very different. Not life-changing. They're like parsley on the 1960s' dinner plate. It was there to make the whole thing more appealing. Fact is, if you promised to take your seven-year-old skiing and you found a product that would save him from snapping his femur while speeding down his first intermediate slope, you'd buy one even if it were purple or green-and-orange striped.

But color appeal alone doesn't affect the Life-Force 8 desires.

- While orange might offend you, it might make me think of juicy citrus fruit.

- While purple might make you think of the giant hunk of dysentery-infected blueberry pie you threw up all over the CEO when attending your first company *"Let's Meet the New-Hires Get-Acquainted Gala,"* it might remind me of the amazing, sweet *Winter Mountain Red* wine from Galen Glen wineries in Andreas, Pennsylvania—which, by the way, is fantastic.

- While black might convey darkness, mystery, or death in some cultures, it might also be the best color to showcase the amazingly delicious new line of "Midnight Dark" chocolate truffles you just created to sell to local restaurants for their dessert menu.

- Although blue is generally used for cleaning products (think laundry detergent), it might work just great for a software product that helps increase your Twitter followers—the primary Twitter color being hex #1da1f2—a pixel-palette blend of 11.4 percent red, 63.1 percent green, and 94.9 percent blue.

WTH?! Is your head spinning yet? Where the heck does this leave us when trying to choose a color for our ad, logo, or color scheme for our website or sales page or other online (or offline, for that matter) promotional materials?

If you've read the original *Cashvertising*, you know that I like relying on study and research for most everything . . . like the color studies I just mentioned. Why not capitalize on someone else's time, effort, and money? You should, of course. But with all things advertising, you simply need to *test*. Let your market be the final arbiter—which it will be, of course.

For example, even though it's been thoroughly proven that a headline starting with the words *How to* . . . is a great way to draw people into your ad, you might be pleasantly surprised that the one word *"GROSS!"* might be even more effective for your particular ad medium, product, and demographic. And while that might be true, I don't know of a single study that ever tested the word *gross* as a standalone headline.

How could this be? How could a simple headline that you dream up while brushing your teeth one morning beat a headline that's been studied and proven effective for decades?

Simply because truth exists outside of the realm of study results. If those researchers tested the headline *"GROSS!"* decades ago—using your choice of ad medium, product, and demographic—they might have included the results in their study. Then people *today* would be writing about how the one-word headline *"GROSS!"* is equally as effective as *"How to."*

Bottom line: You and I should use studies to *inform* and *guide* us, but never to *restrict* us. Always be open to testing another approach.

Back to color. Look at the studies, and then use your best judgment. Then test your control (your currently best-performing ad) with an A-B split, trying a different color. You wouldn't use pink for a man's cologne nor would you use green for a tooth whitener. But, hey, what's the harm in trying and seeing if there's much of an effect in going counter to your intuition? After all, who says that your results wouldn't one day be the basis for "updated research" that others would come to rely on?

ONLINE AD-AGENCY SECRET #3:
How to Ramp Up Your CTAs So People Respond

It's one thing to get people to your ad or web page but quite another to get them to take the action that ultimately results in a sale . . . or gets them closer to it. Behold your *CTA,* or *call to action.* In its simplest form, it's plain text telling people to do something, like "Order Now!" You're calling them to act. Of course, online, it could also be hypertext or a simple button.

Comparing the CTA to in-person selling, it's the salesperson telling the prospect how to get the stuff he or she's offering. It's the last step in the old advertising-success formula: AIDPA (Attention, Interest, Desire, Persuasion, Action). Without persuading them to actually do something, your salesperson is having a nice chat with your prospects and—when done talking—just stares at them with big open eyes, hoping they know what to do next. No good. Sales is a process of leading people by the hand—like painting by numbers—and taking them step by step. Only until you've successfully taken them from Step #1 can you next take them to Step #2, with one of the last steps being the call to action. Okay, with this in mind, let's take a look at some research.

According to *Unbounce*, 90+ percent of visitors who read your headline also read your CTA copy.[16] You could argue that this percentage would be affected by exactly how your CTA is "physically" positioned. And this is where we see a big difference over hard-copy advertising.

For example, if you have a web page with a strong headline that gets good readership, but your opening paragraph and copy bore readers to tears, and your CTA doesn't appear until much farther down on the page, those same readers wouldn't ever arrive at your CTA. So, for this 90 percent stat to make sense, you'd have to assume that both your headline and the copy (which were both read *before* your CTA) were indeed effective. *Why?* Because if your headline and body copy *weren't* effective, readers wouldn't have read deep enough in your sales message to ever arrive at your CTA, which most often comes much deeper into the sell . . . after you've attempted to convince them that what you're selling is worth buying!

Fact is, many advertisers (you, too?) don't state their CTA until well into the pitch. In other words, they don't ask readers to buy until they've delivered what they consider to be the words necessary to get the readers in the buying frame of mind.

Back to hard-copy ads—think a printed sales letter, magazine or newspaper ad, or brochure, for example. With these in hand, your eyes can quickly dart a few inches and see the order form or other type of CTA. It's right there; no scrolling or clicking required. You instantly know the price and how to buy: call the 800 number, fill out the form, clip the coupon—it's right in front of your eyeballs.

Not so with online advertising. Most ads, emails, and web pages require you to scroll or click to learn the price, what forms of payment are accepted, the guarantee, and any other details needed to buy. In other words, you don't get the whole buying picture up front. This affects your potential buyers negatively on two fronts: 1) If they're ready to buy, they need to scroll or click (or, worse still, watch until the end of your "no-player-control" video) to get to what I call the "buy zone"; and 2) those who aren't ready to buy aren't given any indication of *how* to buy should they arrive at the *"I'm ready to buy right now!"* place in their heads while reading your pitch, even though they haven't completed reading.

Phooey! I have a simple solution to this, and every time I've tested it, it works ridiculously well.

> ✓ **DO THIS:** Give your readers the opportunity to buy right in the beginning—*far earlier than your copywriter intuition would otherwise tell you*—long before you've sold them on buying. (Yes, this tip sounds counterintuitive.) Tell them you want them to buy right at the beginning of your pitch.

Meaning? You put your *BUY NOW, ACT NOW, CLICK HERE* button or link (or whatever other wording is appropriate for your situation, and we'll discuss some good options later) right up front, long before you get into the brunt of your selling message—right after your headline. I call it the *Quick-Buy* button. The thinking behind this follows my exact same "long copy versus short copy" advice that says that good long copy sells stronger than good short copy. (If you're one of those who still believes otherwise, please stop here and read "Ad-Agency Secret #26" in the original *Cashvertising*.)

This simple "put your CTA at the top" idea satisfies both audiences: first, people who need lots of convincing and will keep reading until they're satisfied to move ahead or not. (These people are *not* going to say, *"Hmmm, I was going to check this out, but since I have the opportunity to order right now—so early in the ad—FORGET IT!"* This just doesn't happen.)

Second, this technique also satisfies those who *don't* need (or want) any more pitch. They'll have the option of clicking immediately and finding out the details of how to buy—price, shipping, guarantee, etc.—without wading through the whole expanded "convince me" process. One online marketer who tested this idea saw a 47 percent increase in clicks to his pricing page.[17]

One key indicator that prospects are getting close to buying is when they ask about the price. In this case, they were compelled sufficiently by the headline to want to know the cost of the product. Result: They clicked the CTA before even reading the rest of the copy. That doesn't mean they're going to buy without going back and reading more, of course, but you don't want to keep hot buyers waiting. Give them what they want when they want it. Otherwise, it's like responding to a prospect's *"How much is it?"* with *"I'm not gonna tell you yet because I have more to say."* Hey, some people want that info now . . . and those might be your easiest sales.

Same for your product or service. If your headline is strong enough and really hits home, a percentage of your readers might be poised to spend money right then and there, so why make them wait? They're already primed to spend—perhaps after doing days or weeks of research before spotting your ad, email, or web page—that they're already thinking, *"How much is it? How can I get it?!"* Why risk losing them through your obstacle course of sales copy when you might be able to snag the sale immediately? You want to encourage the sale, not slow it down or do anything to possibly *discourage* it.

I've used this same simple "Quick-Buy" idea in hard copy (postcards, magazine ads, sales letters, etc.) by plastering "Order Now" language and an 800 number right in the subhead), and it only helps produce success.

Interestingly enough, one study cites that a CTA above the fold decreased conversions by 17 percent because *"People like to learn about the product before buying."*[18] Well, of course, they do! But a CTA placed above the fold doesn't *force* people to buy. It gives them the opportunity to do so and plants in their heads where to quickly go to order should the mood strike them early on. What's more, it's a subtle *"buy"* message, which, by the very nature of the ease of clicking a button, suggests that buying is easy.

Of course—as is the case with many advertising topics—the experts are all over the map on this CTA placement issue. Some say, *"Put it at the bottom!"* Others say, *"Put it at two points of the lazy Z eye-flow pattern!"* Others rant, *"Use heatmaps to determine eye-dwell locations!"*

Come on, guys. Let's not make this so damned complicated! Advertising is a salesperson in print. A good salesperson would give the prospect multiple opportunities to buy. Trial close after trial close. Give some info, try to close. Give more info, try to close. Handle rebuttals, try to close. It's a continual process, not a do-it-once event. Put a button at the top, at least one in the middle (more if your presentation is extensive), and one at the end. Give multiple opportunities for people to click and buy. Trust me; they'll figure it out.

Ask for only one thing? A Wordstream study noted that emails with a single call to action increased clicks 371 percent and sales 1,617 percent.[19] Such numbers can be reflective of many factors, and I've also seen studies that say that including *multiple* CTAs increased response. Ah, direct-response: it's all about testing.

Fact is, if you know little about your market (which is sometimes the case, particularly if your product appeals to a broad market versus a more narrowly defined demographic), you might offer a few different choices and see which one is most popular. For example, let's say your web page offers a free report and another link drives them to a video . . . and your video crushes it and your report is a dead fish. In that case, your next effort could focus on the video alone.

QUESTION: What would you do if you're getting better click-through on your video but higher conversions from those who download the report?

ANSWER: You'd keep the video as your lead generator and add those prospects to your funnel and keep working them. They're the ones that'll take more effort. And, hey, who are we to tell them not to want to watch a video over downloading a report? It's likely they're what those involved in Neurolinguistic Programming (NLP) would refer to as "visuals"—people whose brains are more wired to *see* than hear or feel—and who need a more active sell involving imagery and visual demonstration. The important thing is the lead capture, no matter how you get it.

Let's be realistic. Some will convert easily, some won't. Why not give people different ways to give you their contact information? One might give it up for a report. Others for a free video seminar. Others for a free trial. Sure, run one ad with just one offer if you want, and try it against an ad that gives two or even three options and compare the numbers. The idea that you'll reduce your response by giving more than one option to satisfy different people makes little sense to me.

"But, Drew!" you might say. *"Doesn't the old saying 'Confusion leads to inaction' apply here?"* It would apply only if you make it confusing. (Who says you *have* to do that?) You probably *would* if you spread all the options apart, if you use confusing language, if you don't make any of those options sound particularly appealing, and if you don't state clearly what they'll be getting as a result of giving you their contact info. Sure, you'll definitely cause inaction. But, really, how tough is it to put a few simple options in a neat little box and put it in several positions on your sales page or email?

Learn More Now! Click Your Choice:
O Watch This Fascinating 2-Minute Video
O Download Our Powerful Free Report
O Try It Free for 10 Days—No Credit Card Required

On the other hand, if you know your market well and you need to direct them more precisely—say, to buy right then and there or download your app, and you have no other options to offer—then sure, go ahead and focus on just that. But don't offer it only once. If you do, you're like a salesperson who asks for the sale one time and quits. In advertising, we don't have the benefit of seeing and hearing our prospects' responses. We can't tailor our pitch in real time while they're reading it. We can't say, *"Okay, they seem to have understood that point . . . no need to elaborate."* That's why we need to give them a *thorough* sell, not just a quick overview. It's why we have to fire all our cannons, unload all our benefits, lay on all our social proof, and, yes, ask for the sale *multiple* times.

Buttons versus Links

What do you think when you see a red traffic light? You likely think, "Stop." How about a green light? "Go," right? How about when you see a hammer? Nailing. When you see a ladder, you know it's for climbing to reach something.

Likewise, when you see an online icon of a button, you think to *click*. The image of a button itself is a call to action. You instinctively know what it wants you to do. Compare this to links—clickable words. They can take you to the same place, right? And the text itself—*CLICK HERE!*—tells you what to do, just like the text on a button graphic.

However, buttons are psychologically more potent as action evokers because the purpose of buttons is understood universally to indicate action: *"Press Me!"* Links are essentially buttons without the subliminal "Press Me!" graphic. They're missing 50 percent of the ingredients that we want to encourage people to act. What's more, they're usually crowded by other text. And since they're only text, they need to be read to be understood.

But does this hold true for all audiences? Ahh, testing once again. The good folks at AWeber tested this for months with their blog. They sent a blog update via email to their subscribers and teased them with a partial article, encouraging them to click a *text link* to finish reading. To encourage more people to read the entire article, they tested a newly created button versus their standard text link.

In their first five split tests, their *Read More* button drew a clicks-to-opens rate that was about 33 percent higher than their text link clicks-to-opens rate. *"Aha!"* they thought. *"The button is the big winner!"* However, after twenty tests, the win-rate changed, dropping down to beating the text link by an average of 17.29 percent. By the time they concluded their testing, they found that the text links outperformed the button nearly two-thirds of the time, as high as nearly 35 percent.

But we shouldn't be surprised because . . .

. . . All their past emails contained only the text link, and those recipients saw that same text link two to three times a week with every mailing. They'd never used a button in their emails before! It was new, different, and graphically striking compared to a standard text link. After a while, the button was a novelty that eventually wore off.

According to Justin Premick, director of education marketing at AWeber Communications,

> *We exposed subscribers to the button often, which may have increased the speed with which they started to ignore it. If you send less frequently, or only use a button for emails where you have a particularly compelling offer, you may find it to be effective.*[20]

Most anything that's out of the ordinary will get fresh attention. If every day you walk to the store and see the same old cars parked along the curb, you eventually wouldn't even notice them. However, park the latest Snow Quartz White Bentley convertible in the middle of the block and—*BOOM!*—an explosion of attention is suddenly paid to that beauty. It's new, and the human mind quickly recognizes differences.

"But, Drew! Why did the old text link—when it replaced the button—eventually become the winner?" Perhaps because the text link itself—after the readers saw the button so many times—became the "new thing." Rather than stopping one and starting the other, I'd prefer to do an A-B split to determine which was more effective. *Make sense?* In other words, half the audience would see the link, and the other half would see your button. Run it for a couple of months without switching. That eliminates the element of introducing something new to the experiment.

Therefore, I draw a different conclusion from AWeber's. My conclusion—and advice to you—is to keep changing your CTA element. Use a button for a while. Change to a text link. Then change to a different button with different wording. Hey, why not get really creative and try some totally different-style buttons that are relevant to your product or service? If the goal is to get them to see the button—and changing it for the same audience helps improve what's called "noting"—then why not really push the envelope—stock button images be damned!

This advice harkens back to a quote from the company founded by psychologist and market researcher Daniel Starch:

> *Create ads that are different and instantly recognizable.*
> *Research finds "something new and fresh" in the headline*
> *or picture delivers higher "Read Most" scores.*
>
> —STARCH RESEARCH

For example, if you're selling *dog vitamins*, how about a button shaped like the vitamin itself? That's as relevant as heck, if you ask me. Selling *muscle supplements*? Click on the flexed bicep! (In each of these examples, you'd include text within the image directing readers to click it. We take nothing for granted when leading prospects by the hand.) Selling *beefsteak tomato seeds*? Then a button shaped like a big, juicy beefsteak tomato couldn't be more appropriate. Ultimately, pit the two winners (the CTA elements with the highest engagement after multiple split tests are run) against each other in a final split test. The winner will reveal itself to you.

OTHER CTA STATS TO CONSIDER

- Adding CTAs to your Facebook page can increase click-through rate (CTR) by 285 percent.[21]

- Forcing visitors to watch a video before presenting your CTA could dramatically increase your conversions. According to *QuickSprout*, conversions were boosted by 144 percent for author Kimberly Snyder in promoting her health and lifestyle products.[22]

- Neil Patel's Kissmetrics found that a CTA placed within a video gets 380 percent more clicks than their normal sidebar CTAs. *The most effective?* One that takes the readers to another web page for more information.[23]

- How about "Share This" CTAs? When *Social Times* added sharing buttons to their emails, they saw a hefty 158 percent increase in their click-through rate.[24] Your CTR is the number of times your ad is clicked divided by the number of times your ad is shown

(**Clicks ÷ impressions = CTR**). Five clicks and 100 impressions equals a 5 percent CTR.

CONVERSION RATE ESTIMATES ACCORDING TO PAGE PLACEMENT

Welcome gates	10%–25%
Feature box	3%–9%
Pop-ups	1%–8%
Sliders and bars	1%–5%
Generic/end-of-post	0.5%–1.5%
Navigation bars	Variable

(Source: Grow and Convert)

According to the creative folks at web services agency Brafton, strategically placed CTA buttons made dramatic improvements in conversions and sales. When Brafton added them to article templates, they experienced an 83 percent revenue increase in one month, e-commerce conversion rates increased 22 percent from one quarter to the next, and their average order value for blog readers jumped 49 percent during those same periods.[25]

▸ Helzberg Diamonds saw a 26 percent increase in clicks by adding an arrow icon to their CTA buttons.[26] In advertising, you use both words and images to direct people. Arrows are directors. We're trained to look where they point. Point to your *headline*, your *price*, your *special offer*, a particularly *important paragraph*, your *guarantee*, and your *call to action*. Don't let people just "happen" to look. Take them by the hand and show and tell them exactly where. Tell them to *click*, to *read*, to *be cautious* of the competition's products (and say why). Tell them to *compare* and to *feel confident* about buying from you (because so many others are now thrilled, repeat customers, etc.). Above all, *tell them to buy*, and give them reasons why.

According to HubSpot:

▸ Anchor-text CTAs increased conversion rates by 121 percent.

- Fully 47 percent to 93 percent of a post's leads come only from anchor-text CTAs.

- 83 percent to 93 percent of each post's leads come from anchor text and internal link CTAs.[27]

Have you tested different wording? Little changes can make a big difference. In addition, CTA wording that is personalized to your offer is more effective than generic CTAs. For example:

- **"Click Here & Learn to Become Deadly"** is better than just **"Click to Order"**

- **"Start Making Fresh Juices!"** is better than **"Buy Now"**

- **"Click Here & We'll Mow Your Lawn Fast"** is better than **"Click to Schedule"**

Or, for the more personal touch:

- **"YES, Chase! Make Me Deadly!"**

- **"YES, Reid! I Want to Make Fresh Juices!"**

- **"YES! Mow My Lawn for Me, Stanley!"**

Aside from the first names (of the advertisers), the last three examples take advantage of the power of using personal pronouns—such as *you, me, I, my*, etc.—throughout your advertising. Remember that your ad copy should never sound as though it was written for a mass audience, but only to the one real human being who is currently reading it.

That's why, when I write, I often imagine that I'm writing to my friend or brother. I'll include his name in the rough copy and imagine him while I write. This approach has a tremendously positive effect on the words I choose and the overall tone of my finished copy. If you don't think it sounds natural for your friend, change it. You'll discover that much of your copy sounds robotic . . . or corporate . . . or simply not personal. Try this simple idea and you'll see what I mean.

Add a Second Deck and Turbo-Boost Your CTA

Don't let what I've previously said scare you away from saying *CLICK HERE* or *BUY NOW*. But don't stop there. If you want to use rocket fuel rather than regular unleaded, add a *second deck* to your CTA and really motivate prospects to click. The second deck is a modifying line of text under your primary CTA wording. You see, the ideal CTA button is one that tells you to click using a bold headline. Underneath that headline, in smaller text, is text that's customized to your offer, like this:

Click Now to Order
Enjoy Fresh, Pure Water for Just Pennies!

Click Now to Schedule
We'll Shovel Your Snow Fast!

Start My Free Trial Today
Learn How to Bake Pizzas Like a Pro!

Watch This "ANTastic" Video!
Discover My Secret for Killing Ants in 23 Seconds

Click for My Shredded-Abs Plan
You'll Download My Free Report Instantly!

Look at it this way: your primary CTA wording, the *BUY NOW* text, is your headline; your second deck copy is your subhead. Your headline tells prospects what to do, and your subhead tells them *why* to do it. Why just say *Register* when you can also tell them the benefit of doing so? So you see, CTAs aren't anything mysterious. They operate on the same principles of effective ad copy that you already know.

MORE CTA RESEARCH AND STATS
TEST THESE IDEAS AND SEE WHAT WORKS FOR YOU

- ContentVerve saw a 90 percent boost in click-through rate by using first-person phrasing, like this: *"Start MY free 30-day trial"* instead of this: *"Start YOUR free 30-day trial."*[28]

- Making CTAs look like buttons created a 45 percent boost in clicks for CreateDebate.[29]

- SAP Software Solutions found that orange CTAs boosted their conversion rate over 32.5 percent.[30]

- Performable (now HubSpot) found that red CTAs boosted their conversion rate by 21 percent.

- Reducing clutter around their CTA increased Open Mile's conversion rate by 232 percent.[31]

- Personalized CTAs convert 202 percent better than non-personalized CTAs—based on an analysis of 330,000 CTAs.[32]

- Easy Response Booster: Place a picture of your product next to your CTA and quickly boost your response. This harkens back to the classic direct-response technique of putting an image of your product inside your coupon. Online marketers have enjoyed big bumps in CTA engagement—a whopping 28 percent conversion in one test.

- FriendBuy increased signups by 34 percent by adding anxiety-reducing content and explaining key benefits next to their CTA.[33]

- Neil Patel found that users prefer to learn more about the offer *before* clicking a CTA, and that placing his CTA above the fold decreased conversions by 17 percent. However, another test placed the CTA above the fold *and* another below it. *Result?* The below-the-fold CTA generated a conversion lift of 304 percent.[34] Test both variations yourself and see which performs best. My test might do better with the CTA above and yours below.

Personally, I'd never restrict my salesperson from attempting to close a deal. It's like saying, *"Hey, go out and sell my stuff . . . but never ask more than once for people to buy."* Ridiculous! Go ahead and put your CTA above *and* below the fold. In fact, I'd sprinkle buttons throughout a long page in various forms with different wording. Why limit the ways in which your prospect might be persuaded? I'll bet you a good pizza (extra crispy, please) that your offer featuring more than one strong CTA will be your winner.

How to Persuade Online Influencers to Respond

FACT: People can't respond to ads they can't see. Truth is, ad-blocker usage is growing fast, and your promotions might not be getting the reach you're expecting. Here are some quick stats to consider:[35]

- 615 million devices now use AdBlock.

▸ 11 percent of the global internet population is blocking ads on the web.

▸ AdBlock usage grew 30 percent globally in 2016.

▸ Mobile AdBlock usage grew by 108 million to reach 380 million devices.

▸ Desktop AdBlock usage grew by 34 million to reach 236 million devices.

▸ 74 percent of American AdBlock users say they leave sites with AdBlock walls.

▸ 77 percent of American AdBlock users are willing to view some ad formats.

▸ AdBlock usage is now mainstream across all ages.

▸ AdBlock users prefer standard display ads.

▸ AdBlock users are more likely to have a bachelor's degree than the average American.[36]

One tried and true solution? *Influencer marketing.*

Ah, yes. *Influencers.* These are people—celebrities for one reason or another—with bigger than average social media followings. They fall into four categories:

INFLUENCER CATEGORY	NUMBER OF FOLLOWERS
Nano Influencers	1,000–5,000
Micro Influencers	5,000–100,000
Macro Influencers	100,000 to one million
Mega Influencers	One million+

Influencers' opinions are often valued more than those of others simply because of their online celebrity status. If you can grab the attention of even one popular influencer whose opinion carries weight in your product niche, their reach can help propel you to success quickly. They already have a huge, established audience that hangs on their every word. The easiest path to success is often to jump into an established, fully constructed system—an operational river—and let the momentum of its current carry you to your destination . . . versus digging miles of canals and building your own boat.

That's why some of the world's biggest brands are jumping into influencer marketing. In fact, international giant Procter & Gamble cut back its digital marketing a few years ago by a whopping $200 million. *The difference?* None. But when they flipped that spending over to different channels, including using influencers to spread their messages, their reach increased by 10 percent.[37]

The concept is simple: You locate a voice or voices that are influential to your audience and encourage them to give you a shout-out, lending "authority credibility" to your offer. Their audience hears their glowing words about your product and assumes, *"It must be true. My idol has spoken."* Funny, right? But on a psychological level, that's just what's going on. All you need to do is take advantage of it.

> *Celebrity culture is an aspirational culture*
> *regardless of how much you don't want it to be.*
>
> —PALOMA FAITH, ENGLISH SINGER, SONGWRITER, AND ACTRESS

But how do you reach these way-too-busy people, and why the heck should they give a damn about you and what you're trying to sell?

The *reason* they do it is easy: money. Shocked? They get paid well for their posts. The ones with the highest engagement rates (and not necessarily the most followers) get the most per-post fee. *How much?* Let's look at the top five social media platforms with the most active influencers.

According to the "The State of Influencer Marketing 2022: Benchmark Report,"[38] the top five social media platforms for influencer marketing are:

SOCIAL MEDIA PLATFORM	INFLUENCER PARTICIPATION
Instagram	82%
YouTube	41%
TikTok	46%
Twitter	23%
Facebook	5%

What do they charge, on average, per post? Check out the following chart:

INFLUENCER MARKETING PER-POST PRICING

	NANO	MICRO	MID	MACRO	MEGA	CELEBRITY
INSTA-GRAM	$10–$100	$100–$500	$500–$5,000	$5,000–$10,000	$10,000+	Variable
YOUTUBE	$20–$200	$200–$1,000	$1,000–$10,000	$10,000–$20,000	$20,000+	Variable
TIKTOK	$5–$25	$25–$125	$125–$1,250	$1,250–$2,500	$2,500+	Variable
TWITTER	$2–$20	$20–$100	$100–$1,000	$1,000–$2,000	$2,000	Variable
FACEBOOK	$25–$250	$250–$1,250	$1,250–$2,500	$12,500–$25,000	$25,000+	Variable

Okay, now you know who they are and what they charge. But how do you interest them in *you*? Assuming you're not going to hire one of the many influencer marketing companies that act as the liaison between you and the influencer (for a fee, of course), here's what you do:

Step #1: Identify the Right Influencers for Your Brand. Not every popular guy or gal online is right for your product or audience. For example, if you're selling a new type of pliers called *OctoGrip*, you don't reach out to Barbara Palvin or Huda Kattan, two beauty influencers, even though they have a combined following of over 50 million. Hey, that's an impressive number, but what's more important is whether or not they can impress the audience for *your* product. And while we're talking about reach, here's a list of some of today's top influencers and their current following:

- ▸ **Beauty Influencers**
  - ▷ Huda Kattan (50.1 million)
  - ▷ Becky G (25 million)
  - ▷ Chiara Ferragni (26.3 million)
  - ▷ Nikkie de Jager (14 million)

- **Fashion and Style Influencers**
  - ▷ Gigi Hadid (73.1 million)
  - ▷ Bella Hadid (50.4 million)
  - ▷ Sommer Ray (26.7 million)
  - ▷ Chiara Ferragni (26.3 million)
  - ▷ Alexa Chung (5.0 million)

- **Food Influencers**
  - ▷ Jamie Oliver (9.0 million)
  - ▷ David Chang (1.7 million)
  - ▷ Salt Bae (43.3 million)

- **Lifestyle Influencers**
  - ▷ Joanna Gaines (13.5 million)
  - ▷ Rosanna Pansino (4.3 million)
  - ▷ Lilly Singh (11.1 million)
  - ▷ Carlinhos Maia (24.7 million)

- **Photography Influencers**
  - ▷ Murad Osmann (3.6 million)

- **Fitness Influencers**
  - ▷ Kayla Itsines (14.1 million)
  - ▷ Simeon Panda (8.0 million)

- **Travel Influencers**
  - ▷ Jack Morris (2.6 million)
  - ▷ Lauren Bullen (2 million)
  - ▷ Murad Osmann (3.6 million)
  - ▷ Chris Burkard (3.6 million)
  - ▷ Jessica Stein (2.3 million)

- **YouTubers**
  - ▷ Zach King (24.5 million)
  - ▷ PewDiePie (21.8 million)
  - ▷ David Dobrik (12.3 million)
  - ▷ AuronPlay (17.5 million)
  - ▷ CarryMinati (14.9 million)

Big numbers. But keep in mind that unless your pockets are extremely deep—or you have a product or service that personally appeals to them in some extraordinary way—attracting giants like these will be a challenge. It's not that you aren't important or that your product isn't relevant. It's just that these people are already up to their eyeballs in lucrative deals. They're being pitched constantly.

Is it even possible to break through? Of course. But could there be a better and easier way? Yes, by going after the smaller (but still very powerful) fish who still can spread the word about your company far and wide, well beyond your current reach. Hey, would you be upset if you landed an influencer or two with *just* 100,000 active followers? You shouldn't be. And here's why . . .

According to a study conducted by Wharton School marketing professor Jonah Berger in partnership with market researchers at the Keller Fay Group, *"Micro influencers have up to 22.2 times more conversations each week regarding recommendations on what to buy versus an average consumer"* and *"82 percent of consumers who were surveyed for the study reported they were highly likely to follow a recommendation made by a micro influencer."*[39]

The ideal plan? Start with the nanos and micros and then—when your sales justify it and your profits can support it—work your way up to the macros and megas. Aside from the steady-growth financial advantages of working your influencer outreach this way, it also gives you experience dealing with them. By the time you've reached macro level, you'll be far more comfortable and confident in both making your initial contacts and also the back-and-forth negotiating.

Continue these steps to land your first influencer:

Step #2: Plan Your Pitch. Remember the classic advertising rule of thumb: *AIDA*: Get their *Attention,* get them *Interested,* build up their *Desire* to get involved with you (how will they benefit from working with you?), and tell them to take *Action* (tell them exactly what you want them to do to start the ball rolling—this is usually a simple email reply).

Step #3: Write a Strong Email. Your email to your chosen influencer(s) is a sales letter. You're selling them on the idea of them talking to their audience about your product. It's no less a sales pitch than your own pitch to *your* prospects. In this case, the influencers themselves are your prospects. All the same rules of advertising apply. After you get their attention, you need to lay on the benefits and push them to reply. See the following sample emails I've provided. And let's talk for a moment about getting them to actually *open* your email. If they don't do that, it doesn't matter whether you're offering to send them huge pallets of cash . . . they'll never see your offer.

First, send your emails on and at the "right" days and times. According to CoSchedule and multiple studies it examined, it's 10 a.m. on Thursdays, Tuesdays, and Wednesdays—in that order.[40]

Looking ahead, what happens after you send your email? Barring any spam-blocking or deliverability issues, we can assume it will be delivered. First hurdle successfully jumped. Next, like an envelope in a traditional snail-mail letterbox, you need to get your prospects past the subject line and inside to read your message.

And here's a super-simple trick that will do exactly that. Your subject line—which is the headline for your offer—should contain nothing more than their first name. Yep, as simple as that. *"Steve"* or *"Jill"* is all you need. If you feel the need to be friendlier, go with *"Hi Steve"* or *"Hi Jill"* and then stop typing. That's all you want to reveal. If just their name doesn't get them inside, it's not likely that revealing details of your offer is going to do any better. In fact, saying more within the subject line is tantamount to plastering an overly wordy teaser on an envelope.

For example, let's say you're targeting homeowners, and you send a letter with the following printed on the envelope: *"HOMEOWNERS! Save 25% on New No-Clog Gutters!"* What happens? Recipients decide right then and there to look inside or—based only on the short teaser—to throw away the letter, unopened, in the trash . . . completely missing the chance that your full sell inside might influence them to consider your offer. No good.

You never want your prospects to make up their minds from the few quick words contained in your subject line. You want to get them inside where you can hit them with all the benefits, all the features, and all the engaging photos. You want to expose them to amazing stats such as how clogged gutters overflow, causing thousands of gallons of water spilling over the edges of the roof and pouring down directly to the base of their house's foundation and possibly leading to serious basement floods and water damage.

"Did you know that a 2,000 square foot roof collects 1,120 gallons of rainwater for every inch of rainfall? With an average rainfall of 25 inches a year, that's a massive 28,000 gallons of water annually . . . gushing like a river through your gutters and downspouts!"

Add your social proof . . . more facts and stats . . . the power of your full sell! How much of that selling can just the few words in your subject do?

Bottom line: Don't use your subject line to advertise why you're writing. Use it only to get them inside. (That's a copywriter's number-one goal.) You can use the first sentence of your body copy inside your email to encapsulate why you're writing.

Step #4: Be Persistent. Influencers are busy. Aside from looking for creative ways to spend their seemingly endless stream of money from their laborious toil behind the camera—<eye roll>—they're usually busy creating more posts. Many stay involved with their own video production, whereas others have pros handle it for them. They're fielding mountains of offers and, like most book agents, have a "slush pile" of unopened communications they just haven't gotten around to. It's likely going to take multiple hits before you get any response.

Step #5: Simultaneously Market to Multiple Influencers. Like any sales effort, it's a numbers game. That's why you shouldn't limit yourself to a small number of possible influencers. Make a big list and send all your emails out at once. Don't think, *"I'll send one and wait."* That's because you'll usually be waiting weeks or months for responses from these people—if they respond at all. This is what you call "snail speed" and—as Moe of the *Three Stooges* used to say—you'll get *"nowhere fast."* On the other hand, if you're lucky and happen to get several responses at once (unlikely, but possible), that's great! You'll weigh which influencer(s) you want to work with.

Now, how do you get these big shots to reply? Here are some tips:

1. **Keep Your Emails Short.** These people are generally very active. They won't wade through your warm-up paragraphs. Like all other good direct-response, cut out the fluff and get right to the heart of your message in your first sentence. (Yes, *that* fast.) *"But, Drew, you always say 'long copy beats short copy!' Aren't you being a hypocrite?"* Yes, well-written *long* copy typically outsells well-written short copy. But these are not the average recipients. While you and I might get hundreds of emails a week, these people get thousands. A large percentage of them are offers to engage them in some form or another. They've built such a valuable brand and audience that their attention is coveted. If they open your email, you'll have seconds to make your point. If it's appealing enough, you might get a reply. And know this: If you don't get a response, that doesn't mean your

offer is no good. The first likelihood is that they never got to it because it's buried under a mountain of others. And, if they did get to it, that doesn't mean it won't appeal to someone else. It's a mass-mailing effort . . . just like your other promotions.

2. **Be 100 Percent Personal.** Emailing influencers is no different from emailing anyone else that you want to respond. Say their name; mention what they said in their video that you liked. Tell them *specifically* why they're a good fit. Tell them how your offer benefits them and their audience. These people have large followings, but they're still just people, albeit busy people. The same things that influence others will influence them. Nothing generic, please.

3. **Give Compliments!** As my dear grandfather Sam used to say, *"Butter them up!"* Stroke their (usually large) egos. Ask their opinion; make them feel important. Don't be ridiculous about it, of course. There's a big difference between saying, *"My audience values your expert opinion because you're a famous thought leader in this industry"* and *"OMG, I can't believe I'm actually writing to you today. You're such a god. I'm dying here!"*

4. **Offer Them Something of Value.** Just because they're big shots doesn't mean they don't like freebies. Everyone does! Ask if you can send them a free sample, if you can collaborate to help them expand their reach, if you can interview them to expose them to your audience. Tell them you need an expert's advice and you could think of nobody more qualified. (You get the idea.)

5. **Don't Try to "Sell Them."** Lest I be ambiguous, your goal is to sell them only on replying . . . softly . . . just to get a response . . . to open a line of communication that you can parlay into a relationship of mutual benefit. Don't be pushy. You'll do much better coming across as humble. Let them play the role of the "big cheese." When you're trying to stroke someone's ego, you don't drive to their office in a Bugatti wearing a $12,000 Canali suit. That would tend to make them either uncomfortable or competitive, depending on the size of their ego. Humility will serve you well with this audience. At the same time, you *do* want to express confidence so they know they're dealing with someone who's worth their time.

6. **Tell Them What to Do Next.** The best way is for them to simply hit *Reply* and say *Yes* or *Tell Me More*. Don't expect a phone call. Or for them to visit your site. Or to fill out a form. Or to tell you their schedule so you can arrange a Zoom call. Make it easy. Require as little effort as possible. In the end, if you don't get the response you were hoping for, you never want to be thinking, *"Are they not responding because I didn't make it easy enough?"* Eliminate any of these post-mailing concerns *before* you send out your emails. This way, you can be more confident that you did all you could to encourage replies.

7. **Be Upbeat, Positive, Confident, and Enthusiastic.** Influencers are go-getters . . . doers. They usually have positive attitudes—a driver of their success—and like to associate with like-minded people. They know that opportunities can bring them even more influence and success. And they'll sense your confident tone. For example, after some personal and sincere intro words that warm them up . . .

✖ **DON'T SAY:** *"I was wondering if you have any time to check out my new lip product that has a lot of people talking whenever I give out free samples. I know you're really busy, but . . . "*

✔ **DO SAY:** *"Suzi, your lips are beautiful! No wonder so many of your followers comment about them. That's why I think your followers would fall in love with LipBeez . . . our new (and crazy popular) lip-plumping roll-on that makes even the thinnest lips look bee-stung sexy in just 15 minutes. I have 50 full-sized, beautifully packaged samples already boxed and ready to send you for your review . . . "*

Try a simple approach like this:

`Hi Steve!`

`WOW . . . what a coincidence!`

`I'm Drew from Drew's Pennsylvania Pretzel Factory. I loved your post about how much you love pretzels—so cool! :-)`

`Because you love pretzels so much, I'm sending you a giant box of 50 of our most popular soft` pretzels ever: our massive 24" Godzilla Pretzels that are taking the country by storm.

They're the B-I-G-G-E-S-T and most delicious soft pretzels in history. Crispy . . . chewy . . . totally mind-blowing!

I know you're a stickler for quality. So you'll be happy to know that we bake them fresh daily—with 100% organic ingredients—in our coal-fired brick ovens here in Pennsylvania in beautiful Amish country.

STEVE: Just hit REPLY . . . shoot me your best shipping address . . . and I'll send you a big box of our freshly baked 24" Godzilla Pretzels within 24 hours—hot out of the oven—just for you!

Thanks so much!

Sincerely,

Drew Eric Whitman

Drew's Pennsylvania Pretzel Factory

Did you notice that I didn't ask for a review or a business agreement or any commitment whatsoever? The purpose of your first email is simply to *open a line of communication.* If they won't respond to an offer for free samples—short of an outright offer to pay them for their mentions—they're likely not going to respond at all. Of course, if you're looking to pay them, they'll likely have a specific individual to contact through which you'll make such arrangements.

Payment, of course, is the fastest way to get them on board. And many will only work that way. But if your intention is to get the others to work with you for free, offering samples up front is likely the strongest deal that you can make . . . and the easiest way to influence them to respond.

Hey, they're human beings just like you and me. The offer of something for free is irresistible if it's something that interests them. If they do respond, great! Send them the products and then do a quick follow-up asking for feedback. If they liked them, ask them to give a shout-out to their peeps. The mere fact that they received something free from you will kick off the powerful *Law of Reciprocity*—the feeling that one needs to return a favor in order to "balance the scales." Reciprocation is discussed in the original *Cashvertising*.

Want to split test? If you're mailing to a large list of influencers—not simply to the smaller number of megas—it wouldn't hurt to try a slightly more direct approach and test the response to your specific offer. (Again, with the bigger guys, I'd stick to the preceding approach that asks for nothing in return.) Here's a different take on that email:

Hi Steve!

I loved your recent [video/post] about [topic]. Wow, very eye-opening! Especially when you said [quote here to make your email more personal and less like a mass-emailed form letter].

I'm Drew from Drew's Pennsylvania Pretzel Factory—we bake the biggest and most delicious soft pretzels in the world 100% from scratch in our little stone cottage in beautiful Lancaster, Pennsylvania. We've been reviewed by [media outlets] and everyone who bites them, instantly falls in pretzel love! ;-)

Can I send you a fresh-baked box of our new 24" Godzilla Pretzels for a possible review? No obligation, of course. But I think you'll love them!

STEVE: Just hit REPLY . . . shoot me your best shipping address . . . and I'll send you a big box of our freshly baked 24" Godzilla Pretzels within 24 hours—hot out of the oven—just for you!

Thanks so much!

Sincerely,

Drew Eric Whitman

Drew's Pennsylvania Pretzel Factory

P.S. **Steve:** Check: [ ] Yellow or [ ] Spicy Dark (or both!) and I'll include several big jars of our amazing, made-from-scratch Whole-Grain MegaMustards with my compliments!

ONLINE AD-AGENCY SECRET #5:

Endowment Effect: How to Make Them Love You

Buyer's Remorse. Ugh. No seller likes those two words. That's because they mean a disgruntled, unsatisfied customer. Fact is, if we're selling products of good quality that do what we claim, our buyers shouldn't experience much of this remorse.

But how about those customers who *are* satisfied? How do we turn their satisfaction—or liking—of our product into a real *love* for it? I'm talking about a love that drives them to become like a noncommissioned salesperson for your company. One who recommends your products to friends, family, coworkers, neighbors—even to complete strangers online.

Enter the Endowment Effect.[41] It's fascinating, and it gives us insight as to how to increase the perceived value of our products after the sale. The Endowment Effect says that people place a higher value on an object *after*—versus *before*—they own it. With me so far? Great. Let's look at an experiment that revealed this bias.

Research on the Endowment Effect has been conducted with items ranging from coffee mugs to sports cards.[42] In the former, three economics professors at Cornell University in Ithaca, New York, conducted a sneaky experiment with their students. Splitting the group of "lab-rat" students into two groups, they "gifted" one of the groups a lovely Cornell coffee mug. The other group got nothing at all. This effectively split the group into a simulated marketplace of "owners" and "non-owners."

The professors then asked the owners, *"What's the least you'd accept if you were to sell your mug?"* Result? The median owner was unwilling to sell for less than $5.25.

Next, the professors asked the non-owners, *"What's the most you'd pay if you were to buy the mug?"* Result? The median buyer was unwilling to pay more than $2.25 to $2.75.

Similar experiments were conducted with different objects—such as pens, for example—and in each case the results were similar: median selling prices are about twice median buying prices. Said another way, buyers are typically willing to pay only half the price that sellers are willing to accept to part with their possession. The theory behind it all is that once ownership occurs, value increases. The standard explanation for this price gap is *"asymmetry in the subjective impact of losses and gains." Meaning?* An equivalent loss feels worse than an equivalent gain feels good; therefore, sellers are typically more hesitant to give away a possession than buyers are eager to acquire it.

Interesting, right? But what does this mean for you and me as marketers? Simply that if we can find some way to make our prospects feel some degree of ownership of what we're selling, they'll 1) assign it greater value, 2) be more willing to buy, and 3) interpret our asking price to be lower than if they assumed no ownership.

"Okay, Drew, but how can people own what they haven't already bought?" Great question, so let's look at . . .

FIVE PROVEN WAYS TO STIMULATE FEELINGS OF PERCEIVED OWNERSHIP

1. **Free Trials Increase Endowment.** Fact is, once you start using something—and liking it—the less likely you are to want to give it up. For example, one great sales technique I've seen used by Xerox photocopier machine salespeople is the *"go ahead and use it for a while and let me know what you think"* deal.

   This is exactly what happened when I worked in a suburban Philadelphia ad agency. Our copy machine was on the blink, and the owner was looking to replace it. In comes the Xerox salesperson. Instead of trying to close the deal right then and there, the salesperson left the machine for a free trial. After we had hassled with a machine that was on its last legs for weeks, having a brand-new, state-of-the-art Xerox machine that made copies three times as fast and didn't shred every other page was a dream come true. The new machine collated, printed on both sides, stapled in a variety of patterns, copied onto envelopes or thicker sheets of paper, lasted longer on one toner cartridge, and offered a zillion other benefits that the old machine did not.

After the entire agency used it for several weeks and oohed and aahed every time the Start button was pushed, what do you think happened at the end of that trial? No way was the owner going to give it back. Once we used it, it was, for all intents and purposes, *ours*, and they'd have to pry it from our cold, dead hands to get it back.

Take video streaming services, for example. With the backing of millions of dollars to test various marketing methods, which do you think the biggest of them use? You guessed it: free trials. For example:

Amazon Prime Video	Free trial period: 30 days
Showtime	Free trial period: 30 days
YouTube Premium	Free trial period: 30 days
Hulu	Free trial period: 7 days
Amazon Kids	Free trial period: 30 days

How about other online services?

Audiobooks.com	3 books free
TIDAL Music	Free trial period: 30 days
ABCmouse	Free trial period: 30 days
Amazon Music Unlimited	Free trial period: 30 days
Curiosity Stream	Free trial period: 7 days

If some of the biggest names in online selling are doing it, you should try it. Watch how it helps turn mere lookers into buyers. It's the old "sampling" method of selling that's worked since the beginning of selling itself. It's why retailers give free tastes: Chick-fil-A gives free nuggets, Auntie Anne's gives pretzels, Cinnabon samples their heavenly scented pastries; Dunkin' Donuts actually has a sample van driving around looking to turn tasters into customers; Sam's Club and Costco give out thousands of samples throughout their stores: nuts, candy, protein bars, drinks, cheeses, meats—you name it! Don't forget ice cream shops with their little sampling spoons . . . wineries that let you taste until you're tipsy. Add to those: Johnson & Johnson, Influenster, L'Oreal, Reebok, McCormick—and the list goes on and on.

Bottom line: Letting someone use your product or service for free makes it feel as if it's theirs. Not only do they enjoy the benefits of its use, but it becomes so ingrained in their daily life that not having it becomes tantamount to a loss. Think about that: a loss of something that was never theirs in the first place . . . but a psychological loss just the same. Can you use this idea for your product or service? Think about it. It's extremely powerful and effective.

2. **Personalization Increases Endowment.** *"Sign Up & Create Your Account for Free!"* is a great way to get people to more closely associate with your brand and feel a sense of ownership or belonging. What can you give them after signing up as a benefit simply for the signup itself? Sure, you're capturing their contact information, and that's important for your follow-up marketing, but how can you engage them *before* you ask them to pull out their credit card or click the PayPal link?

It could be as simple as having them create an account for future purchases and receiving a discount coupon by email. What's more, signing up could give them access to additional features that someone who does not sign up would not receive. Once they visit your website, you personalize their experience by using their first name in several areas. Welcome them back by name each time they visit. Do you have their city and state information? Can you include this somehow in your copy? The idea is to make the communication as personal as possible to set the Endowment Effect in motion.

3. **Giveaways Increase Endowment.** Put a simple coupon or gift certificate in their hands that conveys perceived value, and they'll be compelled to hold it—own it—until they use it. Holding it gives future ownership of the experience of your brand. It causes them to think about using it . . . to think about the experience of getting more involved. Just seeing that coupon—ideally marked with a deadline date for its use—causes them to re-experience interacting with you until they actually do. It's like a repeat commercial that

doesn't end until the certificate is redeemed. And what does it cost you? Not one penny until they actually give you their business.

"But, Drew! People really don't use coupons anymore! They're so old school." Au contraire! Check out the latest stats:

▷ 92 percent of shoppers in 2020 searched for coupons or offers before buying online.

▷ 60 percent of online shoppers reported that discounts were even more important during COVID-19.

▷ Digital coupon redemption was on course to surpass $90 billion in 2022, up from $47 billion in 2017.

▷ 96 percent of Millennial parents reported using digital coupons in 2020.

▷ 86 percent of Millennials in 2020 reported that they could be persuaded to try a new brand if offered a discount.

▷ 80 percent of all coupon redemptions were projected to occur on a mobile device in 2022, and still growing.[43]

4. **Free Versions Increase Endowment.** Are you selling a product or service that could be offered for free with limited features so as to engage users first and then ultimately razzle-dazzle—or simply convince—them enough to upgrade to a more premium service or model? It's just another version of sampling, but occurring within the digital space.

For example, a while back I took advantage of an online portfolio offer that allowed me to upload scores of writing samples to showcase my work. I named the portfolio, added my bio, uploaded scores of photos plus their associated thumbnails as separate files, included an overall summary of my writing philosophy, and then spent a long time captioning each of the thumbnails that represented each particular writing sample.

Whew! It was a lot of work And they knew it. And I came to rely on it. Eventually, they began to offer premium services which, unless I upgraded my account, wouldn't be available to me, such as expanded capacity and the ability to upload more samples. Without these extras, anytime I wanted to add more of my work (and move the most current ones to the top of the page), I'd have to delete previously uploaded samples because I had reached maximum capacity. Then they added the ability for people to contact me directly after viewing my portfolio. They also added the ability to more easily reorganize, sort, and update the photos I had already uploaded. Plus the ability to add professionally designed cover pages. And more.

Believe me, they wasted no opportunity to continually advertise all the new premium services that would be available to me if I simply upgraded. Having invested so many hours establishing the portfolio, what was I to do? Having used the platform for so long and become so comfortable with it, I regarded it as *my* online portfolio. To start with another platform would be too time-consuming. Even the thought of doing so was too much to bear.

Result? Upgrade I did! It was really the next natural step. They suck you in with an attractive and very-easy-to-become-engaged offer and then—when you're all set and comfy—upsell you to the point of making what you currently have look crummy by comparison. **Bottom line:** It works.

5. **Expressing Their Opinion Increases Endowment.** Always encourage people to give feedback and ideas for improvement. What would they do if they were the president of your company? Not only can you get invaluable comments that could help you fine-tune your product or offer, but you'll be encouraging them to take more time thinking about you and their purchase. If they're happy and satisfied, you'll have a fresh source of powerful testimonials to boot.

The Buffer Effect of Social Support and How It Saves Your Customers

Ugh . . . it's really bad. According to *Forbes*, poor customer service costs businesses up to $75 billion annually. And the following five reasons are mostly to blame:

1. Customers don't feel appreciated.
2. Customers say employees are rude and not helpful.

3. Customers hate being passed around from person to person.

4. Customers are put on hold for way too long.

5. Customers aren't able to speak to a human to get their questions answered.

These reasons foment both buyer's remorse and the urge to never do business with the offending companies again. In fact, of the customers who experienced poor service, 39 percent said they'd never patronize the company again. (That's a hefty chunk of lost business.) Plus 36 percent of the disgruntled customers would complain by letter or email. (And who knows how many of them would be gone forever?)

The silver cloud in all this gloom? Of the customers surveyed, 86 percent said that if they had some *emotional connection* with a customer service agent, they'd continue doing business. Unfortunately, only 30 percent of the customers felt that the companies were effective in establishing such a connection.[44]

Enter researchers Nuckolls, Cassel, and Kaplan and their 1972 study of pregnant women experiencing a variety of complications. From preeclampsia to ectopic pregnancies, these women were stressed! And what the researchers found is eye-opening: 91 percent suffering from high stress and low social support (meaning few friends and/or family members there to comfort them) suffered complications. By contrast, of those with a good social support system, only 33 percent suffered complications. The mere presence of the support—the availability of it itself—dramatically reduced the stress they felt and, likewise, the complications they suffered.[45] This is only one of a number of studies in what's currently called *social marketing*—using commercial marketing techniques to help solve social problems.

Interestingly enough, we can use social marketing in reverse: taking what works in the social context and employing it in our advertising. How? By powerfully and repeatedly playing up your customer support. Not as an afterthought. Not in just a sentence or two hidden on some page deep inside your site map. Not buried in one of the last questions in your FAQ. But by giving it star treatment. Mention it on your home page. Create its own tab and page on your site. Write a full and thorough paragraph about how customer service isn't just a nice phrase; it's a commitment your company lives by. How you survey your customers after the sale. How you want only honest replies so you can improve your current process. According to *Forbes*:

> For a company that provides good service, 66 percent of customers would be more loyal, 65 percent would be willing to recommend the company to others, and 48 percent would spend more money.[46]

Do you offer post-sale service by email, telephone, live chat, and social media messaging? This is called "omni-channel support" and it's critical—especially for Software as a Service (SaaS) companies—because one of the most common complaints of customers of this type of product is their inability to reach a live human being when they need assistance. In fact—in many cases—someone from support contacts them only after they've already figured out the problem themselves! (How many times have you filled out a support request, waited for a response, and ultimately Googled or YouTubed for the solution before anyone got back to you?) Frustrating! Research shows that 83 percent of U.S. consumers prefer dealing with human beings over support via digital channels.[47] No doubt a similar sentiment is felt by consumers worldwide.

Customers expect quick replies to their concerns. *Don't you?* In fact, according to Sprout Social, 13 percent of U.S. consumers expect brands to respond within the first hour of reaching out on social media, while 76 percent expect a response in the first 24 hours.[48] Do you experience this kind of responsiveness from the companies you do business with? How does it make you feel—after having spent the money—being left to twist in the wind until they finally get around to helping you? Would you say it makes you *more* or *less* likely to renew, keep the subscription going, or buy again?

Now for the—*gulp!*—hot seat question: How many of these things are *you* currently doing? Many? A few? *None?* Surely, you have a good reason for your answer, right? Or, like many other businesses, have you just not given it enough consideration? Have you been too focused on the sale and profit? Unfortunately, most businesses today spend far more time thinking about how to make money than they do about how to make and keep their customers happy. In the U.S. alone, the result is a loss of $1.6 trillion due to poor customer service, with 52 percent of customers switching providers and giving their money to the competition.[49]

FIVE EASY WAYS TO INCREASE FEELINGS OF SOCIAL SUPPORT

1. **Power Up Your FAQ.** Instead of just listing Q&As in the standard linear fashion, also add a search box so prospects and customers can find the information they need fast without having to scour through scads of information that's irrelevant to them. Have it anticipate questions and pop them up for easy selection and access.

2. **Add Video Demos.** Don't just tell. Show them as well! There's nothing more helpful than a concise video to demonstrate a product before the sale and also to help solve customers' problems *after* they buy.

For example, I bought two bicycles online for my kids, and the bikes needed some assembly when they arrived. The company didn't just stuff some paperwork into the box, but they pointed me to a series of step-by-step how-to videos that showed me exactly what to do. It would have taken three times as long if I'd had to interpret the text and line art descriptions! Each video was less than one minute—which Trustpilot recommends—and got right to business without fluff or nonsense. (Keep your viewers' state of mind when producing your videos. If it's to solve problems, forgo the long introductions and cross-sale nonsense. Your viewers are already on edge. Just solve their problems and let them get on with life.)

Video is also critical for showing how to use new software, a new app, or an online service. Remember, you want the whole process—from ordering to post-sale use—to be as smooth and easy as possible. Think about this: if your buyers aren't happy with your product, it's not just your product they'll turn against. It's your company too, if they get even the slightest inkling that resolving their problem isn't a priority.

What else does video do? Featuring yourself, an employee, or other human being (as opposed to simply showing text) instantly begins a much warmer and personal relationship with your company that likely didn't exist before. Now, your prospects or buyers will know you better. Your company has a human face. They will know that real people are behind your logo . . . real people who are available (and interested) to help. If there are issues, they now know they can contact "Bob" or "Eileen"—actual people!—and they'll get the answers they need.

3. **Monitor Your Social Accounts.** Your prospects and customers are just as socially active online as the rest of the population. They often turn to social media to contact you rather than check your website for the support tab and contact information. Make sure you're checking your messages frequently and responding

in an upbeat, positive manner, even to the crabbiest comments you might get. The way you reply actually helps shape present and future prospects' opinions of you.

Take Yelp, for example. On that platform, I often give high praise and biting criticism to restaurants that make me happy and make me sick. Interestingly enough, considering the great value of hearing what your customers think of how well you're doing (and how it can steer you to make even more money by tweaking where necessary), in 99 percent of the cases, nobody replies. Not the owner. Not the manager. Nobody. Just crickets.

Why? I consider this a form of business insanity. You'd pay a consultant thousands of dollars to tell you how to improve your operations, but you don't press a few keys on your keyboard or phone to reply to people who are paying to keep your lights on. They're doing you a favor—taking their time to tell you how to improve—and you're ignoring them? *Ridiculous!* So keep your eyes open for feedback and questions. They're a free source of new information for your FAQ page—things that you might not have ever thought about but are of prime interest to those who open their wallets for you.

4. **Add Chat Support.** There's nothing like interaction with a live human being to instantly start building a relationship with prospects and customers. In fact, 44 percent of online consumers say that having questions answered right then and there by a living, breathing person while they're in the process of considering an online purchase is one of the most important features a website can offer.[50]

Think about it! It's possible that more people aren't buying from you not because of your product, but simply because there's something they don't understand, or they just need more information to pull the trigger. Now consider this stat: *68.8 percent* of online shopping carts are abandoned.[51] *Meaning?* For every 100 people who were just moments from sending you their money, nearly 69 of them will—*POOF!*—vanish.

Without a chat feature, they'd have to hunt down your contact information and email or phone you. Think that will happen?

In most cases, it's unlikely. With a chat pop-up—typically and conveniently placed on the lower-right side of the current page they're viewing—they're just one click away from getting the info they need to turn indecision into sending you a payment. Otherwise, you're always gambling that you've done a good enough job with your copy and left absolutely zero questions unaddressed. That gamble—without a doubt—is costing you money.

Pinching pennies? Add a chat feature for just the first six months and see what questions come up. This approach will help you fine-tune any new sites/pages and give you the immediate feedback you need to polish your site on the fly. If the questions keep coming, keep the chat running and keep on polishing. If the chat requests dramatically taper off, you could always quit the service. (And then check to see if your conversion rate tapers off too, due to the removal of this one comfort-enhancing social buffer.)

5. **Add Photos of Your Support Team.** People, people, people. Knowing they're there to help when we need it makes us feel comfortable and more secure in our purchase. Even if your support team consists of only one person, show them! Positioning a paragraph of text (in quotes) by this person tells the reader that someone is standing by ready to help. I'm not talking about a generic stock photograph either. These are as authentic as a Walmart frozen pizza. Instead, opt for a real picture of a real person who works for your company—even if it's your partner or family member. The image doesn't have to be fancy. Dramatic backgrounds—like soaring Roman columns or majestic mountains—aren't necessary. If it's fitting with your brand, even some smiling guy in a baseball cap taking a selfie is fine, as long as the image is authentic. I don't care what the support person looks like, as long as that person is capable of helping me quickly and professionally.

Buffer-Effect Bottom Line: Give your prospects the impression that someone is there for them to support them both before and after the sale. Don't just imply this. Actually *say it*. Demonstrate it by having the associated online features available for their use. One secret of successful selling is making the prospects so comfortable that they believe you'll actually give them what you're promising. Remember, *Fear* is always on the other side of *Desire*. Only when your advertising overcomes your prospects' ever-present state of *"I'm afraid of getting ripped off"* will your cash register ring.

ONLINE AD-AGENCY SECRET #7:
The Psychology of Online Photos and Images

Advertising master John Caples once said, *"Of all the kinds of photos you can show in your ads, it's the human face that gets the most attention."* That's because ever since we were little babies, we were trained to look at faces for information. Even as adults, how exactly do we know when people are happy, sad, angry, afraid, or the twenty-three other human emotions scientists say we exhibit? Before your boss even speaks, you can see that annoyed look on their face indicating that you goofed up big time. Even before your mother hugged you as a child, you could see the expression of joy and love on her face.

During one study, psychologist Robert Frantz and colleagues discovered that infants looked at images with human faces for twice as long as photos without faces.[52] In my seminars I describe another classic study called "Visual Cliff." Babies were placed on one side of what looked like a steep hole in the floor (safely covered by a sheet of clean glass). Their mothers were positioned on the other side. The babies thought they were separated from their mothers by a dangerous drop, and they wouldn't dare crawl to the mother if she had a worried look on her face. But when momma shifted to a happy look, immediately the baby crawled bravely over the "cliff," across the glass chasm, right into the mother's arms. *The lesson?* The baby looked at the mother's face for information.[53]

How does this natural appeal of human faces affect our marketing? According to research, *social media posts on Instagram that include human faces of any kind actually increase likes by 38 percent and comments by 32 percent more than similar posts without the faces.*[54] From a user's perspective, photos are also the most engaging type of content on Facebook, with a whopping 87 percent interaction rate from fans. No other type of post received more than a 4 percent interaction rate. Photos are the primary type of content posted and shared on Facebook.

Photos are powerful on social media even without faces. Look how posts with photos were *shared* as compared to those without them:

POST WITH ONLY	PERCENTAGE OF POSTS SHARED
Photo	87%
Link	4%
Album	4%
Video	3%
Status	2%

(Source: SocialBakers.com)

According to Sprout Social, photos and videos accounted for 62.9 percent of content posted by Facebook pages worldwide.[55] In fact, according to HubSpot, across all social channels, posts consisting primarily of photos and other types of imagery (as opposed to posts that are mostly text) are the types of posts that most increase audience engagement.[56]

Not surprising when you learn that according to various researchers conducting studies (primarily questionnaires), the majority of the population learns most readily by the "visual mode." Others learn best by what they hear. Others need hands-on experience to fully grasp the context.

For example, let's say you're selling a *Pro Pizza-Making Course.* To appeal to the visual learners, you provide a video that will satisfy those who need to only *see* and/or *hear* the directions. The kinesthetic learners, on the other hand, can watch and listen until the cows come home, but until they get their hands covered with flour and sink their fingers into that fresh dough, they're just not going to "get it." Having said that, it's important to note that people aren't all one system of learning or another. There's a crossover, and many people unconsciously use a blending of styles to learn and understand. The key word here is *unconsciously.* People typically have no idea why they're not comprehending. They just know that the information isn't sinking in. They might rationalize their failure to grasp as *"It's just confusing!"* or *"It doesn't make sense!"*

So what's the lesson for you and me as marketers and advertisers? *Simply this:* Be sure to cover all modes of learning in your sales materials. Go heavy with videos because they cover both the visual and auditory learners. Heck, you can even put a video on your FAQ and About Us pages. Why not? Did you ever consider a video for your order page—the last page in the sales process on your site? What better place to give that extra push, knowing that cart abandonment hovers around a whopping 70 percent. If appropriate for your product or service, offer seminars or demos that let prospects get a hands-on trial. This also provides the Buffer Effect we discussed earlier, giving prospects an opportunity to build a relationship with your company by personally interacting with you or another employee.

Back to the star of our ads and posts: *visuals*. What kinds are best? Do certain images cause people to share more often? If we studied thousands of ads and posts, would we find a common denominator that we could put into practice that would help put more green into our pockets? Yes, indeed. So let's look at a comprehensive study that examined thousands of posts on both Twitter and Instagram and discover how we can use its findings for our benefit.

The authoritative *Journal of Marketing Research* presented a powerfully extensive study conducted by Yi Yi Li and Ying Xie, assistant professors of marketing at the University of Texas, where they examined the effects of image content on social media posts on different product categories. Their goal was to authoritatively answer these two questions: 1) is it true that including pictures in a post always leads to higher user engagement on social media platforms such as Twitter and Facebook, for example, as some industry studies have suggested?[57] And, 2) do pictures with certain image characteristics induce more interaction and propagation than others? And if so, what are these characteristics?

Three data sets were used:

Data Set 1: Twitter—*consisted of a whopping 18,790 tweets that mentioned at least one of the nine major U.S. airlines: American, JetBlue, Frontier, Southwest, Virgin America, Delta, United, Alaska, and Spirit Airlines. Why airlines? Because many people use social media to tweet about their vacations, business and social trips, and to voice their complaints about their travels. In addition, all nine of these airlines maintain their own Twitter accounts and regularly post content.*

The researchers were clever. They tossed out thousands of tweets that included hyperlinks to other web pages (except those hyperlinks going to photos alone). Why? Because the engagement received by these tweets could have been affected by the content of the web pages rather than the tweet alone. Compare this to the results you get from your posts. Close the deal from a link to a single web page—which contains every-thing they need to order—and you know which page was responsible for making or breaking the sale. Alternatively, send people to a page that links to multiple other pages and—argh!—you'll have a harder time figuring out which page changed their mindset from "This looks interesting" to "Uh, I think I'll pass" when your conversion ratio heads down the toilet.

Data Set 2: Twitter—*consisted of 14,959 tweets (occurring the same month as Data Set #1) that mentioned at least one of the ten major com-pact sport utility vehicle (SUV) models available for purchase.*

For both of these Twitter data sets, the researchers measured the total engagement using the standard industry practice of counting the number of likes and retweets.

Data Set 3: Instagram—*consisted of a random sample of 2,044 Instagram photos posted between January 16 and February 15, 2018, concerning the same nine airlines in the airline tweets data set. For this data set, the user-engagement level was measured in likes, as sharing was not as readily available on Instagram as it was on Twitter.*

The two researchers, Li and Xie, conducted an exhaustively techni-cal study and relied on the most current data-collection tools available, including Google Cloud Vision API with manual coding to categorize the images in each tweet. They looked for the amount of color used in the images; the picture quality (pro or amateur, brightness, colorfulness, clarity, visual balance, and amount of focus); the category of object in the image; if the image was a screenshot versus a "directly shot" photo; and if a human face was featured. To accomplish this Sisyphean task, they relied on the magic of high tech: a deep convolutional neural network model mysteriously named *Inception-v3*.

Those into the technical nitty-gritty will be interested to know that the performance of the model used to interpret the results *"has been verified in the 2012 ImageNet Large Visual Recognition Challenge (Szegedy et al. 2016): it beat the then-state-of-the-art models including AlexNet, Incep-tion (GoogLeNet), and BN-Inception-v2 by achieving the lowest failure rate of 3.46% in predicting the correct label for an image as one of top five guesses."*[58]

Next, the text! The researchers looked for words in six different categories:

1. **Affect**—Words describing feelings

2. **Social**—Words expressing thoughts and interpretations of ourselves and others

3. **Cognitive**—Words relating to thinking, reasoning, or remembering

4. **Perceptual**—Words relating to or involving sensory experiences

5. **Biological processes**—Words related to functions vital to life

6. **Needs**—Words expressing wants, desires, and necessities

Next, Li and Xie counted the numbers of mentions, emojis, and hashtags and coded them using a standard keyword search, while the word count was generated using the Carnegie Mellon University tweet part-of-speech tagger. Sentiment, topic(s) discussed, and two behavioral drivers were coded using machine learning models.

Whew. Frankly, it would take up too much space on these pages to share with you the brain-twistingly complex mathematical formulae used in this research. Most look like hieroglyphics requiring the Rosetta Stone for deciphering or something created by blobby-brained aliens from planets not yet discovered.

Study Results

Okay, it's time to get practical. Let's codify the results of this painstakingly thorough research into a series of valuable "Always Do/Never Do" rules. Remember, these aren't based on conjecture, or what sounds good, or a quick study done to crank out a new blog post. Instead, they're the result of profoundly deep research by two highly qualified data scientists who studied literally thousands of posts using the most sophisticated research controls available. Each "rule" should be taken seriously . . . and adopted without delay. (Ignore them at your own peril.)

NINE RULES CONCERNING IMAGE CONTENT

- **Rule #1: Always, Always Include Images.** The mere presence of directly viewable image content—regardless of size—significantly increases both types of engagement. This has also been confirmed by researchers Pieters and Wedel.[59] In other words, always include photos or images in every ad or post. *What kinds of images?* Keep reading:

ENGAGEMENT	AIRLINE POSTS	SUV POSTS
Likes	+87.36% When hyperlinked = 66.2% fewer than tweets with no pictures	+151.56%
Retweets	+119.15% When hyperlinked = 78.18% fewer than tweets with no pictures	+213.12%

(Source: Pieters and Wedel, *Journal of Marketing Research*)

- **Rule #2: Never Hyperlink Your Images.** Research shows significantly negative coefficients of linked images for both liking and sharing. *Meaning?* Show your image directly in your post with your text. Don't make people click a link to see your pictures. Satisfy them right then and there without them having to lift a finger to see them.

- **Rule #3: Crank Up the Colors.** Bright and colorful images encourage maximum retweets. This is consistent with findings in previously published visual marketing literature.[60] Look for striking images that pop off the page. Remember, the whole game is *grabbing attention.* All other advertisers and "personal-social posters" are battling you for readers' attention, of which there's a limited supply. Both your words and images have to pull their own weight if you're to win any of the available attention. Fact is, someone is going to get more attention than someone else. Colorfulness helps both attract your readers' attention and helps them understand the meaning of your ad during their frequently "brief and blurred" exposures.

- **Rule #4: Always Include Faces in Tweets.** The presence of a human face accompanying your text in Twitter posts increases both likes and shares. This finding agrees with research conducted by Cyr and colleagues and by Xiao and Ding.[61] Statistically, pictures with a human face led to an increase of 80.40 percent in sharing and 38.76 percent in liking. Interestingly, because Instagram posts feature far more human faces, these increases aren't noticed on Instagram. And don't make the mistake of saying, *"But Drew, these studies were conducted a few years ago. Times have changed. They don't really apply today!"* Keep in mind that the topic here is human psychology. The human brain doesn't change according to calendars—certainly not those from just a handful of years ago. People want the same things today as they did thousands of years ago when they slept in caves in animal skins. Those things just take different forms, but—and get ready for this—*they satisfy the same exact human needs!*

It was *decades* ago that master copywriter John Caples made the quote that I included at the start of this section . . . and it's worth repeating: *"Of all the kinds of photos you can show in your ads, it's the human face that gets the most attention."* Times have changed, but the things that influenced people decades ago still do so today: models' faces, average faces, interesting faces, odd faces. Include any of them and reap the rewards of enhanced noting, liking, and sharing. It's just that easy.

▸ **Rule #5: Happy Isn't Always Happy.** This rule seems counterintuitive, but the research showed that pictures with happy faces tend to induce significantly fewer retweets than pictures containing other facial expressions, but they do not significantly affect the number of likes expressed. *Strange, right?* However, if you dig deeper into the research, you'll discover that images with "happy" facial expressions are mostly selfies. Selfies typically contain only personal information that's generally not useful or relevant to readers outside of the original poster's own base of followers. *Result?* These tweets are less likely to be shared. Whether you agree or disagree, this is what the study found after dissecting thousands of posts.

▸ **Rule #6: Post Professional Photos.** Posts containing professional photos versus amateur shots tend to boost retweets. Like the counterintuitive "happy face" discussion in Rule #5 above, amateur shots are usually accompanied by personal info and contain details about the poster's private life. This type of post might be interesting to immediate friends and family, but the general public tends not to share them as enthusiastically. This finding is consistent with prior research conducted by Hagtvedt and Patrick and by Zhang and colleagues.[62]

▸ **Rule #7: Scrap Your Screenshots.** Tweets containing screenshots receive a significantly lower number of retweets than those containing professional photos. The reasoning is that screenshots are typically less interesting and informative than other types of pictures.

▸ **Rule #8: Make Your Images "Text-Relevant."** Known as *image-text fit*, relevant-image content has a statistically positive effect on the number of likes your posts receive. This result is consistent with earlier studies of print advertising—by Heckler and Childers and by Lee and Mason—which found that relevant pictures in newspapers and magazines, for example, led to more favorable attitudes toward the ad, product, and company. Researchers Heckler and Childers showed that an irrelevant visual stimulus *"creates difficulty for the reader to make sense of the ad information and therefore may lead to frustration rather than resolution."*[63] The (correct) thinking is that irrelevant imagery can detract from the information you're trying to convey with your text.

▸ **Rule #9: Make Banner Ads Purposefully Obtrusive.** Use bold colors, dramatic professional photos, loud text and, yes, animation. Researchers Bruce and Goldfarb and Tucker confirmed what I call the *Principle of Obtrusiveness*—making attempting to be "too noticeable" a primary objective of your design.[64] Regarding animation, Bruce stated:

Our research found that animated formats are superior to static formats in most settings. It confirms that they can improve engagement, since they can generate higher recall, attract user attention, and create favorability for the advertised brand. Yet, static formats can still be effective when it comes to price ads and retargeting. Most interestingly, we found that retargeted ads are effective only if they offer price incentives.[65]

FOUR RULES CONCERNING TEXT CONTENT

▸ **Rule #1: Keep Posts Positive for Stronger Overall Engagement.** Focusing on the good and happy increases shares and likes. Interestingly enough, negative content boosts sharing but reduces likes. Researcher Berger discovered the same thing.[66] This makes sense. Assume you liked a post that someone made complaining how the airline ruined their vacation. Your like seems to make you unsympathetic . . . as if you liked their misfortune.

▸ **Rule #2: Make Your Ads and Posts Informative.** This is the most-shared type of content. Tan, Lee, and Pang find that the informativeness of the tweet (measured by the number of words, hashtags, and mentions) performs the best in predicting the popularity of social media content.[67] *Why?* People have the tendency to "self-enhance" and provide useful information. They use the sharing of valuable information to boost their own self-value by appearing smart and helpful.[68] (Read those last two sentences again. Are *your* posts helpful and informative?)

▸ **Rule #3: Share High-Emotion News Items.** Looking to go viral? Latch onto news stories that already have people talking. According to researchers Berger and Milkman, news articles that are packed with emotional intensity are more likely to spread quickly.[69] Just ask yourself, *"How can I link what I'm selling with one of today's hot news stories?"* It's like jumping onto a speeding train and taking advantage of the great momentum that's already chugging along.

▸ **Rule #4: Crank Up the Emotions and Descriptions.** Packard, Moore, and McFerran found that online engagement is enhanced by the use of emotional, social, cognitive, and descriptive words.[70] The whole idea is to engage your readers. Remove them from their current trance and put them into yours. The sharper, clearer, and more colorful your words are, the more you'll engage them.

Do you recall my discussion about this point in *Cashvertising*? I talked about using *powerful visual adjectives*, or *PVAs*, to create mental movies inside people's heads. Remember, people first buy in their heads before they buy in reality. For example:

> Strong emotion-producing words engage people. *"OMG! He scared me to death last night!"* Strong (social) words expressing thoughts and interpretations of ourselves and others engage readers: *"She has such an amazingly thin body and great hair. I used to be sooo jealous of that skinny b#%!@! But now I know exactly how she got it!"*

> Strong cognitive words expressing thought processes engage people: *"I always felt weird in public . . . like people were always staring at me . . . thinking weird stuff. Then I figured out what was really going on."*

> Strong descriptive words engage people: *"Ouch! Today Josh was running . . . tripped . . . and fell brutally hard onto the rough cement—BAM! He tore up his right knee so badly on the cement that it left a 7" wet skid of blood and skin—UGH! So glad I had QuickKlot spray and . . . "*

ONLINE AD-AGENCY SECRET #8:

How to Use the "Frequency Illusion" to Appear to Be Everywhere

For years, old man Joe bought the same brand of car. Ford, Ford, Ford, Ford. One day, his best friend said, *"Hey, Joe, you've been driving Fords since you could remember what you had for breakfast each morning. Why not try a different brand and model?"*

So Joe got to thinking. He did some research and surprisingly broke out of his decades-old F-150 shell. *Hallelujah!* He bought a brand new, high-tech, 100 percent electric *Nissan Surf-Out* pickup truck and—boy oh boy—did he ever feel cutting edge. *"Nobody . . . simply nobody has anything like this!"* he said to himself, admiring its sleek lines and futuristic "space-age" styling. Ol' Joe felt young again!

But . . . huh? What's this!? NO! It can't be! Suddenly, Joe began seeing lots of *other* people—even those *his* age—driving Nissan Surf-Outs. His neighbor down the block, his brother-in-law, . . . heck, even his own grandson started yakking about getting one. Suddenly, TV commercials were popping up. Full-page newspaper ads. Even the billboard that formerly advertised roach killer was changed to feature the new Surf-Out!

Argh! Was this some kind of gaslighting operation to drive ol' Joe crazy? How's it possible that everyone is suddenly talking about the super-unusual new car that he thought that only *he* knew about?

Truth is, those Nissans were always on the road—not as many as the old reliable Fords he's been driving—but they were there, just the same . . . and more every day since the model was released. It's just that good ol' Joe never noticed them through his Ford-fixation filter. Suddenly, after buying the new Nissan, he's seeing them everywhere. *What's going on?*

Enter the *Baader-Meinhof phenomenon,* also known as the *frequency illusion,* or *frequency bias*—all fancy names for the phenomenon of frequently noticing something after you notice it for the first time. Like when you hear a song for the first time and suddenly you hear it everywhere. It was always there, just not in your field of consciousness.

Interesting how our brains work, right? But can we use this unusual phenomenon to our advantage as advertisers to make it *seem* to consumers that our brand is more dominant in the market than it really is? Indeed, we can, . . . and it can be done in these ways:

1. **Textual and Graphic Consistency.** Look at most companies' ads—perhaps yours included—and you'll see a whole smorgasbord of colors, typestyles, design elements, and conceptual positionings that would be sufficient for any dozens of other companies and brands. In short, all of their ads look different from each other. There's no consistency of message or design. Each looks as if it was created by a different team of account managers, copywriters, and designers. With such differences in every ad, it's like they're seeing you for the *first* time. *The result?* Zero snowballing of recognition among your readers.

   What you need to do is what today's most successful brands do . . . and that's just the opposite. Instead of making your ads look different from each other, *each ad should look like the next in a series.* Decide on one strong layout. And that means your headline and subheads should appear in the same places in relation to your graphics across all of your ads. Choose two or three relevant fonts. Use the same type and quality of images.

   In other words, if you're using photos, then don't suddenly start using illustrations. If you're showing people using your product, don't start showing close-ups of just the products themselves without showing people. Choose an appealing color palette—perhaps pulling it from your logo—and stick with it. **Bottom line:** Make your ads all look like they're from the same company. Consistency across all your channels creates the frequency illusion. This helps make your brand appear bigger and more established.

2. **Front-Loaded Flighting.** Flighting is a media-placement strategy that entails running your campaign for set periods of time and then backing off—sometimes completely—particularly when demand for your product might be lower, such as for winter coats in the spring. But it also instructs advertisers to run ads heavily when launching a new product and then to use periods of lower activity to stay top of mind.

In other words, if you're continuing to advertise in the same market—Facebook, Twitter, or Instagram, for example—you can give the illusion that you're "all over the place" by first making a big splash with heavy frequency and then tapering off with a steady but lower rate of impressions.

According to research conducted by Janiszewski, Noel, and Sawyer, repeated exposures strengthen a consumer's memory for an ad even though the time between each exposure to the ad increases. *Why?* Because ads seen the first time leave a "memory fragment," which is made stronger each time the ad appears due to retrieval of the memory fragment created by the first ad.[71]

Of course, the passage of time will, ultimately, cause readers to recall less about you. But the good news is that it's not as long a time as you might think. (That's good news if you're on a particularly tight budget.) For example, research conducted by Wansink and Ray showed that up to 70 percent of the subjects exposed to advertising could recall the target brand after three months.[72]

A more recent study by Aravindakshan and Naik suggests three weeks of ad memorability even after advertising is pulled entirely.[73] By flighting your advertising within these periods of recall, you'll maximize your ad budget while, at the same time, strengthening the memory fragment and building brand recognition.

3. **Pulsing.** This is another media placement strategy based on running ads continuously with a number of planned frequency spikes to accomplish different objectives. There are six primary types of pulsing:

   A. **Steady Pulse.** You run your ads on a fixed schedule for twelve months.
   B. **Erratic Pulse.** You run your ads irregularly, a strategy often used for changing old patterns and determining whether your current, most-used media-scheduling might be in need of a change.
   C. **Start-Up Pulse.** You run your ads heavily initially and then switch to a different pulsing model after your splash.
   D. **Promotional Pulse.** You run "single-use" ads promoting date or deadline-specific special offers or events.
   E. **Seasonal Pulse.** You run your ads based on your product's seasonality.
   F. **Regular Period Pulse.** You run your ad continuously, bursting it with heavier frequency on a regular basis.

   Keep in mind that while flighting and pulsing are implemented to keep a brand top of mind, they're not strategies that direct-response marketers would use to keep the orders flowing. Rather, they're used to keep the public aware of the *existence* of your brand so that when they're ready to buy, they'll think of you.

   Yes, people prefer brands they're familiar with, but awareness itself isn't a catalyst for immediate purchases. Ads in front of eyeballs stimulate sales. If you're not advertising, there's no catalyst. To get the order *today*, you need to advertise *today*.

4. **Retargeting.** This is a great way to foster the frequency illusion. Joe Prospect visits your site and—*BOOM!*—suddenly you're everywhere he goes. And today's stats make a great case for it. According to MailChimp, 97 percent of website visitors never return. Studies and surveys from 2020 reveal that in the United States, the average e-commerce website conversion rate is 2.63 percent, as compared to a global conversion rate of 4.31 percent.[74] So getting someone back to your site after they visited but didn't buy is a great strategy to keep you and your

offer in front of them and to attempt to convince them to give you another shot.

Consider these impressive stats:

✓ **Retargeting beats** *all other ad placement strategies with a 1,046 percent efficiency rate.*

✓ **Three out of five** *potential buyers recognize product ads they previously saw on other sites.*

✓ **Ads are three times more likely** *to be clicked by retargeted customers than new ones.*

✓ **Website visitors who are retargeted** *with display ads are 70 percent more likely to convert on the retailer's website.*

✓ **Engagement retargeting with video** *increases conversion rates by 70 percent. And on holidays, it's been shown to boost conversion rates by 30 percent.*

✓ **25 percent of consumers** *love retargeting ads.*

✓ **Marketers utilize** *Google Display Network to retarget over 90 percent of internet users worldwide.*[75]

With stats like these and others equally impressive, it's worth adding retargeting to your mix. Check out the Google Display Network and Facebook for retargeting instructions—they're simple and straightforward. Choose *Meta Pixel Retargeting* on Facebook—while it's still available—and you'll install a snippet of JavaScript code on your site that causes a cookie to be placed on your visitors' computers so the retargeting network can display your ads to them when they're busy browsing other places.

Alternatively, choose *List Retargeting,* which uses the email addresses of people who've visited your site and have expressed enough interest to provide their contact information but haven't purchased . . . *yet.* You simply upload these lists to the retargeting platform of your choice, and the network will show your ads to only those folks. Nice, right?

Not using retargeting? You should! Think of it this way: these prospects visited you in the first place. Something you said or do interests them. Good salespeople make more than one attempt to close the sale, don't they? And since it's likely that your prospects' initial visits were prompted by something you did to get them there (as opposed to an organic search), why not keep the snowball rolling and try to convert them? They're not strangers to you, so keep the relationship going! Get to it!

What a Study of 100,000 Facebook Messages across 800 Companies Revealed

FACT: Less than 1 percent of the typical company's Facebook fans (users who have liked their Facebook page) ever engage with the company by adding a comment, sharing, or liking their posts.[76] *Ugh.*

Reason? Most posts suck. They're dull, lifeless, emotionless. They contain nothing to move you, to make you think, to persuade you to do anything differently. Truth is, unless you know what works, you're wasting time that could be spent more effectively doing something else. (Like reading books to learn what works.) Fact is, we need some real, hard-core research to instruct us—once and for all—as to the right way to post on Facebook for results.

But even if you and I had an exceptionally good breakfast—followed by multiple pots of strong coffee—we'd likely not have the gumption to personally research, say, 100,000 Facebook messages to determine what caused the most successful of them to be liked and commented on most often.

Fortunately, three qualified and serious researchers, Lee and Hosanagar of the Wharton School and Nair of Stanford Graduate School of Business, did the work for us. In their exhaustive eleven-month-long study, "The Effect of Advertising Content on Consumer Engagement: Evidence from Facebook," they content-coded more than 100,000 unique messages across 800 companies and employed a combination of Amazon Mechanical Turk (AMT) to assist with pure brute-force data collection, highly sophisticated natural language processing (NLP) algorithms, and some of the most freakishly complex mathematical equations I've ever seen. As a creative type, I thank God that there are people who actually enjoy doing this work; the amount of detail is mind-boggling.

According to the authors of the study:

> *This algorithm uses the 5,000 AMT-tagged messages as the training data-set. Best practices reported in the recent literature are used to ensure the quality of results from AMT and to improve the performance of the NLP algorithm (accuracy, recall, precision). The resulting NLP algorithm achieves around 99% accuracy, 99% recall*

and 99% precision for almost all the content profiles we consider with 10-fold cross validation.[77]

(I told you they were serious.)

So, with the number-crunching finalized, they presented sixteen key findings from a painstakingly researched real-world study. Next, I translate these findings and convert them into practical how-tos you can begin using today.

THE SIXTEEN KEY FINDINGS OF DISSECTING OVER 100,000 FACEBOOK ADS ACROSS 800 COMPANIES

1. **Six Days and Done.** Both comments and likes fizzle out to zero after two and six days, respectively. Impressions fade more slowly. To stay top of mind, strive to repost before your last message vanishes into the six-day internet ether.

2. **The Fifteen-Day Fade.** Once you post, more than 99.9 percent of all your engagements and impressions will be accounted for within fifteen days.

3. **Go Photo-Heavy.** Messages containing photos receive the highest average likes and comments over their lifetime. Don't post text-only messages. Take a few seconds more and include a photo for significantly higher engagement.

4. **Status versus Videos.** Typically, company status updates get more comments than videos, but videos tend to encourage more likes. **Remember:** Clicking thumbs-up takes little effort. Comments are far more valuable to you and your followers. They're proof of much greater engagement/involvement with your company. Plus each positive remark acts as social proof of your popularity, which positively affects all your other followers! **HOT TIP:** Getting great comments? Ask for permission to use the very best in your advertising. Hardly any businesses do this. It's crazy! It's a free source of more great reviews than you could possibly ever want. It creates a snowball effect that helps put cash in your pocket.

5. **Links Are Losers.** Links draw both the lowest likes and comments. Add your content, both text and imagery, directly to your post rather than sending readers elsewhere.

6. **Emotions Are Winners.** Emotional messages win the most number of likes. So don't hold back! If something makes you happy, angry, sad, or otherwise, just say it . . . but *powerfully!*

✖ **WRONG WAY:** *"I was so mad I couldn't think!"*

✔ **RIGHT WAY:** *"ARGH! I was so %#$@# FURIOUS my head was about to—BOOM!—EXPLODE!"*

You're competing with thousands of others. Inject *power* into your posts. People want to be *moved!*

7. **Go Heavy with Persuasive Content.** The Lee, Hosanagar, and Nair study revealed that content that attempts to persuade has a positive and statistically significant effect on both types of engagement: likes and shares. *Best types?* Emotional and philanthropic. Don't fear trying to convert people to your point of view. Give facts, evidence, and social proof to support your claim. Lay on the emotions, too, and you'll engage them even more and boost shares for even greater effect and response.

8. **Don't Use Product Info Alone.** Mentions of price, product features, and availability have been shown to actually *reduce* engagement when you feature this info by itself. However, when you team it with persuasive content, you'll reverse the negative-engagement tendency. **Bottom line:** Persuasive content appears to be the magic key to effective engagement on Facebook.

9. **Avoid High Reading Complexity.** Difficult reading decreases both likes and comments. Use simple words and language with short sentences and paragraphs. Cut out buzzwords and slang that could be misunderstood. Chop out unnecessary words. Write to *express*, not to impress.

10. **Use Shorter Messages.** They encourage more likes and comments. Like, uh, this.

11. **Including Links Is Worse for Engagement.** Put your message right there. Include links only for additional information, but not because you didn't deliver your full sell/message in your ad. In other words, give prospects enough information in your post to consider whether they want to like or share what you're

discussing. If you ask them to click and go elsewhere to make this determination, many won't.

Here's a quick comparison. I called the company *Instant* to ask a technical question about their rice cookers. I was put on hold and waited about ten minutes before a recording came on saying, *"If you don't want to hold, we'll call you back at a convenient time. Simply visit our website at . . . "* and they gave a long URL. How many people—after waiting on hold—are going to write down the URL, hang up, and go through the whole "set up your convenient call-back" process using a form on their site? Few, I imagine. While some elements are different from the social media posting situation, some similarities hold true. Simply this: I want the info now. Don't make me work to get it.

12. **Ask Questions and You'll Significantly Increase Comments . . . But at the Cost of Likes.** Likes are nice, but comments take more energy and thought—that's why they're more valuable. Heck, anyone can click a thumbs-up button in a fraction of a second. However, not everyone is inclined to 1) consider their thoughts, 2) mentally edit what they want to put in the public eye, and 3) structure the words to make a good impression on those reading their comment. So *ask, ask, ask.*

"What do you think?" "What's your experience?" "Am I right or wrong?" "What would you do?" "How could we improve this?" "Did you ever try_____?" "Would you rather _____ or _____?"

. . . and countless other engaging questions. Plus, when you get prospects to engage more fully in this way, the ones with the positive comments are setting the stage for the Endowment Effect, discussed earlier.

13. **Include Fill-in-the-Blanks to Encourage Comments.** *"My favorite _____ is _____," "The best coffee you ever drank was in _____," "If YOU were the CEO of our company, you would _____,"* and scores of variations. This has a similar negative effect of asking questions as it simultaneously depresses likes. The odds ratio of comments increases by 75 percent if a post asks

a question and increases by 214 percent if blanks are included. This outcome strongly suggests that blanks are more effective than questions if the goal is to increase comments. *Likely reasoning?* The response has already been started for them. As opposed to constructing complete sentences and paragraphs, all they need to do is pop in a few words and move to the next post. Always remember, humans want ease and speed.

My Suggestion: Ask readers to click the Like button *before* commenting. Such a simple instruction might be all it takes to get just as many likes as comments. Remember, this is sales. You need to lead people by the hand and *tell* them what to do.

14. **Always Ask for Likes.** Doing so increases both your likes and comments, whereas asking for comments alone increases comments . . . but at the cost of likes. Remember, comments are considered the "gold standard" of social media engagement. They suggest to others that your business is legitimate, credible, popular, and worth checking out.

15. **Avoid Mentioning Holidays.** Seems counterintuitive, doesn't it? But shooting out happy holiday messages has a negative effect on engagement. Lee, Hosanagar, and Nair speculate that this could be caused by excessive holiday messaging, especially by consumer product companies. When I get holiday emails, I usually don't even open them. A handwritten card? Yes. A personal email from someone I have a personal or business relationship with? Yes. A mass-mailing? Nope. And especially not a social media post. How much more impersonal could you get? It's like your dentist bulk-mailing Christmas postcards. It's just insurance to drill more of your teeth. Ugh.

16. **Test Multiple Content Strategies.** Lee, Hosanagar, and Nair conclude that *"There is no one-size-fits-all content strategy and firms need to test multiple content strategies."*[78] This advice refers specifically to the informative/persuasive effectiveness dichotomy. You might find that informative posts about your particular product or services are more interesting than the industries these researchers examined. If so, then providing interesting feature and benefit information (without particularly persuasive

content) might be all you need to rake in the likes and comments. My suggestion? Test *both* types of ads and posts and see which works best for your business, keeping yourself prepared to make the tweaks necessary guided by this study.

ONLINE AD-AGENCY SECRET #10:

The Power of Polarization—A Daring Way to Stand Out

Merriam-Webster's Dictionary defines **polarizing** as "causing strong disagreement between opposing factions or groupings."

Take Donald Trump and Elon Musk . . . two masters of the game. Do they do it by accident? No, they play the polarization game like the famed Niccolò Paganini (1782–1840) played the Stradivarius. Truth is, being polarizing online can attract a massive following of like-minded supporters. The recipe is simple:

> **Make a controversial statement that supports your cause → Post it to the masses on social media → Which effectively splits your audience into those that DO and DON'T support your cause → Market to your newly found, self-identified market segment who support you more than ever as they've now emotionally aligned to your purpose.**

How can you use this technique for your business? Here are some examples for other industries to give you the flavor of the messaging you're after:

Pizza Shop: *"Ugh! I'm sick of other pizza shops downright LYING about their frozen dough as being "Fresh Daily." What a scam! Here at Lamberti's we're up at 6 a.m. making our dough from only the freshest organic ingredients. Same for our sauce and cheeses. We love our customers! Come taste the difference!"*

Web Designer: *"Crappy Web Design Sucks! Good business people are getting RIPPED OFF by lousy web designers using overworked, generic templates that look cheap and amateurish! I design all sites from SCRATCH and they pull customers like wildfire. What's the UGLIEST website you've seen . . . comment and tell me!"*

Cafe: *"We're Not Idiots! Charging customers $4.15 for a venti caffè latte is insane. Our award-winning coffee shop serves an even fresher and more* *amazing venti Latte Supreme for just $2.95 . . . and includes our home-made fresh chocolate biscotti! (Take THAT, Charbucks!)"*

How do you stir up emotions and bring people to your side? What can you rail against in your industry? What do you know that people *already* dislike? (You don't need to create anything new . . . it's already out there!) What are they already battling that you can latch onto and ride their wave of emotions? What can you say in your posts that let people know that you're looking out for them, effectively putting them on your side, supporting your brand?

It's a great (albeit sneaky) tactic. Not only does it convey a strong sense of consumer advocacy—which produces instant positive appeal—but it's also injected with emotions, which are one of the primary ingredients that encourage people to like and share.

Are there risks? Few, if any. Of course, you don't want to get so out-rageous as to intentionally offend or alienate your readers. Look at the examples I provided here. Do any of them offend you? Or do you naturally associate with them because they're espousing things that anyone with good sense would agree with? That's the key. You're expressing your emotions powerfully, but—aside from my "Charbucks" quip—there's really no identifiable suspect. Sure, the lousy coffee shops, bad pizza shops, and template-loving web designers won't love you, but they're your *competition*. Who cares? *Let them up their game!*

ONLINE AD-AGENCY SECRET #11:
Ethical Bribes: The Psychology of Buyer Incentives

"Capture the contact information!" is the mantra of every direct marketing manager leading a sales team. Of course. If you can't message prospects, you can't persuade them to buy from you. But, let's face it: not everyone willingly gives up their name and email (let alone their phone number and more) just to be nice to you. Nope, they often need to be "ethically bribed" with some kind of incentive.

Enter our researcher friends at SocialVibe (then TrueX, Inc., and now Infillion), a US digital advertising company, and KN Dimestore, one of the top fifteen market research companies in the United States.

The aim of their study of more than 30,000 consumers viewing the ads of multiple U.S. brands—including entertainment, consumer packaged goods, e-commerce, financial, and technology—was to find out three things: 1) if and why incentives influence people to become more engaged with the ads they read; 2) how incentives, freebies, discounts, premiums etc., affect consumers' perception of the brands; and 3) if the incentives they offered persuaded people to visit the companies' websites and/or pass the deal along to others in their social network.[79]

HERE'S HOW THE INCENTIVES CHANGED CONSUMER BEHAVIOR

- ▸ 48 percent of those interacted *because* of the incentive *but* paid attention to the brand.

- ▸ 12 percent interacted purely based on brand.

- ▸ 31 percent interacted for brand *and* incentive.

- ▸ 9 percent interacted purely for the incentive.

- ▸ 36 percent of respondents were more likely to buy the brand's products in physical stores after taking the incentive.

- ▸ 23 percent increase in likelihood, post-incentive, to *consider* the product over the competition.

- ▸ 32 percent increase in likelihood, post-incentive, to *buy* the product over the competition.

This research shows more than simply the fact that people are subject to "ethical bribery" or incentivization. It also shows that engaging with the ad increases the odds that consumers would ultimately buy the product being advertised. (This speaks to the Endowment Effect, discussed earlier.) Incentives do still more: They boost website traffic and drive people through retail store doors.

Infillion calls the strategy "value-exchange brand advertising"—aptly named because you're asking for your readers' attention in order to get something they want. If they pay attention, they'll be rewarded. The variety of incentives is virtually endless. Here are some incentives to consider (the more expensive ones reserved for high-ticket items, of course):

1. **Exclusive Sneak Previews.** From new tech, designer clothes, and sporting goods to educational seminars and more—people like to be first! What could you offer as an incentive that they'll get to see before it's "released to the public"?

2. **How-To Guides.** Assign a believable dollar value for the perfect incentive to buy now or to exchange their contact info.

3. **Free Seminars.** These seminars have high value and cost you next to nothing.

4. **Donations.** They help buyers rationalize spending money.

5. **Discount Coupons.** Everyone loves a discount.

6. **Buy-One-Get-One-Free Offers.** Tests prove this approach is better than saying, "50% Off!"

7. **Free Memberships.** People want to belong. Memberships convey high value, too.

8. **Loyalty Programs.** They give customers more reasons to return.

9. **Free Returns.** This incentive makes buying easy and reduces the risk.

10. **Free Gift Wrapping.** This incentive is ideal for gifty products because it reduces work.

11. **Free Expert Consultations.** How much is a consultation worth? $50? $100? $500?

12. **Tickets to an Event.** Tickets convey high value and you can buy in bulk at a discount.

13. **Restaurant Gift Cards.** Full-service restaurants, cafés, and fast food. Everyone loves eating out.

. . . and many others.

How to Use Tested Design Psychology to Create Irresistible Facebook Business Pages

Do you already have an "official" page set up for your business on Facebook? Like your personal page, your business page—formerly called a "fan page"—is a great way for the "fans" of your business to interact with you while you keep them informed with updates, specials, and offers.

The benefits are many: 1) It allows you to have unlimited business follow-ers. 2) Your status updates appear in the newsfeed, keeping you top of mind. 3) You can add an unlimited number of photos and videos promoting your brand and products. 4) You can promote your page with Facebook tools. 5) It gives you an added SEO boost. 6) It's a great way to encourage and respond to customer feedback. 7) And it's a valuable funnel directly to your own web-site. And—to top it off: 8) It's 100 percent free. *How can you lose?*

Well, there's one way to lose: You ignore what has already been learned about how to create the most effective Facebook posts and struggle doing your own trial-and-error experimentation. (Aren't you glad you're reading this book?)

Fortunately, research has been conducted concerning how key design features affect consumers' liking and commenting on Facebook business pages. For example, does the size of the posting get you more likes? Does longer text get you more comments? Does the number of graphic ele-ments—photos, videos, etc.—get people more engaged? And is it better to ask people to comment, or does this just annoy and scare them away? *Lass es uns herausfinden . . .* er, *let's find out!*

What Three Researchers Discovered in Germany

Researchers Rauschnabel, Praxmarer, and Ivens of the University of Bam-berg, Germany, studied 369 postings for four car manufacturers: Opel, Lexus, BMW, and Audi. Their hypothesis was that larger ads with more images (rather than fewer) and less text (rather than more) would increase engagement.

They recorded the number of likes for each posting. The number of likes per posting was divided by the number of likes for all postings of the corresponding brands. They next recorded the number of user comments for each posting, counting only one comment per unique follower.

They counted pixels to measure the size of the postings using the Firefox plug-in named MeasureIt. They next counted text by the number of letters used and divided the result by the number of pixels the posting contained. If text had to be expanded, they counted only the text that was visible before the expansion. Next, they counted the number of graphic elements (photos, videos, etc.) between one and three (due to Facebook's settings). Finally, they checked all postings and identified those that included a message asking the reader to respond in some manner—comment, like, or vote for any options presented (e.g., *"If you like this information, please click on the Like button below"*).[80]

The following table shows the setup and breakdown of likes and comments:

BRAND	POSTINGS	LIKES	COMMENTS
Opel	129	59,230	10,360
Lexus	46	75,850	12,890
BMW	99	271,770	34,470
Audi	95	328,230	44,670

The next table shows the result of each hypothesis and its bivariate correlation. Sounds impressive, but it's simply a statistical technique used to determine the relationship between two variables, like X and Y, for example. It shows how much X will change when there is a change in Y. It's the change and its effect that's meaningful.

In the following table, a positive number shows that when that independent variable is increased, a corresponding increase in the dependent variables was shown. The higher the number, the greater the effect of increasing that independent variable. You can see that when size is increased, there's a significant correlation in the number of likes received, but not so much for comments.

INDEPENDENT VARIABLE	DEPENDENT VARIABLE: LIKES	DEPENDENT VARIABLE: COMMENTS
Size	.253	.070
Amount of Text	−.403	−.306
# of Media Elements	.365	.178
Invite vs. No Invite to Engage	.204	.411

In summarizing the data, the results show:

► Size is not significantly related to the number of comments received.

- ► The greater the size of the ad, the greater the liking.

- ► The greater the text length, the less the liking. Does this argue against long ad copy, as I always espouse? No. This study did not look at ad effectiveness whatsoever. A more-liked ad isn't necessarily the more persuasive ad when it comes to converting prospects into buyers. I contend that people who are interested in buying will click to learn more and already be off reading sales copy on the company's own website rather than hitting a thumbs-up icon to express their "satisfaction" with the post.

- ► The effects of size, amount of text, and media elements are stronger on the number of likes than on the number of comments, as comments take more thought and effort.

- ► Inviting readers to comment/respond powerfully motivates them to do so.

Remember, in direct-response advertising—no matter how much data you have—testing is always your best friend. Even though Facebook stats say that the average user clicks on eleven ads per month, that mobile-optimized videos deliver a 27 percent higher brand lift, and live videos on their platform result in six times greater user engagement, you still need to test to see whether these stats play out for *you*.[81] Let research guide you to craft your campaigns in the most efficient and effective manner. Just a few key points taken from someone else's hard-fought study could save you months of trial-and-error experimentation.

The Psychology of Persuasive Websites: Twenty-Point Action Checklist

FACT: Forty-eight percent of people view a website's design as the number-one factor in deciding the credibility of the business.[82]

Not surprising, really. They think, *"Lousy website . . . crappy business. Confusing website . . . disorganized business. Sloppy website . . . sloppy business practices. Website filled with technical glitches, spelling and grammatical errors . . . forget it!"*

But it's not much different from the *offline* world, is it? Walk into an important job interview with a half-eaten slice of pepperoni pizza hanging off your new dress shirt, and the immediate impression is, *"OMG, what a slob!"* First impressions on the web matter, too.

So let's look at a few "action suggestions" for improving a handful of ingredients in your current site—some technical, some design, and others psychological. Each suggests what you need to do to make your site more effective. Put an actual or virtual checkmark in the boxes if your site already addresses each issue.

1. **Pile on the Reviews.** Seventy-two percent of people trust online reviews as much as personal recommendations from people they know. Social proof is key to satisfying consumers' "convincer strategies," as Richard Bandler, the co-creator of neuro-linguistic programming (NLP), would put it. What's more, on average, the conversion rate of a product can increase by as much as 270 percent as it accumulates reviews.[83]

2. **Tap into Authority Persuasion.** Positive reviews by influencers and recognized experts rank high on the persuasion scale because the influence from an expert is competence based "through implicit assurances, by virtue of the authoritativeness of the source, that the opinion has adequate justification in fact and logic."[84] Multiple testimonials have a snowball effect, actually *crafting*—like a skilled potter working clay—a positive perception in consumers' minds.[85] Who in your industry can you get an endorsement from? Who can you "gift" your product to for a quick review? Remember, it's a two-way street: you're giving them something and they're helping you. But for most influencers, it's not the *product* you send them; it's the *extra publicity* you promise in exchange for their review. That taps their ego and gets them listening.

3. **Make It "Not Always Available."** Conveying scarcity works to boost sales.[86] It's like the used car salesperson telling you that two others are considering the same car you're admiring, and— *YIKES!*—suddenly you want it more. It's the armrest on the airplane that you couldn't care less about until the guy next to you suddenly plops his arm on it. Scarcity, or the FOMO—fear of missing out—causes anxiety and leverages the fear of a shortage

in order to sell more. Approximately 60 percent of millennial consumers report making a reactive purchase—usually within 24 hours—after they experienced FOMO.[87] *Unethical?* Not if you're selling a helpful, quality product and your claims are true. Discounts really *do* expire. Quantities sometimes really *are* limited. Scarcity also implies that your product is popular. Such claims can encourage consumers to do less central route processing—deep thought, as described in *Cashvertising,* page 54—and buy with less careful consideration.[88]

Methods? Scarcity in stock claims . . . Countdown timers (accounted for a 9 percent increase conversion in a split-test by *WhichTestWon*) . . . Real-time buyer behavior notices such as recent-sale pop-ups like *"Joe from La Quinta, CA just signed up 20 minutes ago"* works like "living" social proof.[89] Sites that spoof these pop-ups lose credibility because they typically overdo it with a barrage of pop-ups for questionable products. Getting eight pop-ups every minute for a smiley face soap dish just isn't believable.

4. **You're Already Mobile, Right?** Sixty-two percent of companies that designed their websites for mobile platforms increased their sales; 64 percent that designed for tablets did the same. *Why?* Because 67 percent of shoppers are more likely to buy from a site they can navigate from a mobile device.[90] No surprise here, but still I see scores of sites that are virtually impossible to navigate effectively on a smaller mobile screen. (And don't get me started on filling out *forms* on non-mobile-optimized sites. Argh!)

5. **Avoid the Three-Second Death Trap.** Most mobile users expect a website to load in three seconds or less. After just three seconds, your non-loaded site will be "dead" to 40 percent who arrived.[91] *Meaning?* They'll click away that fast. That's nearly *half* of the people who actually got to your site! (How much are you spending on advertising to get them there?) It's like having the world's most powerful sales letter, but the recipients can't get the damned envelope opened! When's the last time you performed a speed check? Do it now! And because your web designer might not be familiar with the terms *progressive enhancement* and *graceful degradation,* you should recheck it regularly.

6. **Top-Load Your Benefits.** Website visitors spend 57 percent of their time above the fold, the part of your site they see without scrolling.[92] Is your biggest benefit above the fold? Are readers hit with a good reason to do business with you? Good direct-response says they should see a strong claim or promise the second they arrive. While those interested will scroll and read deep if your copy is good and suggests value, it's your biggest benefit that will grab the attention of your true target audience. Those not interested won't read past the first few words.

7. **Bulletize All Lists.** Fifty-five percent looked at lists. Add bullet • symbols and that figure jumps to 70 percent. Easy win.

8. **Get It UX Tested.** Forty-four percent of mobile users reported that navigating a web page was difficult, and 6 percent complained of difficulties interacting with it.[93] Has your site been user-experience (UX) tested? There are scores of services that can help . . . cheap. Put some fresh eyes on your site and be prepared for things you never realized. It's a forest-for-the-trees situation. You just need other eyeballs and brains to check it out. It could pay for itself with just the first few findings.

9. **Navbars Get Six.** Consumers spend approximately 6.44 seconds looking at a website's navigation bar when they first arrive at your site. That's the second-longest viewing time of any common individual page element after the logo.[94] It can either suggest an easy or difficult-to-navigate site. **HINT:** *This isn't the place to get creative!* Visitors expect horizontal navbars across the top or vertical bars along the left side. So give them what they expect.

10. **Drop the Drop-Downs.** Drop-down menus slow readers and force them to search for information that they don't even know they'll find. Make locating things on your site more certain with descriptive links that they see without needing to "unfold" your main tabs.

11. **Strategically Load the Left.** Users spend 80 percent of their time viewing information on the left of the page.[95] This suggests that your most important information should be located in the left column if your web pages are formatted this way.

12. **Anchor the Preferred Option.** Imagine that you're reading the menu at BiCE, a (very) high-end Italian restaurant in Midtown Manhattan. The first dish—the renowned Bice Tagliolini Pasta with Lobster and Truffles—is $1,950. The second dish—an equally appealing Valentino Uovo al Tartufo—is "just" $295. By contrast, the second dish—still outrageously expensive—is now considered "cheap." That's anchoring, and it's powerfully persuasive. Use it on your website by setting pricing tiers, with one being significantly higher than the other. *The effect?* Like the Tartufo, the less-expensive choice seems dramatically cheaper. The higher-priced tier causes readers to believe that the lower-priced tier has greater value. This effect is magnified if both products/offers are similar.[96]

13. **Choose an Appropriate Color Scheme.** A study from the University of Toronto revealed how people using Adobe Color—a free web tool for color combination creation and sharing—preferred simple combinations of only two to three colors.[97] Colors convey meanings and feelings, so simple combinations might make it easier for consumers to understand the message being conveyed. Four primary color schemes are popular with web designers today: *monochromatic, analogous, triadic,* and *complementary*. And here's when to use each:

   ▷ **Have a simple message or product?** Going for a high-end look? A *monochromatic* color scheme might be right for you. This palette uses different variations of the same color—varying shades of purple, for example. It's a simple, clean look that's ideal for communicating simple, straightforward ideas. **Examples:** 1) dark blue, slightly lighter blue, and light blue; 2) black, gray, and white; 3) brown and beige. High-end sellers adopt the monochromatic color scheme to convey sophistication and refinement.[98] Check *rolls-roycemotorcars.com* for a great example.

   ▷ **Looking to convey harmony?** *Analogous* schemes use colors close together on the color wheel, like blue and violet, for example. Or red, red-orange, and orange. Because of their similar hues, they're ideal for expressing harmony and cooperation.

▷ **Need to make a splash?** *Triadic* palettes use three colors positioned at a 120-degree interval on the color wheel. **Examples:** 1) red, yellow, and blue; 2) purple, green, and orange; 3) blue-violet, red-orange, and yellow-green; and 4) red-violet, yellow-orange, and blue-green. Ask your designer to use one color for the background—preferably the lighter one for easy reading—and the other two for high-contrast text and features. Or, choose one dominant color (usually a primary or secondary color), a supporting color (a secondary or tertiary color), and a third color that's a mix of the first two colors . . . or a totally different color for an eye-popping splash for elements you want to really stand out.

▷ **Need to shake things up?** *Complementary* color schemes can do it with high-contrasting colors from *opposite* sides of the color wheel. **Examples:** 1) red and green; 2) blue and orange; 3) yellow and purple, and 4) yellow-green and red-purple. Our eyeballs love these choices. *Why?* Because when two opposite colors enter the human eye, they simultaneously stimulate both low- and high-frequency photoreceptor cells in our retinas. The result is an "optical massage" of sorts, as the contrasting colors create a sort of "harmonious rivalry" while balancing each other's intensity. Complementary colors are often used to call attention to specific page elements, such as a CTA, sale price, or button.

14. **Don't Assume Red or Green Is Better.** *Ah yes, the ol' green versus red CTA button debate.* I'm familiar with the studies: HubSpot, Bing, Monetate, RIPT, VWO, and others. Before you drive yourself nuts, know this: when it comes to generating responses, *it's not the* **color** *of your button, but, instead, the* **degree** *of which your button contrasts with the rest of your web page.* That's because the human eye is naturally drawn toward stimuli that are most noticeable.[99] High contrast increases what scientists call *processing fluency,* which is our willingness to do something depending on how well we understand it and how easy or difficult it is to perform.[100] To click a button, we must

first see it. The greater the likelihood of us seeing it, the greater the chances we'll click it . . . *but only if we want the stuff.* Makes sense, right?

Think about it! The button itself—unless it contains persuasive text within it (such as a discount offer or deadline, for example)—has no inherent power to make your prospects want to buy what you're selling! They don't read your sales copy, see your button, and suddenly have a mysterious and unconscious change of heart due to its color. They don't say, *"I'm not interested in this slop! Oh, but, wait! Look at this bright green BUY NOW button. Uh, hmmm, actually, I DO want to buy it!"* Doesn't happen. Similarly, they don't say, *"Hey, I want this! Wait, what's this? A bright red BUY NOW button?! Hmmm, something's not right. Oh, FORGET IT!"*

Yes, color influences on a subconscious level, but color itself isn't going to *decrease* your prospects' desire for a product that they've already decided can add value to their life. Nor will it *increase* the desire for a product for which they see no need.

Bottom line: *Buttons don't make people want stuff.* Instead, they 1) suggest the idea of buying and 2) give the opportunity to buy. Choose any color you want with high contrast to the background and the rest of your page. Make it pop! Test colors for sure. But don't restrict yourself to red and green. Over 300 million people worldwide are color-blind to those two colors. Whatever color you choose, just know that all things being the same, *the button that's most noticeable on your page will likely be the winner in your tests.*[101]

15. **Scatter Your CTAs.** How many times would you ask your salesperson to ask for a sale? Would you say, *"Hey, Bill, make sure you ask the prospect to buy only one time, okay? If they don't buy, just leave."* Ridiculous! Well, your website is your salesperson. To feature your call to action on your site only once is ridiculous. That's why your primary CTA should appear multiple times on your website. The more times it's seen, the greater the chances of getting attention. If viewers miss it at the top, they might click it in the middle or bottom. Also, they might not be ready to buy wherever you first place it, but they might be ready to whip out their credit card a minute later.

16. **Center and Label Your "Most Popular" Option.** If you offer more than one choice, put the one you'd most like prospects to choose in the visual center of the others, with a corner flag or burst saying, *"Most Popular!"* Or Amazon's *"#1 Best Seller"* flag. This takes advantage of the old Bandwagon Effect—present since the beginning of time—tapping into the human desire to follow the most "socially acceptable" path.[102] When you position one item in the center of other choices, it attracts more attention and persuades consumers to choose them over others.[103] Enlarging it a bit amplifies this effect.

17. **Direct Them Where to Look.** We humans are social creatures. We like to—no, we're *programmed* to—look at people's faces. And we also look where they're looking. For example, in my seminars, I prove this point in fifteen seconds. I suddenly stop talking and look at the blank ceiling. When I look back at the audience, the majority of them are looking at the blank ceiling, too. Talk about easy control. But it's natural! We have an inborn tendency to follow people's gazes. It's an evolutionary trait that helped us learn about the world. It's programmed into our brains.[104] Take advantage of this by featuring photos of people looking at your CTA button. If they're pointing to it, that's even better. If they're looking, pointing, and smiling, it's a triple whammy. You're showing them where to look, showing them how to feel, and increasing the impact of the placement of your response mechanism.[105] Psychology is wonderful.

18. **Number the Steps.** Tell your buyers exactly what to do and in what order to do it. Numbering the steps helps improve their understanding of the process and reduces their anxiety. In addition, one study showed that labeling each step of the checkout process with a number can increase the checkout completion rate by up to 8.6 percent. Consumers prefer to know the number of steps within any online sequence of events.[106] That means if you're asking them to complete forms or any activity that requires them to navigate multiple pages, always number each step and show your readers where they are in the process. Shadow or checkmark the completed steps, or use a progress bar to denote that they're moving forward. This gives them a sense of progression and finality and reduces the stress inherent in spending money.

19. **Force Them to Reject Your CTA.** Consumers never want to miss out. They also want things they can't have. You'll recall we discussed both of these psychological phenomena earlier. So rather than just allowing your readers to overlook the CTA on your upsell page, ask them to *reject* it if it's not for them.[107] Give them two options: "[ ] *YES, Drew! Give me a bonus 60 minutes consulting time for just $99—an instant 67% discount"* and also "[ ] *NO THANKS, Drew—I'll pass on this one-time upgrade offer."* *The effect?* Research shows that providing these options causes them to take a thoughtful moment to reconsider and also triggers FOMO, what psychologists call *loss aversion.*[108]

20. **Limit the Options.** More choices means more brainwork needed to make a decision. *"Do I pick A or B or C or D? Ugh!"* We've known for decades that with more options, people are often less likely to make a decision.[109] *Solution?* Break your CTA into steps. For example, for the first step, they provide only their name and email address. *Easy, right?* Next, they click a link that takes them to another page that captures more information such as their company name and phone number.

The effect? Dramatically better compliance than putting everything on the first page. What looks easy when formatted over two pages looks like *"Ugh, lots to type"* when shown on just one page. But upon arriving at page two, they're faced with a slightly uncomfortable dilemma. *"Gee, I got this far. I want the thing. How can I quit now?"* You've successfully created *cognitive dissonance,* the state of discomfort felt when two or more modes of thought contradict each other.[110] So spread your options apart to make choosing psychologically easier.

ONLINE AD-AGENCY SECRET #14:

Seven Key Findings to Maximize Your Online Video Ads

Ahhh, who doesn't love watching online videos? No matter what your interest—from baking chocolate-fudge zucchini cake to tying the tightest-gripping trucker's knot—there are thousands of online videos waiting to teach you how to do it, or do it better. Videos educate, persuade, entertain, and—probably most of them—just kill time.

What about video advertising? How does it compare to the effectiveness of blog posts and typical "static" social media ads? Most videos are more effective than most blog posts for 1) grabbing attention and 2) driving action. *Why?* For the same reason that movies are more engaging than your hometown newspaper. Sound and motion . . . music and effects . . . demonstrations of products right in front of your eyes.

But how effective are video *ads?* Unlike the television infomercials and direct-response print ads in, say, your local newspaper, today's online ads don't typically drive prospects to their phones to call an 800 number, where their effectiveness can be immediately measured. That's the essence of "pure" direct response.

Let's compare your ads to a real live salesperson. Your ad is essentially one salesperson—one ad—doing the work to grab the prospects' attention. However, unlike a salesperson who attempts to close the deal on the spot, most online ads send readers to yet other "salespeople"—websites—where those websites are now charged with closing the "real" deal—the one that makes the cash register ring. Your ad influenced them to click. *Great!* But now those prospects, all primed to learn more, often get turned off—or not sufficiently motivated—by that "second salesperson"—the website that doesn't have the same closing "skills."

Meaning? You can have the greatest video ad in your industry that's producing leads-a-plenty, but if your website doesn't close those leads, your work needs to be focused on your weak-closing site, not your ad. There are plenty of practical how-tos in this book to help you do that. But for now, let's talk about boosting the response from your video ads if they're not the star closers you'd like them to be.

What specific things make video ads effective? There are many metrics to consider, and a high CTR helps put the $$$ in our pockets. But first, you need *views*. Indeed, for any video ad to be effective, it must first be *watched*. The longer people watch, the more likely they're interested. The more they're interested, the greater the likelihood they'll buy.

Enter Professor Ramesh K. Sitaraman of the College of Information and Computer Sciences at the University of Massachusetts at Amherst, along with S. Shunmuga Krishnan. To find out what keeps people watching, they conducted the first in-depth scientific study of video ads and their effectiveness. The data set employed is one of the most extensive cross-sections of varied enterprise videos ever used in a scientific study of this kind. Namely, they studied data from thirty-three video providers—consisting of 362 million videos and 257 million ad impressions—watched by 65 million unique viewers located across the world.[111]

Let's get practical and look at . . .

THE SEVEN KEY FINDINGS PROFESSOR SITARAMAN DISCOVERED IN AMHERST

1. **Mid-Roll Wins.** "Mid-roll" ads placed in the middle of a video had the highest completion rate of 97 percent, whereas "pre-roll" ads placed in the beginning and "post-roll" ads placed in the end resulted in dramatically smaller completion rates of 74 percent and 45 percent, respectively. *Reason?* Viewers are more engaged during mid-roll ads, causing them to be more patient. Your ad is 18.1 percent more likely to complete when placed as a mid-roll versus a pre-roll. It's 14.3 percent more likely to complete when placed as a pre-roll versus a post-roll.

2. **Twenty-Second Ads Lost . . .** and had the lowest completion rate of 60 percent. Scoring better were fifteen-second ads at 84 percent completion and thirty-second ads at 90 percent. In his quasi-experiment—an attempt to establish a cause-and-effect relationship by using criteria other than randomization—Sitaraman showed that longer ads are in fact *less* likely to be completed because viewers would have less patience to sit through them. Of course, the flip side is that—like long *written* sales copy—only those interested in the topic would watch anyway. I'll take fewer watchers and more buyers any day. (Wouldn't you?)

3. **Ads Played Within Long-Form Videos,** such as TV shows, movies, documentaries, and similar, were completed at 87 percent. By contrast, ads played within short-form videos completed at 67 percent. Ads are 4.2 percent more likely to complete when they appear within a long-form versus a short-form video.

4. **Time of Day No Influence.** Some marketers proclaim that because people are generally more relaxed at night and overall viewership peaks (which is true), they're more willing to watch video ads to completion. That thinking is reasonable; however, this study found no supporting evidence for this hypothesis.

5. **Repeat Visitors Watch Longer** for all subcategories of ad placements—pre-rolls, mid-rolls, and post-rolls—with a completion rate of 84.9 percent versus first-time/one-time visitors at only 78 percent.

6. **Greater Impatience for Videos to Start**—Slow-loading videos drive people nuts. In fact, they're more likely to complete a video than wait for one to begin. For example, at the ten-second mark, 45.8 percent of the viewers abandoned a slow-loading video (meaning nothing is playing yet) versus only 13.4 percent of viewers watching a pre-roll ad. *Lesson?* Give them something to see while your video loads, or you might lose nearly half of them just ten seconds in!

7. **People Abandon Early** . . . with nearly one-third leaving in the first quarter of the video and two-thirds at the halfway point. According to Facebook, 65 percent of people who watch the first three seconds of a video will watch for at least ten seconds; 45 percent of them will continue watching for an additional thirty seconds. **TIP:** Hook viewers in the first few seconds with a powerful benefit statement and strong, emotional words. Make your claim immediately. **IMPORTANT REMINDER:** Your first few words are actually your video ad's all-important *headline,* so write your script that way!

Plus . . . Always Add Captions to Easily Increase Viewing Time. Video ads with captions enjoy an average 12 percent increase in view time.[112] *Why?* A joint study by Verizon Media and Publicis Media finds that 69 percent of users watch videos with the sound turned off.[113]

Multiple Studies Reveal the Best Days and Times to Post

Decisions, decisions, decisions. As if writing the copy and choosing the graphics aren't challenging enough. Now you have to decide which days and times to post for the highest noting, interaction, and response. Fortunately, there's no shortage of data, but even some of those who conducted extensive tests don't agree. So test your own ads, using the following to guide you. (**NOTE:** All times shown are assumed to be "local time" unless otherwise stated.)

THE BEST TIMES TO RUN FACEBOOK ADS

- *Social Intelligence Report:* Brands are targeting Facebook users on Fridays because that's the day with the highest engagement rates, with 17 percent of all comments, 16 percent of likes, and 16 percent of shares occurring on Fridays. Sunday posts get the lowest engagement.

- A Buffer study reports the best time to post to Facebook is between 1 p.m. and 3 p.m. during the week and Saturdays. Engagement rates are 18 percent higher on Thursdays and Fridays.

- HubSpot says: "Thursdays and Fridays from 1 p.m. to 3 p.m. are the best times to post on Facebook."

- CoSchedule says that they "analyzed 37,219,512 social media messages from more than 30,000 organizations" and found that 1–4 p.m. late into the week and on weekends is best.

- Hootsuite's findings show that 8 a.m. to 12 p.m. on Tuesdays and Thursdays are the best times and days.

- Oberlo reports that the best days to post are "3 a.m. on Mondays through Fridays and 10 a.m. and noon on Tuesdays, with the best days being Tuesday through Friday."[114]

THE BEST TIMES TO RUN TWITTER ADS

- Sysomos says: "Twitter's peak times are between 11 a.m. and 3 p.m. EST."

- Buffer says: "The early morning hours appear to be the time in which tweets receive the most clicks, on average. Noon to 1 p.m. local time, on average for each time zone, is the most popular time to tweet. The highest number of clicks per tweet occurs between 2 a.m. and 4 a.m., peaking between 2 and 3 a.m."

▸ Hootsuite says: "The best time to post on Twitter is 8 a.m. on Mondays and Thursdays."

▸ HubSpot says: "23% of marketers surveyed say 9 a.m.–2 p.m. is the best time to post on the platform, followed by 12 p.m.–3 p.m., then 3 p.m.–6 p.m." Fridays and Wednesdays are equally the best days to post.[115]

THE BEST TIMES TO RUN INSTAGRAM ADS

▸ HubSpot says: "The best times to post on Instagram across industries are in the mid- to late afternoon, specifically between 6–9 p.m. . . . 3–6 p.m. . . . and 9–12 p.m."

▸ Hootsuite reports that 11 a.m. on Wednesdays is the best posting time.

▸ Later—the social media scheduler—says they conducted a study of 35 million global posts and determined that "Saturday and Sunday at 6 a.m. local time is the best time to post."

▸ Sprout Social says: "The best times to post are Monday at 11 a.m. . . . Tuesday and Wednesday 10 a.m.–2 p.m. . . . and Thursdays and Fridays 10 a.m.–noon, with Tuesdays and Wednesdays edging out Mondays."

▸ Oberlo data shows that 11 a.m. on Mondays, 10 a.m. to 2 p.m. on Tuesdays and Wednesdays, and 10 a.m. to 12 p.m. on Thursdays and Fridays are best.[116]

THE BEST TIMES TO RUN LINKEDIN ADS

▸ Hootsuite says: "The best time to post on LinkedIn is 9 a.m. on Tuesdays and Wednesdays."

▸ HubSpot advises: "Aim to post on LinkedIn between 6–9 p.m., 3–6 p.m., or 12–3 p.m. The best day to post is Saturdays, Sundays, and Wednesdays."

▸ Oberlo suggests posting on Tuesdays, Wednesdays, and Thursdays between 10–11 a.m. for best results.

- Sprout Social: Wednesdays from 8–10 a.m. and at 12 p.m.; Thursdays at 9 a.m. and between 1–2 p.m.; Fridays at 9 a.m.

- Quintly: 7–8 a.m., 12 p.m., and 5–6 p.m.[117]

THE BEST TIMES TO RUN YOUTUBE ADS

- HubSpot advises to post between 6–9 p.m. (31 percent), 3–6 p.m., and noon–3 p.m. They also say that 25 percent of marketers surveyed recommend posting on Saturdays, while 23 percent say Friday is the best day to post. Monday through Wednesday are the worst days to post on the platform, along with early mornings from 6–9 a.m.

- SocialPilot cites four studies:
  1. Frederator Networks suggests posting between 2 to 4 p.m. (EST) on weekdays and between 9 to 11 a.m. (EST) on weekends.
  2. Boosted concluded that posting on Sunday, either at 11 a.m. or 5 p.m. (EST) is best.
  3. HowSociable favors 2 to 4 p.m. (EST) as the most effective time and Thursday and Friday as the most effective days.
  4. InVideo suggests posting between 12 and 4 p.m. (EST) on weekdays, and 9 and 11 a.m. (EST) on weekends.[118]

THE BEST TIMES TO RUN TIKTOK ADS

- HubSpot: The best times to post are 6–9 p.m., 3–6 p.m., and 12–3 p.m. For B2B brands, Saturdays and Thursdays are the best days to post. For B2C brands, it's Saturdays and Sundays. Although transportation and financial services brands seem to find success in posting between 6–9 a.m., most marketers don't recommend it.

- Influencer Marketing Hub reports that in their study of over 10,000 TikTok posts, the highest levels of engagement happen at 9 a.m. on Tuesday, 12 p.m. on Thursday, and 5 a.m. on Friday, all times EST.

- Hootsuite says: "Based on our experiments and analysis of 30,000 posts, the best time to post on TikTok for maximum engagement is Thursday at 7 p.m."[119]

THE BEST TIMES TO RUN PINTEREST ADS

> ▸ HubSpot reports: "The best times to post on Pinterest are between 6 p.m. to 9 p.m."
>
> Second best: noon to 3 p.m. "22% of B2C brands say Sundays are the best days to post on Pinterest, compared to only 6% of B2B brands. Conversely, only 2% of B2C brands chose Mondays versus 13% of B2B brands."
>
> ▸ Public Sector Marketing Institute says: "The best times to post on Pinterest are 12:00 p.m., 6:17 p.m., and 8:02 p.m. on Friday, Tuesday, and Thursday."
>
> ▸ CoSchedule analyzed 30,000 accounts and concluded, "The top 5 best hours to post on Pinterest are 8:00 p.m., 4:00 p.m., 9:00 p.m., 3:00 p.m., and 2:00 p.m. The top 3 best days to post to Pinterest Sunday, Monday and Tuesday."[120]

It's clear: Some companies and researchers agree on post timing, and some don't. One says post on Instagram on Wednesdays, and the other likes weekends. *Argh! Who's right?* Well, test results aren't based on empty ads. *Meaning?* The "best" results come from the best ads containing the best copy, offer, targeting, and the same factors you consider when you run ads *anywhere*, online and off. However, these suggestions are guidelines based on extensive data, in some cases thousands of ads. Following their recommendations *first*—rather than testing random placements—will likely save you a huge amount of time and frustration.

ONLINE AD-AGENCY SECRET #16:

The Illusory Truth Effect and the Psychological Power of Repetition

What would you think if your best friend sent you the panicked text: *"OMG! Aliens just landed 2 miles from your house. Get in your car and get out of town NOW!!!"* You'd probably think your friend was cuckoo, nuts, or just messing around with you, right?

But what if a close family member sent you a similar text just five minutes later? You'd probably think that was pretty weird, right? Would it get you wondering a bit? Or, maybe you'd think it's a setup—a "conspiracy" to freak you out. In any event, you'd likely scratch your head and move on with your day. (Unless you did a quick Google news search . . . uh, just in case.)

But it doesn't stop there. Just fifteen minutes later, *another* friend (who didn't know the first friend) and then also a coworker (who didn't know *any* of the people who already contacted you) both texted similar messages: *"Hey, you saw the news, right??? If you're home, leave the area now and come to my place!"* and *"GET OUT OF THERE. They're hostile!!!"* At what point would you begin to think there's some real substance to their warnings?

While studying neuro-linguistic programming (NLP) under cofounder Richard Bandler in San Francisco and Robert Dilts, Todd Epstein, and Judith Delozier in Santa Cruz, I learned of something called the *convincer strategy*, something each of us has. Simply defined, it's how a person believes something is true. Different people have different convincer strategies.

For example, to believe something, some people need to *see* it; others simply need to *hear* it. (There are others, but let's focus on these two primaries.) There's also a *frequency* component. Some people believe it the first time they see or hear it; others need to see or hear it three, four, five times, or more to be convinced. Lastly, there's a *time* component. Some need to see or hear the same message or event over the course of several days, weeks, or months before they believe it's true.

Whatever convincer strategy a person uses to process information in their world, one thing is consistent: *repetition*. The more something is repeated, the greater the likelihood is that the message will be believed.

> *If a lie is only printed often enough, it becomes a quasi-truth,*
> *and if such a truth is repeated often enough, it becomes an*
> *article of belief, a dogma, and men will die for it.*
>
> —ISA BLAGDEN, AUTHOR, *THE CROWN OF A LIFE*

Back to advertising. If you repeat your ad and its claims more often, will your message gain credibility, an essential ingredient for consumer trust and positive buying behavior? Yes, indeed. This finding is known as the *Illusory Truth Effect*. It happens because repeated information increases what's called *processing fluency*—the ease with which information is processed. We humans process an average of 74 gigabytes of information daily—the equivalent to watching sixteen full-length movies—and we've learned to use processing fluency as an indicator of truthfulness. Most studies of the phenomenon have used three or fewer repetitions. For the purposes of advertising, it would be far more beneficial if we knew what the effect was with a greater number of repetitions.

Enter researchers Hassan of the Department of Psychology, San Francisco State University, and Barber of the Department of Psychology, Georgia State University. In their study, "The Effects of Repetition Frequency on the Illusory Truth Effect," they examined how a larger number of repeated exposures affects our judgments of truth.

In a nutshell: Hassan and Barber conducted two experiments, showing participants two statements such as "The gestation period of a giraffe is 425 days." In the first experiment, the statements were shown either one, three, five, seven, or nine times. In the second experiment, the statements were shown either one, nine, eighteen, or twenty-seven times. One week later, the researchers repeated the statements and added new facts, and asked participants to rate their truthfulness. In both cases, the researchers discovered that the more often the participants read the statements, the more truthful they rated them to be. *Results?* "The largest increase in perceived truth occurred when people encountered the statement for the second time."[121]

What's more, research has also shown that repeated information is perceived as more truthful than new information, even if the repeated information is false and the new information is true! This *Illusory Truth Effect* has been shown to influence perception using a variety of different sources, such as trivia statements, products, fake news headlines, statements of pure opinion, outright rumors, and misinformation about personally observed events.[122]

Does it matter how much time elapses between repetitions? Not according to research. It could be just minutes, weeks, or even months apart. In fact, the effect even happens when the listener is told that the source isn't reliable, which is both fascinating and scary at the same time.[123]

Remember what I mentioned about processing fluency? That information that's easier to understand is more readily believed? Change to a more easily readable font on your website, and more people will believe your claims.[124] Switch to simpler, more easy-to-understand language, and more of your visitors will accept what you say is true.[125]

Easier Font = Easier Exercise (Huh?)

When two sets of identical exercise instructions were presented to study participants, the version set in an easy-to-read Arial font was judged to take only 8.2 minutes to complete. For the version set in a more difficult-to-read font, participants assumed that it would take twice as long to complete the exercise, over 15 minutes.[126] Fascinating, isn't it?

Interestingly enough, not only does repetition increase belief, but research has shown that when ads are repeated, people believe that the product is of higher quality.[127]

While the second repetition increases believability the most, results of a meta-analysis suggest that positive attitudes increase with up to ten exposures to an ad, after which there's a decline in positive attitudes.[128] *"An advertisement is 'worn in' when the repetition initially garners a positive effect and is 'worn out' when the repetition produces no effect or even a negative one."*[129]

Keep in mind, however, that simply repeating your ad doesn't mean it's repeating in *everyone's* brains. The *Illusory Truth Effect* occurs only in those individuals who actually *saw* your ads. And every time you run an ad, only a fraction of the total potential audience sees it. I say this merely to dissuade you from thinking, *"Oh no! I'm running my ad too often, and people will stop liking us!"* Typically, when you start becoming sick of seeing your own ad, that is when others are just beginning to see it.

Finally, according to research:

- Consumers who saw an advertisement ten or more times had greater purchase intentions than consumers with less exposure.

- Purchase intentions were driven more by *emotional* motivations for consumers who had seen an ad one to two times . . .
  - ▷ By *cognitive* factors for consumers who had seen an ad three to ten times, and again . . .
  - ▷ By *emotions* for consumers who had seen an ad more than ten times.[130]

How to sort this out? Keep your ads running, test each one against new creatives changing limited variables so you know the cause of any change in response, and let your market decide when your ads stop working. In the meantime, know that each repetition helps increase the credibility of your claims. You are making claims, aren't you? (And hopefully your first and strongest claim is in your headline.)

Killer Slogans: These Six Ingredients Make People Like and Remember Them

"Got milk?" . . . *"Just do it"* . . . *"You're in good hands with Allstate"* . . . *"Finger-lickin' good."*

Sound familiar?

How about: *"Melts in your mouth, not in your hands"* . . . *"Good to the last drop"* . . . *"Packed with peanuts, Snickers really satisfies."* These and scores of other company slogans have burned themselves into our brains.

Companies often spend millions of dollars in development and to have them do exactly that. Not only do they promote the products they're created for, but they also stick like glue in our heads—often causing us to unsuspectingly repeat (or sing!) them for "no apparent reason"—setting off the *Illusory Truth Effect* described in Online Ad-Agency Secret 16.

Many online companies considering creating a slogan for their business will sit down and just conjure up what they think are cute or clever lines. They'll play with rhymes, alliteration ("Big Bob's Bubba Burgers Boast a Bounty of Bodacious Beef!"), silly plays on words, and a mix of whatever else they think would be catchy. Too bad they're not reading this book—like you are right now—because an extensive and little-known study was conducted that tells us which of nine key elements are most important in crafting a winning slogan.

The insightful research included the examination of nine qualities embodied by company slogans and determined how important each is in creating one that's ultimately successful, likable, and memorable. The study included 220 respondents who, via survey, whittled down 241 nationally known slogans to retain only the 150 that were most familiar. A wide variety of industries were represented, including breakfast cereals, cars, financial services, cosmetics, laundry detergents, and fast food. Phase two included 595 participants who then answered questions about the 150 "finalist" slogans and determined which of nine key ingredients most contributed to their being both liked and remembered.[131]

SLOGANS: WHICH OF THESE NINE INGREDIENTS LEADS TO GREATER LIKING AND RECALL?

INGREDIENT	PREDICTION	OUTCOME
1. Clarity	More clarity = greater liking	✓ Supported
2. Benefit	Benefits emphasized = greater liking	✓ Supported
3. Creativity	More creativity = greater liking	✓ Supported
4. Brand Appropriateness	Brand appropriate = greater liking	✘ Not supported
5. Product Relevance	Product relevant = greater liking	✓ Supported
6. Jingle	Slogans with music = greater liking	✘ Not supported
7. Rhyme	Slogans with rhymes = greater liking	✓ Supported
8. Inclusion of Brand Name	Slogans without brand names = greater liking	✓ Supported
9. Length	Shorter slogans = greater liking	✘ Not supported

More findings: Are older slogans liked more? *No.* Those backed by bigger budgets? *No.* Do males like slogans more than females? *No.* How about younger people: do they like them more? *Yes.* And lastly, do lower-income respondents have a greater liking of slogans? *No.*

THE TOP TEN SLOGANS RANKED

MOST LIKED	MOST RECALLED
1. Melts in your mouth, not in your hand	1. Just do it
2. The few, the proud, the Marines	2. I'm lovin' it
3. What happens in Vegas, stays in Vegas	3. Have it your way
4. The happiest place on Earth	4. Melts in your mouth, not in your hand
5. Easy, breezy, beautiful, CoverGirl	5. Got milk?
6. Eat fresh	6. Eat fresh
7. Red Bull gives you wings	7. M'm! M'm! Good!!
8. Think outside the bun	8. You're in good hands with Allstate
9. Got milk?	9. Think outside the bun
10. Get in the zone	10. The ultimate driving machine

Finally, look at the preceding chart, and you'll see that of all the 241 slogans initially included in this study—boiled down to 150 finalists—the top 10 most liked of all of them with the highest recall have an average length of 3.9 words.

Meaning? If you want your slogan to be better remembered, in addition to considering the nine key ingredients, *keep it short!* The old rule for copy length for highway billboards serves us well with slogans too: *seven words or fewer.* But better remembered doesn't necessarily mean your slogan will be liked more, of course, but hopefully, if you incorporate all the "true" elements from the first chart here, your new slogan will stick in your prospects' heads like hungry flies to a big slice of wet-bottom shoofly pie.

The Psychological Power of Self-Referencing Headlines

In seminars that I conduct in the United States and overseas, I always ask my audiences the same simple question. (And I'll ask *you* too, right now.) I point to an ad that's projected on the giant screen behind me and say: *"If I asked you to point to the most important part of this ad, where would you point?"* People shout out a variety of things: *"The phone number!"* . . . *"The price!"* . . . *"The offer!"*

Wrong, wrong, wrong. Your answer? It's your *headline*, of course. That's because your headline is actually "the ad for your ad."

> *On the average, five times as many people read the headline as read the body copy. When you have written your headline, you have spent eighty cents out of your dollar.*
>
> —DAVID OGILVY

Just remember this: No matter how great your product, offer, price, creativity, copy, graphics, slogan, response device, and whatever other elements you can list, if your headline doesn't stop them, then it's—are you sitting down?—no different from having absolutely nothing under your headline, meaning an entirely blank page! *Comparison?* It's like pulling your car backward out of a driveway without first looking for possible cars or people behind you. *That's no different from having no eyes in your skull and backing out!* Okay, I think I made my point.

Let's now talk about making your headlines more effective and appending what we already discussed in the original *Cashvertising* on pages 92, 96, and 98. Rather than just play guessing games—which, as a direct-response guy, you know I don't do—are there any hard-core studies we can benefit from?

Researchers Lai and Farbrot—both of the BI Norwegian Business School in Oslo, Norway (the largest business school in Norway and the second largest in all of Europe)—set out to discover whether the inclusion of simple *questions* can significantly boost readership of your current headlines and, as a result, drive people into your body copy.[132]

For example, which of these two headlines do you think might be more effective: *"Easily Defend Yourself Against Attackers!"* versus *"Do You Want to Easily Defend Yourself Against Attackers?"*

How about: *"Train Any Dog in Just 1 Hour!"* versus *"Do You Know How to Train Any Dog in Just One Hour?"*

Could there be a measurable difference in readership by simply including a question and a personal reference—the word *you*? Can this be standardized for any product or service? Could it really be this easy? Well, way back in 1914, the famed advertising researcher Daniel Starch—a name I mentioned earlier—wrote the following:

> *The interrogatory form of heading tends to heighten interest. A question naturally stimulates a response as a matter of habit.*
>
> —DANIEL STARCH

Fact is, multiple studies have been conducted on the topic. Some theorized that "self-referencing," or mentioning the reader (typically by including the words *you* or *your*), boosts your ad's influence.[133] Other studies state that such pronouns make your message seem more relevant and useful when contrasted to words like *he, she, they,* and *them.*[134] Other researchers said that including questions actually enhances how the brain processes your message.[135]

The four-month study conducted by Lai and Farbrot used Twitter as their advertising lab. Farbot had 6,350 followers during the course of the experiment, with the bulk of her followers being news media employees. Four types of tweets were created with the following characteristics: 1) Tweets with declarative headlines, i.e., straightforward statements (this was the control), 2) question headlines *without* personal pronouns, e.g., *"How Important Is Family?"* (my example), and 3) question headlines *with* personal pronouns, e.g., *"How Important Is Your Family?"* (my example). They posted each message twice: first, the control condition (declarative headline), and subsequently, after one hour, by using one of the two experimental conditions (question headline with and without self-referencing cues).

Results: In 100 percent of the cases observed—no matter what the topic—headlines *with* questions generated higher interest in the target message compared to the non-question (control) headlines. How much greater? Between 10 percent and 533 percent for question heads *without* self-referencing cues, and between 49 percent and 350 percent for question heads *with* self-referencing cues. The mean increase of those *with* the cues was 25 percent higher than those without, as shown here:

HEADLINE VARIABLE	INCREASE OVER CONTROL*
Question Headlines *without* Self-Referencing Cues	**10%–533%** (Mean = 150%)
Question Headlines *with* Self-Referencing Cues	**49%–350%** (Mean = 175%)

*Declarative-Statement Headline

That's pretty darned impressive, right? But how would these results hold up when a similar test was conducted using consumer products as the topic?

To find out, the researchers placed ads on the auction site FINN, the Norwegian equivalent to eBay. They advertised an iPhone, a washing machine, a couch, and an LCD TV. The same types of headlines were tested as in their first test: 1) *Declarative:* "For sale: Black iPhone4 16GB"; 2) *Question without self-referencing cues:* "Anyone who needs a new iPhone4?"; and 3) *Question with self-referencing cues:* "Is this your new iPhone4?"

Results? Both types of question headlines—with and without self-references—boosted readership for all but the washing machine. For the three other products, a positive effect from 53.85 percent and 361.11 percent for headlines *without* self-referencing cues, and a boost of between 101.71 percent and 744.44 percent for question headlines *with* self-referencing cues. And now the mean increases:

MEAN INCREASES ACROSS ALL FOUR CONSUMER PRODUCTS

HEADLINE VARIABLE	INCREASE OVER CONTROL*
Question Headlines *without* Self-Referencing Cues	**137.30%**
Question Headlines *with* Self-Referencing Cues	**257.03%**

*Declarative-Statement Headline

The bottom line is clear: According to Lai and Farbrot's research, headlines that included questions with self-referencing cues beat declarative-statement headlines by a substantial margin.[136] Will these results hold up for you and your product and market? Nobody knows for sure, but here's a real-world study showing statistically significant differences in the three headline types that's worth putting to the test. *My advice?* Take your current headline, alter it only so much as to turn it into a question, add the word *you*, and see if you get the same big boost as this researcher. You might end up writing all your headlines this way.

The Psychology of Online Credibility and How to Boost Yours Fast

What would you do if a sloppy-looking stranger stopped you on the street and said—in equally sloppy English—*"Yo, uh, if ya gimme ten bucks . . . like, uh, today . . . I'll give ya back one thousand dollars tomorrow. Er, okay?"* What would you do? You'd probably keep walking, right? Most people would.

Okay, *now* imagine that a *different* guy stops you and makes the *same exact offer.* This time, however, it's Bob Stanley, the always well-dressed and beloved Bentley-driving multimillionaire philanthropist who owns the massive 4.5-million-square-foot shopping center in your own hometown. *Now* what do you do? Chances are, you'd start digging in your wallet for the cash.

Two different scenarios with two different likely outcomes. *But why?* Both guys asked you for the *same* amount: $10. Both promised the *same* reward: $1,000. But in the first case, you walked. In the second, you drooled. *Why?*

"That's simple, Drew; the first guy was a complete stranger. He might be dead broke! Plus, I know nothing about him. The second guy, however, was a millionaire . . . a big shot . . . a guy everyone around town knows and loves."

I agree with your logic, but even though the second guy is rich, that doesn't mean he's going to give you $990 of his own money just because he *said* he would. Truth is, it's a combination of many different elements that caused you to *believe* that rich Bob's deal would go through.

It's no different online. People arrive at your site. They read your words. They see your pictures. But do they *believe* what you're communicating? If they do, *why?* If they don't, why not? What's wrong and/or what's missing? Something must be! What, exactly, are the factors that make one website more believable than another, regardless of what they're selling? This is no small question. That's because it's *belief* that moves people from reading to buying. **The hard truth is:** If they don't believe you, they're not giving you their money.

The greatest thing to be achieved in advertising, in my opinion,
is believability, and nothing is more believable
than the product itself.

– LEO BURNETT

Stanford University's Web Credibility Project conducted a three-year study involving 4,500 participants that ultimately identified ten easy-to-implement guidelines that can help any online business boost consumer belief in their claims and, therefore, the likelihood of engaging and buying.

Incorporate as many of these ten suggestions in your site as possible, knowing that each one incrementally boosts your site's believability and, therefore, your chances of making the sale. Here are their findings, with my elaboration:

STANFORD UNIVERSITY'S GUIDELINES FOR WEB CREDIBILITY

1. **Make It Easy.** Make your site easy to use and as useful as possible.

2. **Tout Your Experience.** Buyers want to deal with knowledgeable experts. Give credentials and mention any awards.

3. **Keep It Fresh.** Frequent updates tell buyers that you're on the ball.

4. **Convey Honesty.** Tell prospects that honesty is key to your way of doing business and that your company is run by trustworthy people. Add employee bios for a believable, personal touch.

5. **Make Contacting Easy.** Don't hide your email and phone number. Give your social media links. Make yourself easily reachable.

6. **Be Verifiable.** Don't make claims without backing up what you say. Provide proof right there. Allay their fears. Provide stats with sources.

7. **Avoid Hype.** Don't overpromise or make wild, unbelievable claims.

8. **Make It Error-Free.** Avoid errors in spelling, grammar, spacing, and site performance such as broken links, buttons that don't click, and forms that don't process.

9. **Convey Solidity.** Are you a "real" company? Show photos of your employees, your headquarters, your people at work, your physical address.

10. **Use Pro Design.** Hire a professional graphic artist to design your site. Nothing says amateur—and kills credibility faster—than a visually unappealing, poorly designed site. Having a hammer doesn't make you a carpenter. Likewise, having web design software doesn't make you a skilled graphic artist. Crowdsource the job and see how dozens of designers would professionally execute your job. Try sites like Crowdspring, 99designs, and DesignCrowd. Let them compete and choose the best. You'll never go back to wasting days fiddling around with web design on your own again.[137]

How to "Discount Frame" and Change Their Perception of Value

You're selling toaster ovens. And you want to move them fast before the new models arrive next week. *It's sale time!* Regular price: $150. Do you express your discount as *10 percent off* or *$15.00 off*? Both amount to the same savings, but which will be more appealing to buyers? Could there actually be a statistically significant difference?

Researcher González and cohorts conducted three studies in 2016 to determine whether or not a dollars-off discount framing (e.g., "Save $15.00") results in greater perceptions of value and leads to increased sales for products priced over $100. Result? It did. Additional studies confirmed that this effect generalizes across higher than $100 price levels.

Conversely, they found that for products *under* $100, your discount is better expressed as a percentage off (e.g., "Save 10%"). Additional studies confirmed that this effect generalizes across lower than $100 price levels.[138]

Did you notice that both types of discounts—when applied according to *The Rule of 100*—express the higher number? Meaning that *under* $100, the discount expressed as a percentage will be higher than the dollars-off number. Conversely, for products priced *over* $100, the dollars-off number will be higher than the percentage. Obviously, higher numbers psychologically convey a higher discount. Clever little strategy, no?

Interestingly enough, a study of items in China tagged in yuan currency amounts conjectured that for high-priced products, including an image of the product could negate the effect of the percent-off discount framing, and therefore, showing no image for such products would be preferable.[139] I've seen no confirmation of this in other markets, however, although it might be something worth testing in your own market.

ONLINE AD-AGENCY SECRET #21:

Do They Trust You? What Consumers Find Most Important When Evaluating Your Website

It's one thing to *notice* elements on a website, and quite another to actively *judge* them and make determinations that will affect whether or not you'll buy. What elements were most noticed and judged, and which made the most difference? Which should you focus on, and in what order?

Stanford Persuasive Technology Lab—leading experts in such research—asked thousands of people to evaluate two websites randomly assigned from one of ten categories, such as e-commerce, entertainment, finance, health, news, sports, and travel. Commissioned by *Consumer Reports WebWatch,* the study assessed a total of 100 sites and analyzed 2,440 participants' comments. These results were combined with results from their collaborative study partners at Sliced Bread Design—a Mountain View, California, user-experience shop with a profoundly appealing and smartly crafted website—who asked fifteen health and finance experts to assess the credibility of sites in their respective industries.

STUDY RESULTS: WHAT DO PEOPLE MOST NOTICE WHEN EVALUATING A WEBSITE?

Website's Design 46.1%	**Writing Tone** 9.0%
Information Design/Structure 28.5%	**Site Functionality** 8.6%
Information Focus 25.1%	**Identity of Site Operator** 8.8%
Company Motive 15.5%	**Customer Service** 6.4%
Information Usefulness 14.8%	**Past Experience with Site** 4.6%
Information Accuracy 14.3%	**Information Clarity** 3.7%
Name Recognition/ Reputation 14.1%	**Performance on Test by User** 3.6%
Advertising 13.8%	**Readability** 3.6%
Information Bias 11.6%	**Affiliations** 3.4%

(Source: B. J. Fogg, C. Soohoo, and D. Danielson, "How Do People Evaluate a Web Site's Credibility? Results from a Large Study.")

As the table shows, the overall *design* of the site—layout, type, colors, fonts—was the number-one most-mentioned ingredient at 46.1 percent. Interestingly enough, the researchers stated that this result didn't comport with their initial expectations. They predicted that the more "substantive" elements (e.g., reputation, usefulness, accuracy) would be considered higher in importance, stating, *"We found that when people assessed a real Web site's credibility they did not use rigorous criteria."*[140]

These researchers cited an earlier *Consumer Reports WebWatch* survey of 1,500 people that claimed that things like "having a privacy policy" were vital to credibility. In the more recent Stanford study, most people didn't give a flying flounder about that. They cared mostly about how attractive the site was. (Talk about a mismatch.) Stanford concluded that what people say and do are often quite different. (No surprise here, right?) On the other hand, the health and finance experts who were surveyed expressed just the opposite. These folks are more interested in substance over looks.

So if you're not in the health or finance field—and/or perhaps similar or related fields—you need to take a second look at your site. Is it strikingly appealing? Did you hire a graphics pro to create it, or are you using sterile templates along with thousands of other sites doing the same thing? If you don't currently have your own go-to designer, crowdsource your job, as I mentioned previously, and see what multiple designers would do. Then award your project to the best. This is the easiest way to totally overhaul your online image—giving your job to someone who eats and breathes design—while you concentrate on the other aspects of your business.

And now that you know how important the *look and feel* of your site is to potential buyers—the number-one element both noticed and judged to determine the believability of your message (46.1 percent)—it's something you really can't afford to put off any longer.

Don't Be Invisible! Choosing the Best Font for Mature Readers

Do you advertise to consumers over age fifty? Then you'd better know about their eyeballs!

According to Pew Research, social media is used by 73 percent of Americans ages fifty to sixty-four. The best platform to reach them? Many believe it's Facebook—62 percent of internet users ages sixty-five and older use it, as do 72 percent of those ages fifty to sixty-four. Facebook has the highest number of users in these age ranges.[141]

To respond to your ad, viewers need to be able to read it. If not, you're essentially invisible to them, and that can crush your bottom line. According to the American Foundation for the Blind, approximately 12.0 percent of Americans ages forty-five to sixty-four, 12.2 percent ages sixty-five to seventy-four, and 15.2 percent of those seventy-five years of age and over report having vision loss.[142]

Meaning? If you promote to this older group, you need to think about the fonts you're using. Researchers Bernard, Liao, and Mills of the Software Usability Research Laboratory at Wichita State University conducted a small-scale study on exactly this topic.

The test was simple: They sat twenty-seven participants—aged sixty-two to eighty-three—in front of a computer screen. Participants were instructed to read four passages consisting of 683 words each. Researchers used text passages set in two different serif fonts—Georgia and Times New Roman—in both 12 and 14 points, and also in two sans-serif fonts—Arial and Verdana—set in the same two sizes. **The goal:** To determine if there was any difference in legibility, elapsed reading time, and the overall general preference when read by older folks.

Quick reminder: A serif typeface is one that has little feet and embellishments on the tips and base of each letter, **such as this font**. Sans- (the French word *without*) serif faces, **such as this font**, have no such serifs. On printed matter, the serifs make each letter more distinct and recognizable.

Next, participants read four *different* 683-word passages set in the same fonts, but set in a larger 14 points. Each test passage contained an untold number of "substitution" words that were not appropriate for the passages. For example, *cake* would be substituted by *fake*. Would participants spot these decoy words? If so, that would help the researchers determine "ease of legibility," along with reading speed. The two measures together considered the "effective reading score." *The calculation?* The percentage of accurately detected substituted words divided by the reading time.[143]

STUDY CONCLUSIONS: THE BEST FONT AND SIZE TESTED FOR THE SENIOR MARKET

▸ **Winning Style:** Sans-serif fonts were preferred over serif fonts. The serif fonts set in 12-point type were significantly slower to read than both the 14-point serif and sans-serif fonts.

▶ **Winning Size:** The 14-point fonts of all four typefaces tested were found to be more readable than the widely used 12-point size. Participants were able to read them faster and preferred them over the same text set in 12 points.

RANKING TESTED FONTS AND SIZES BY PREFERENCE MOST TO LEAST PREFERRED

1. 14-point Arial (Most Preferred)

2. 14-point Verdana

3. 14-point Georgia

4. 14-point Times New Roman

5. 12-point Verdana

6. 12-point Arial

7. 12-point Georgia

8. 12-point Times New Roman (Least preferred)

ONLINE AD-AGENCY SECRET #23:

Studies: How Uncertainty Reduction Saves Your Web Visitors

"I want it . . . and I want it NOW!" said every internet user in history.

Fact is, today's consumers have little patience waiting for your page to load. You're literally just a few eyeblinks away from losing a sale. *Yikes!* Could it really be that fast? Let's look at some research.

Referred to by researchers as TWT, or *Tolerable Waiting Time*, their big question was, *"How long are users willing to wait for a web page to load before abandoning it?"* (My own interpretation of the same question is, *"How long before I lose the sale?"*) Also, does providing some kind of on-screen feedback (while the page loads) help increase your prospects' tolerance?

Unfortunately, today's consumers hate waiting. For example, in 1997, Danish computer researcher Jacob Nielsen said that consumers' TWT was ten seconds. In 1999, Zona Research proclaimed it was eight seconds. A 1999 Selvidge study showed that people are as likely to wait for one second as they are for twenty seconds, but at thirty seconds—BAM!—all bets are off. And in 2000, Hoxmeier and DiCesare said consumers' TWT was twelve seconds.[144]

Lots of research. Lots of different study results. But there's one point nobody's debating: *The longer we have to wait—online or off—the more frustrated and sometimes angry we become.*[145] Therefore, to placate prospects before they become too antsy, Nielsen proposed that users should always be kept apprised as to the system's status—or "what's going on" during the delay—to diminish the negative repercussions of the waiting experience.[146]

Multiple researchers agree that the negative effects of waiting can be *"neutralized by effectively managing waiting experiences."*[147]

For example, system feedback can be provided in the form of a moving status bar. The mental process that occurs while they're watching the animated moving bar is called *Resource Allocation Perspective and Uncertainty Reduction.* Essentially, the moving progress bar serves as a distraction and reduces the uncertainty of "endless" waiting. Instead of thinking, *"Is anything happening here? Is this site messed up? Will this page ever load?!"* they think, *"Okay, we're moving along . . . almost there!"* When mental activity is increased, the "empty" time spent waiting appears to move forward more quickly.[148]

"Providing feedback during the wait reduces stress and uncertainty, thereby increasing Tolerable Waiting Time."[149]

Interesting stuff . . . and makes perfect sense, but how much longer would users really wait if a progress bar is shown? Dr. Fiona Fui-Hoon Nah, Professor of Business and Information Technology (BIT) at the Missouri University of Science and Technology asked this exact question.

Seventy web-savvy students were divided into two groups. Each had to look up the names of ten online tools and were given ten hyperlinks—all displayed on one page—to find the answers. Only seven of the links actually worked. (How sneaky!) One group of participants was provided with a moving progress bar that displayed after each link was clicked prior to the page loading. The other group had no such bar and no indication of page-loading progress. To stop the "progress" of pages that seemed to never load, participants simply needed to click the browser's

Stop button. All times were recorded and calculated and produced the following results:

AVERAGE TOLERABLE WAITING TIMES

With Progress Bar (More patient)	**38 seconds** Average abandonment @15–46 seconds
Without Progress Bar (Less patient)	**13 seconds** Average abandonment @ 5–8 seconds

Notice how including the progress feedback bar significantly increased the Tolerable Waiting Time, the users' patience. However, as each *successive* non-working link was clicked, users' tolerance decreased because they were then not expecting the slow pages to load; their patience began to wear thin. Ultimately, after experiencing three non-working links, the total average TWT decreases.

According to Professor Nah, *"Overall, the results suggest that Web users' TWT peaks at approximately 2 seconds. This is in line with Shneiderman's (1986) and Miller's (1968) proposition that users are willing to wait for about 2 seconds before shifts in focus or interference with short-term memory occur."*[150]

And don't get thrown off by the dates of the older studies. Human tolerance for waiting hasn't changed much and even early pre-web studies are consistent with today's research on the topic. Psychologists have found that *continuity of thought* is necessary for effective problem solving. Break or delay that thought for longer than two seconds, and attention wanes and turns elsewhere. *Meaning to us advertisers?* We've lost the potential sale.

ONLINE AD-AGENCY SECRET #24:
How the Decoy Effect Encourages Higher Spending

Want your customers to choose a more expensive option of whatever you sell? Introducing the Decoy Effect—an interesting, and somewhat controversial, marketing phenomenon caused by your introduction of a less favorable option (higher price, fewer features, lower quality, etc.) that makes your more expensive option more attractive.

A classic test conducted by *The Economist* magazine—a British publication founded in 1843—presented three subscription options on their website:

1. **Web Only Subscription: $59.00**

2. **Print Only Subscription: $125.00**

3. **Print & Web Subscription: $125.00**

Huh? Why the heck would *The Economist* sell the combo Print & Web subscription for the same price as just Print? Psychology Professor Dan Ariely at Duke University wanted to find out. He conducted two tests. In Test 1, he made the same three offers to his students: the three subscription choices listed above:

Test 1 Results: *Sixteen percent of buyers chose Web Only, none chose Print Only, and 84 percent chose the Print & Web combo.*

Test 2: *Next, to see what effect the distractor option (Print Only) had, Ariely removed it from the choices, offering only the Web Only and Print & Web options.* **Test Results:** *Sixty-eight percent picked the Web Only option, and 32 percent chose the Print & Web option.*

Bottom line: *Adding the distractor helped increase subscriptions of the more expensive option by 52 percent. That's because it made no sense to get a Print Only subscription for $125 when you could get the Print & Online combo for the same price. When the distractor was removed, buyers went more toward the cheaper option.*[151]

Let's get practical. Let's say you sell knives for the serious home chef. You offer two options of knives:

1. Zwilling J. A. Henckels Professional S Chef Knife @ $119

2. Henckels Classic 8" Chef Knife @$56

Alas, your sales records indicate that far more people are buying the $56 Henckels. But what would happen if you offered a far more expensive choice—one that you don't expect your market to buy (with a price point that's more "pro chef" territory) but would make the cost of that $119 knife look cheap by comparison and, at the same time, make the $56 knife look inferior (even though it's still a quality product)? Now your web page shows the following three choices:

1. Zwilling J. A. Henckels 34891-203 Chef's Knife @$429

2. Zwilling J. A. Henckels Professional S Chef Knife @ $119

3. Henckels Classic 8" Chef Knife @$56

According to the Decoy Effect, more people would be compelled to buy the $119 knife because—now that the $429 "super-pro" knife is inserted into the mix—the $119 slicer looks far more affordable. Again, the decoy isn't a product you're *expecting* your prospects to buy. Its only purpose is to psychologically lower the price of the target product—the one you're really hoping to sell. But, hey, if some people buy it, that's icing on the cake!

Now, it must be said that the Decoy Effect is less effective when buyers have an already-established brand preference. *Meaning?* If you're offering similar products of different brands and your buyer already has a brand preference for one of them, the asymmetric pricing strategy wouldn't be quite as effective.

Some people use the heuristic of "that's my brand" (e.g., *"I only buy Whirlpool washing machines!"*) and dismiss all others. Still, others who are intimately familiar with the products' attributes and advantages might not be swayed because their knowledge of the competitive advantages could make the price difference insignificant (e.g., *"Of course, they're priced differently; these knives are in completely different classes!"*)

Additional studies by other researchers contend that products requiring tasting, smelling, or in-person handling might not be able to pull off the decoy because its effect is most likely when differences of choices are presented numerically or graphically, especially in the absence of extensive text descriptions.[152] Still others assert that the Decoy Effect occurs if the buyer is generally indifferent about the products (no pre-existing preferences), if the products' features are equally important, if the decoy product isn't outright disliked (such as one of exceptionally poor quality or repute), and if the superior attributes of the better product(s) are clear.[153]

What additional options can you add to cause the Decoy Effect? Can you create a new product? Bundle products together? *The Economist* made thousands more in subscriptions by simply adding one simple line to their order page. Why not add this to your testing and see whether it beefs up *your* bottom line?

How to Maximize Profits: Seven Studies on Psychological Pricing

When it comes to money, the way you express it in your ads matters. Here are seven easy-to-implement principles derived from psychological pricing studies that looked at how the *expression of cost affects the interpretation of value.* Are you taking advantage of them? Each affects the consumer brain to make your pricing seem less expensive or more appealing.

1. **Fewer Syllables "Means" Less.** What would you rather pay, $1,295.00, $1,295, or $1295? Most consumers would choose the last. *But why?* Researchers Coulter, Choi, and Monroe call it *auditory representation* and hypothesized that the "verbal encoding" of written prices can affect how consumers assess whether prices are high or low. *"Consumers non-consciously perceive that there is a positive relationship between syllabic length and numerical magnitude."*[154]

2. **Gentlemen Prefer Red.** Remember the discussion of heuristics in *Cashvertising*? In it, I wrote: *"Heuristics pertain to the process of gaining (or discovering) knowledge, not by critical thinking and reasoning, but by intelligent guesswork."* In sports, teams wearing red uniforms are more likely to win due to the color's effect on referees.[155] Men viewing photos of women wearing red or against red backgrounds are more likely to ask them on a date and are subsequently more willing to spend money on them.[156] Crazy, right? It's what the great personal-development speaker Jim Rohn called *"mysteries of the mind."*

    Of particular importance to us marketers is the fact that there's a growing body of evidence suggesting that color itself serves as a heuristic cue. Specifically, the color red tends to cause male buyers to be less conscious of price and, therefore, leads them to spend more.[157] Male study participants say that prices set in red reflect more of a bargain than those in black. Female subjects demonstrated no measurable preference regarding price color.[158] Are men your primary market? This technique couldn't be easier. Give it a shot!

3. **Bigger Font = Bigger Expense.** Slashing your price? Don't shout it too loudly. Research indicates that prices set in *smaller* text lead consumers to believe the price is low and thereby increases your chance of winning the sale.[159]

4. **Bigger Font = More Confidence.** The *Size Congruency Effect* described in principle 3, above, applies when you display two prices close to one another.[160] However, what if you're showing *only* the sale price and not the original price as well? A 2021 study concludes just the opposite—that the *larger* you show your (one and only) price 1) the more attention you'll gain and 2) the more confidence you have that your price is attractive and the performance of your product is greater.[161]

5. **Drop the Symbol.** Would diners spend more money in restaurants if menus were printed without dollar signs next to the prices? The answer was a resounding *"Yes,"* according to 2009 research conducted by Yang and colleagues. Guests at the Culinary Institute of America's St. Andrew's Cafe in Hyde Park, New York, who were given numeral-only menus spent significantly more than diners who received a menu with either 1) prices containing dollar symbols or 2) prices written out in words, e.g., "Seventy-five dollars" rather than "$75.00."[162]

6. **Anchor Your Deals.** Need to make your prices look more attractive? Anchor them next to extraordinarily expensive choices. For example, let's say I'm looking to buy a new high-frequency amateur radio transceiver. I see a web page with an ICOM 2300H in the dead center of the page with a price tag of $219.95. *"Hmmm, not sure if I want to spend that much,"* I say to myself. Flanked on both sides of the unit are two other models: the ICOM 7300 at $1,499.99 and the ICOM IC-7610 at $3,499.99, respectively. By simple contrast, the $219.95 looks like a downright bargain!

Does it matter that the least expensive option doesn't have the full array of features that the other models boast? Not really. At such a disparity of price points, no reasonable person would expect it. But the price difference is so conspicuous that the immediate reaction is, *"Wow, this is cheap by comparison!"* Do you see what it does? It supplies a seemingly logical rationalization for the expenditure—one that might not have ever existed otherwise. *It actually helps your buyer make an excuse to spend money.*

Another example: Master pizza chef Reid Landon offers one hour of professional pizza-making training for $299. *Sounds steep?* Then consider his other two offers, conveniently displayed on opposite sides of his $299 deal: Ten hours at $2,850 and twenty hours at $5,695. Now—next to those bigger figures—that $299 doesn't seem so high, does it?

So, think! What can *you* offer to psychologically make *your* prices seem easier to pay? *What more expensive options could you offer . . .* even if you expect few to choose them? Every business can come up with something. Even funeral homes offer package deals to boost their average sale. They'll sell you their "entry-level" Bronze deal for $4,995 that delivers only standard services; their Silver special at $6,995, which includes a temporary grave marker and memorial blanket; or the Graveyard Gold at $8,995, and they'll toss in more death certificates, a bunch of memorial cards, and a dramatic balloon or dove release to commemorate your demise, just shortly after dropping you into the ground. Heck, if they can do it, so can *you.*

7. **More Benefits = Lower Perceived Cost.** Let's jump back to our previous pizza-training example. You might think $299 is a lot, but that's only because I haven't yet built up the benefits to convince you that the value exceeds the cost. You see, *people spend money only when they want the "thing" more than they want the money that's in their pocket.* When the product has equal or greater perceived value than the money, they'll trade the money for the product.

In my seminars, I tell participants to imagine an old apothecary scale. On one side of the scale is *Skepticism.* On the other side of the scale is the *Desire to Believe.* Only until the Desire to Believe side is heavier—and subsequently equal to or exceeding the weight of the Skepticism side—will the purchase happen. Well, the *benefits* you enumerate are the "weights" that push down on that scale to overtake the gravity of Skepticism. Few benefits = little weight, and the scale's needle still tilts to the Skepticism side. Sufficient benefits, clearly and appealingly described, and that needle tips to the Desire side. Suddenly, the value of the product—in their mind—exceeds the value of the money that you're asking them to pay. *Result?* Sales.

Expert Ways to Turn Cart Abandonments into Cash Orders

It's crazy! Prospects researched the product, found your site, found the product they wanted, decided that your price was satisfactory, checked your About Us page, achieved a satisfactory level of comfort to "risk" sending you their money, typed in all the checkout information, and suddenly, poof, they're gone forever. *What went wrong?*

Fact is, 68.6 percent of online shoppers abandon their carts just seconds before clicking the final Submit Order button. *Yikes,* that's two out of every three shoppers. There are a few primary reasons why this happened. The following chart shows the top eight causes, according to an eleven-year research project involving a whopping 10,721 participants. According to this study, 58.6 percent of them said they just weren't ready to buy.[163] Nothing much we can do about these folks. So, taking them out of the mix, we learn the following:

TOP EIGHT REASONS SHOPPERS ABANDON THEIR CART

1. **Extra costs** too high (shipping, handling, tax, etc.)	48%
2. Site required users to create an **account**	24%
3. **Delivery** quote too slow	22%
4. Don't **trust** site with payment details	18%
5. **Checkout** process too long/complex	17%
6. Couldn't see/calculate **total** order	16%
7. Website **errors**	13%
8. Unsatisfactory **return policy**	12%

(Source: Baymard Institute, 2022)

Baymard Institute—a quality research organization whose work is worth every marketer's attention—has reviewed over 37,000 checkout site elements from many of today's top-grossing U.S. and European e-commerce sites. They've identified scores of ways to make the checkout process smoother, easier, and more successful. Here are just a handful of the findings that you should implement without delay:

1. **Make the Guest Checkout Option Easier to Find.** If you offer this option, don't hide it. Put it right next to the current customer login so it's immediately visible to those who haven't registered before.

2. **Simplify Your Password Creation Process.** Forget listing a dozen rules! Almost 19 percent of users abandoned the site just because of this. Baymard recommends the minimum password requirement be simply six lowercase letters. Your users are smart enough to determine how much security they want, aren't they? Your job is to sell them products and services they want. Make it easy.

3. **Provide an Estimated Delivery Date . . .** rather than only stating the "shipping speed." Your customers want to know when they'll get the stuff, not simply when you'll send it, or how fast the shipping company's planes and trucks move.

4. **Let Buyers Edit Order Data.** When they arrive at the Order Review step, many companies don't allow editing of products, quantity, color, shipping address, and other variables. *Result?* Buyers need to start all over again—or have to go back more steps than necessary—causing frustration and abandonment. Instead, put edit links in each separate data field so they can adjust only what's necessary.

5. **Mark Both Required and Optional Fields.** Don't indicate just your *optional* fields. Also mark your *required* fields with a tiny red asterisk, which follows the statement (*"Required field"*) also set in small text above your first field. Show (*"Optional"*) where relevant. Your goal is to remove as much guesswork as possible from checkout. This lessens the stress shoppers already feel by spending money. Don't add to it.

6. **Accordion Checkout? Let Them Go Back.** The Accordion style design is used by approximately 32 percent of today's top e-commerce sites. It's neat, clean, and (sometimes) easy

to navigate. When used in forms, it collects the buyer's data (name, address, etc.) and—as each section is completed (shipping address, billing address, payment info, etc.)—it collapses to show only the info that the buyer typed. The style is often seen on FAQ pages where just the questions show. Next to each question is a downward-pointing arrow that, when clicked, reveals the answer.

One problem: Many sites don't allow buyers to hit their browser's Back button and move back to the preceding step. Instead, buyers are pulled all the way to the beginning of the form, causing them to start all over again, or, in many cases, leave the site forever. *Ugh, what a hassle!* Be sure to have your web designer or tech incorporate functionality that gives users what they expect when they hit their Back button—that they are taken to the last-viewed checkout step.

ONLINE AD-AGENCY SECRET #27:

The Psychology of Email Subject Lines— Fourteen Facts and Stats

Did you know that 47 percent of email recipients open email based on the subject line, whereas 69 percent of email recipients report email as spam based solely on the subject line? Check out the following facts and stats, all based on real-world experimentation by numerous online-sales companies worldwide:

1. **News? Humbug!** The word *Newsletter* in the subject line decreased the open rate by 18.7 percent.

2. **Less Is More.** Emails with an empty subject line get opened 8 percent more often.

3. **Sweet Spot.** The best number of words in a subject line for the highest open rate: six to ten. Lowest: twenty-one to twenty-five.

4. **Get Personal.** Emails with the recipient's name in the subject line enjoy an average 18.30 percent open rate.[164] Experian says "26 percent more likely to get opened." Other studies say it's a 50 percent open rate.[165] Non-personalized email is like what used to be called "bulk mail" from the post office. When it arrived, you knew it was a solicitation, so you often dumped it before

opening it. With email, the "dump" is the little trash can icon. Don't think more about this one. If you have their name, just use it. Better still, if you mention their name and *another* fact about them in your subject line—company name, location, something you read about them, e.g., *"Hey, Scott, great article in Onion Ring Journal!"*—they'll likely open it before anything else.

5. **Don't Forward.** Emails with *Fw:* in the subject line reduce opens by 17 percent.

6. **No Name = Fewer Opens.** Emails without the recipient's name get an average 15.50 percent open rate.[166]

7. **"Free" Boosts Opens.** Include the magic word *Free* in your subject line and boost opens by 10 percent. *Spam trap bait?* Testing by HubSpot showed no issues with deliverability. Nowadays spam killers look at more than just keywords to score potential spam.

8. **Urgent?** *Say It!* Add emotion to your subject line by expressing how exclusive or urgent your communication is. Research showed a 22 percent higher open rate when this strategy was used.[167]

9. **"Pssst . . . Your Cart!"** Remind shoppers about items they haven't yet bought—and say it in the subject line—for an up to 48 percent open rate.

10. **Discount Don't**—Subject lines that push discounts received below-average performance at 38.31 percent.[168]

11. **Length ≠ Strength**—The length of your subject line and your open rate are inversely proportional. *Meaning?* The longer your line, the lower your open rate.[169]

12. 😃s **Add Personality.** But will they add to your response? That's debatable. According to OptinMonster, adding emojis to your subject lines can boost the effectiveness of your marketing by 70 percent.[170] In 2017, *Business Insider* also saw a response boost in their promotional holiday emails. *Klaviyo* says emails with subject line emojis have an average 39 percent open rate.[171] *Search Engine Journal* tested 3,893,391 emails over seventeen campaigns. That's quite a test. **Their results:** Subject lines *without* the emojis

won, with a higher open rate of 52.94 percent versus the "emoji-included rate" of 47.06 percent.[172]

My suggestion: Test with *your* audience. What's suitable for one market, brand, and product might not be for another. Maybe your prospects think they're cute, funny, or charming. Maybe they hate the damned things. *Test!*

13. **Follow-Ups Rev Up!** If you had a salesperson who outright *refused* to ask for the sale more than once, what might you say to that salesperson? This is a question I ask in my seminars. No matter where I am in the world, the audience shouts out, *"You're FIRED!"* I urge you to always think of your advertising like a salesperson. It's a salesperson in print (or pixels). So why would you ever send just one email and not follow up? Boston-based *Yesware* examined 10 million email threads of salespeople to determine the optimal number of follow-ups to send and the best time intervals between them.[173] **Conclusions:** 1) Send *six* emails within three weeks of the first contact. 2) Space your follow-ups apart by *three* or no more than *four* days. 3) Reps who follow up within *twenty-four hours* of their first contact receive about an average 25 percent response rate. Use email automation tools to help put the process on autopilot.

14. **Best and Worst Words**—According to *Boomerang* (formerly *Baydin*) and their study of over 5 million emails handled by its users, the following words should be **avoided** in your subject lines: *Invite, Social, Speaker, Press, Join, Confirm* and *Assistance*. Words you **should use** for greater response are *Demo, Connect, Opportunity, Apply, Conference, Cancellation,* and *Payments.*[174]

CHAPTER 6

Fifty Powerful Opt-in Headlines to Boost Your Subscriber Base

Your "house list" is invaluable! These people are already in your "fold" and—assuming you satisfied their needs previously—are exponentially more likely to do business with you. By staying in touch, you build tremendous credibility with a group who sees you as a more trusted source for whatever you're selling. Plus, they begin to feel as if they know you. You're no longer just a company, no longer a stranger.

But it doesn't matter how good your products or services are if you can't get them to subscribe. So here's a list of strong opt-in headline ideas you can use for most any offer, product, or service. Use them as a springboard for your own headlines, or copy word for word!

1. [XX]-Point Success ___ Checklist. Learn How to Create ___ with Amazing ___.

2. [XX] Steps to Skyrocket Your ___. Get Motivated by My ___ Examples. BONUS: Free Printable!

3. [*Report Title*] Grab My Free [XX]-Page Report & Start _____ Today!

4. [*Report Title*]. Learn to Be _____ the Fast & Easy Way.

5. Announcing My Proven Step-by-Step System to Double Your ___ in Just Days!

6. ARGH! Are You Fed Up with __? Join My Hard-Core___ Bootcamp 100% Free!

7. YES—You Really Can Boost Your ___ in Just ___ Minutes a Day. Click & Learn How.

8. Want to ___ Faster Than Ever? I've Done It & I'll Show You How. Download My Free No-B.S. Report [*Your Report Title*] & Start Today.

9. ARE YOU Looking for a Sure-Fire Way to ___ with Less Work & Aggravation? Click Here for My Eye-Opening Free Report [*Your Report Title*] That Shows You How.

10. [XX] Ways to ___ with ___. Shockingly Effective & Works Every Time.

11. [XX] Tricks for Quickly & Easily ___. My Free Report [*Your Report Title*] Teaches You Step-by-Step Exactly How.

12. ___ Is Easier Than Ever When You Use My Quick, No-Brainer Method. Click to Learn More.

13. IT'S CRAZY! Why Spend [*TIME*] [*ACTIVITY*] When You Can Get Better Results in Just [*TIME*]? Click & I'll Teach You How, for FREE!

14. Do You Know the Secret of Getting People to ___? Enter Your Email & I'll Send You My New Report [*HOW-TO TITLE*] Absolutely Free.

15. YES! You Really Can ___. My Free 5-Day Video Course Teaches You How. Enter Your Email for Your First Lesson Sent Immediately!

16. ARGH! It's So Hard to ___ When You (Don't Know How to/Can't)___! I've Done It Successfully for [XX Years] & I Can Teach You. Download My FREE Guide: [*TITLE*]

17. ANNOUNCING the Fastest & Easiest Way to ___? This Free [XX]-Page Report Shows You How.

18. GREAT DEAL! Send Me Your Name & Email and I'll Send You ___.

19. LIMITED TIME OFFER: Send Me Your Name & Email to Join My Exclusive Private Coaching Club—Only 47 Spots Remaining!

20. Join Our VIP List to Get Updates On ___.

21. Give Me Just [XX] Days & I'll Personally Teach You How to ___.

22. BOOM! My FREE Guide Teaches You How to Totally Explode Your____.

23. WHAT?! Can You REALLY ___ in Just [*TIME*]? Yes . . . and My New Online Course Shows You How.

24. [XXX] Ways to ___ Without ___. Click for My Free Guide Showing You How.

25. DISCOVER How I Made ___ with Just One Simple ___.

26. OUCH! Learn How to Avoid the One Little Mistake That Can Cost You $___ Every Time You ___.

27. YOU'LL LAUGH at People Who Say You Can't ___. I Just Did It and It Took Only [*TIME*]. Enter Your Name & Email and I'll Show You What Really Works.

28. I'll Give You [XXX] Foolproof Ways to ___. Get Started with My Powerful [*Course Name*] Course.

29. FACT: My New [*NAME*] Formula Helps You ___ in Just [*TIME*] . . . With Absolutely No ___ . . . No . . . and No ___. Click to Get It in 2 Minutes.

30. Free ___ That Gives You ___. Plus Get Actionable Tips Sent to You Every Week! No Spam or Chatter. Just Solid Info You Can Use Right Now to ___.

31. "I DID IT!" Learn My "Easy-as-Pie" 4-Step Process I Used to Build ___.

32. WHAT?! Can You REALLY ___ in Just [*TIME*]? Hell, Yeah . . . If I Did It, So Can YOU! Click to Sign Up for My Free Lessons!

33. SAVE __ Off Your Entire Order When You Sign Up Today. Simply Enter Your Email Below . . .

34. WHAT THE #^*%@#! This Is Crazy. (No Kidding.) Wait Until You Hear What [*NUMBER*] of Today's Top ___ Say About ___. Enter Your Email & I'll Send You This Truly Shocking Report.

35. Give Me [XXX] Days & I'll Show You EXACTLY How to ___. (Without All the B.S. You See Nowadays from Noobs Trying to Impress You.)

36. FREE [XX]-Minute Personal Consultation—For the First 50 Signups. I'll Help You ___with Less _____ & Greater Success.

37. JUST RELEASED: My Top ___ Tips for ___. 100% Tested & Proven . . . They'll Work for You, Too!

38. How We Created Our Best ___ . . . and How You Can Do the Same or Better! Click Here for Details>>>

39. IMAGINE: Achieving ___ in Just [XX] Days. You CAN & I'll Help You! Sign Up for My Free ___ & See How I Do It!

40. Ready to Double, Triple, Even Quadruple Your ___? Cash In on My [XX] Years of Experience & Success. My Top Secrets & Advice for Beginners.

41. Join Over [*XXXX*] Subscribers Who Receive [XX] Fresh Ideas Every [Day/Week/Month] for ___.

42. Want to Learn How We Went from [$XXX to $XXXXX] in Monthly Revenue in Less Than a Year?

43. Pssst! Become a ___ Insider! Sign Up Here & Get Our Latest Video Tips . . . Before Your Competition Sees Them on YouTube.

44. Hey, YOU! (Yes, You!) Want $[XX] Off Your Next ___? No Catch! Enter Your Email for Our Biggest Discount Code Ever>>>

45. Learn My Top [XX] Ways to Crush Your ___. (They Work Like Crazy in Most Any Industry.) Subscribe & Download My ___ Cheat Sheet!

46. Here's My Proven-Successful Gameplan for ___. It's EXACTLY How I Built a ___ in Less Than [XX] [Days/Weeks/Months.] Enter Your Email Below & Start Watching 3 Minutes from Now.

47. Watch Us Build Your ___ Fast! Enter Your Email for Free Video Demo>>>

48. Over [XXX] People Can't Be Wrong! Subscribe & Get 100% Practical Weekly Emails That Teach You Powerful New Ways to ___.

49. Shhhh! Learn [XX] Secret Ways to Hack Your Way to ___ Mastery. My Free Video Breaks the Code & Actually Demonstrates How It's Done.

50. "OMG . . . WHAT?!" Did You Ever See How Millionaires ___? You'll Kick Yourself When You Learn How They Do It. Enter Your Email for a Mind-Blowing Exposé.

CHAPTER 7

Cashvertising Checklist:
Twenty-Nine Things to Make Your Ads Go *KA-CHING*

We've covered a lot of ground in the previous chapters, but how do you put it all together when it's actually time to construct your ad? After you incorporate as many of the ideas you've already learned, next "score" your ad against the following *Cashvertising Checklist*—tips based on what's been learned by examining many of the most popular, most viral social media ads.

Each tip is worth one point. Add up your total points and, with an appealing and well-priced product, you'll get a good sense of your chances for a winning ad no matter which social media platform you choose. Get as close to 29 as possible. *Low score?* Rework your ad according to the recommendations, rescore, and move your chances up the success ladder. It's a simple way to take the guesswork out of creating ads with the potential to profit.

CASHVERTISING TIP #1: Make It Relevant! You wouldn't try to sell a big book of fancy milkshake recipes to people living in South Korea, a population nearly 100 percent lactose intolerant. (Poor targeting.) Because no matter how great your copy is, if you're not reaching the right audience, you're not going to be relevant. And relevant simply means you're reaching the audience that's most likely to buy what you're selling.

Advertising on *Twitter?* Of their global users, 38.5 percent are between twenty-five and thirty-four years old. *Facebook* is most popular for both men and women aged thirty-five to forty-four. *Instagram?* 61 percent are twelve to seventeen years old. *Pinterest?* 30.3 percent are between twenty-five and thirty-four, the largest age demographic on the platform. *LinkedIn?* 59.1 percent are twenty-five to thirty-four.[1]

Of course, age is only one factor. There are location, income, education, interest, and many other demographic options. So, first, make sure you pinpoint the specific audience that's going to be right for your particular product or service. And then make your copy speak to them in their language. Ask yourself, *"Who is the ideal candidate for my product?"* Then describe them in detail. With all the demographic targeting options available, especially on Facebook, pinpointing them is simply a matter of clicking the boxes.

Take advantage of the Facebook pixel and create your own custom audience. Do it now before Facebook retires it, which they're considering at the time of this writing.

TIP #2: Make It Dramatic! Unless there's something new about your product, you want to add some excitement, emotion, and energy. Get creative here! What emotions apply to your product or service? Fear, happiness, anxiety, surprise, anger, jealousy, suspense, relief? Convey it through video, imagery, and words. Drama fuels an ad's virality.

TIP #3: Use Personal Language! Scatter your pronouns liberally! Personal pronouns: *you, I, we, he, she, it, they, me, us, her, him, them, mine, ours, yours, hers, his, theirs, myself, herself, himself, ourselves, itself, yourself,* and more. Remember, social media is social, human, personal, warm, and friendly. People are sharing with friends and family.

Remember the Squatty Potty: *"This unicorn change the way I poop."* Other ads say: *"I can't believe this," "This freaked me out," "Wow, I didn't expect this to work," "Look what happened to me when I tried,"* and similar. This style of copy fits into the whole idea of "camouflage" discussed by direct-response copy master Eugene Schwartz in his classic, *Breakthrough Advertising*, which is included in the "Recommended Reading" appendix in the original *Cashvertising*. The idea is to make the ad look like the content around it.

In newspapers, for example, you make your ad look like an article. You use the same fonts, the same leading (vertical spacing between sentences), the same column width, and the same voice.

In social media, camouflage means making your ad similar to personal posts. The best way to do this is with your copy voice—writing like a friend, instead of a business or corporation. Use casual language. Simple words. Short sentences. Short paragraphs. Lots of pronouns. Heavy on emotion.

Photos? Keep them unique. Nothing's worse than a stock photo to give your business that unmistakable generic look. You know, the perfectly polished professionals—in impeccably selected businesswear—sitting behind a giant boardroom table, all smiling with perfectly spaced, snow-white teeth, and not one hair out of place. You've seen the variations. Stock photos *can* work, but do you know what can work even better? A quick phone-camera shot of your team with imperfect lighting, clothing, and teeth. It says "real." And that engenders confidence. And confidence encourages trust. And trust leads to sales.

TIP #4: Emphasize Newness! People are neophiliacs. We love new things. They're exciting, intriguing, and they're, well, news. Interestingly enough, many of the ads that go viral are for newly introduced products. New tech products . . . new kitchen products . . . new beauty products . . . new software that solves your latest problems: can't sleep . . . can't set goals . . . can't relax . . . can't make time to read . . . can't remember . . . can't manage your money . . . can't get your teeth white enough . . . and more. If your product is new, you don't need to simply play up its benefits (which you should always do, of course), but you also have the unique opportunity to capitalize on the story of its newness, too, and make a big introductory splash of it.

For example, imagine you're selling an amazing new hands-free toothbrush—the amazing *iTooth*—that works with its own equally amazing app (available for both Apple and Android, of course). Just launch the app, pop the *iTooth* in your mouth, bite down gently, select your choice of up to ten custom brushing patterns, and enjoy the sound of your choice of twelve nature sounds (via Bluetooth) while it automatically scrubs your chompers to pearly white perfection.

But it's more than that, right? That's because it's also *new!* So you use powerful words like *"Introducing," "Presenting," "At Last,"* and *"Announcing."* Then you go on about how people have been brushing the same way for about eight hundred years when, during the Tang Dynasty, the Chinese invented the first natural bristle toothbrush made from coarse hair plucked from pig necks. (Nice.) Eventually, in 1939, the first electric brush was invented. But still, manually brushing is so tedious. *"No more! Because thanks to a brand new invention by a couple of genius Phoenix dentists working with two college tech nerds . . ."* Get it? The news is a big part of the appeal, not simply that it exists. If there's something new about your product, play it up big, and you'll be fueling your ad's viral engine.

TIP #5: Use Video and Promise Benefits for Watching. Don't just feature a video and assume they'll click. You want to *sell* them on the idea of watching. If the bulk of your selling happens in your video, then your body text (not contained in the video, but in the ad text itself) is actually *the ad for your video.* Make sense? *"In this video, you'll learn how to . . ." "Click here and watch how . . ."* Sell them on clicking that Play button and pour on those adjective-rich benefit bullets!

TIP #6: Create a Dynamic Still Shot. Remember that the first still image in the video shouldn't be a bland, boring shot. If you're selling mountain bikes, don't just have a picture of a bike. Instead, have a person skillfully "flying" over a log and having a blast. Show action, movement, and product usage!

TIP #7: Always Ask for Action. Never assume people know what to do. Tell them to click, tell them to go here, tell them to look there, tell them exactly what you want them to do. Lead them like a child, step by step.

TIP #8: Use Director Words. Say *"This New Product" . . . "These 3 Men" . . . "Here's How You" . . . "Look How This . . ."* and other such words to direct your readers' attention. It's not *any* amazing product. It's **"This** *amazing product"*—the one you're showing them right now.

TIP #9: Start with Benefits! Looking for a clever way to start your ad? Forget it! Instead, do the smart thing and start with *benefits.* It's as simple as that. Just tell them the biggest benefit they'll enjoy if they buy. They'll read on if they're a good prospect for that benefit. If not, they're just not the buyer for that item.

TIP #10: Say "Order Here!" Most good Facebook ads contain a CTA link. And while it's clear what they should do, it doesn't hurt to also *tell* them! *"Order Here" . . . "Click Here" . . . "Join Here" . . . "Watch Here" . . .* and scores of other directive variations. Selling is leading. Leading is telling. Don't be afraid to make it "too clear" how to buy from you.

TIP #11: A.B.S.: Always Be Selling! *Many web pages simply don't sell.* They're little more than oversized business cards. I don't care that you're in business. I want to know what your products will actively *do* for me. Don't make me guess. And start telling me right away, or I'll click away forever. Every single square inch of your advertising should be charged with selling and moving the customer to Step #2.

TIP #12: Share with "[X] Lovers!" Tell readers to share with cat lovers, dog lovers, with your wine-loving friends. Suggest why and to whom they should be sharing your ad. Give them excuses to help your ad go viral. Guide them every step of the way.

TIP #13: Show the Play Button! Always include the little "play triangle" to plant the click suggestion in their heads. Yes, they know it's a video, but this is sales. Assume nothing. Leave nothing to question.

TIP #14: Include Text Within Your Video! The best videos don't sell only with sound and imagery; they incorporate text as well. Also, add *captions* to reinforce your message. Remember that most people watch with the sound off. With captions, your ad still sells. Plus, the text acts as a constant reinforcement of your message.

TIP #15: Employ Benefit Stacking! "Bazooka" them with benefits! You can't overdo benefits. Remember, your product has a certain price. And in their head is a certain value. Your job is to *increase* the value in their heads so that it's at least equal to the value of the money in their pocket. Until you do that, there's no sale. By the time they're done with your video, they should be exhausted with benefits. Watch a good late-night infomercial and you'll feel the exact same effect.

TIP #16: Strive for Sales, Not Just Shares! Your focus should be on sales, not just likes and shares. Your goal isn't to be a social media entertainer. You don't want millions of shares and no money in your pocket. Strive first for a strong, fundamentally sound sales message. Then, if you want, add some bells and whistles. (Even a rainbow unicorn, if you wish.)

TIP #17: Sell Against Your Competition! Remember, unless you're a monopoly, people will check to see if your competitors' products might satisfy their needs, so always sell against them! Comparative charts are a great way to do it. Even a simple bullet list. How is yours better? Different? Why is theirs not as good? You're not selling in a vacuum. They're selling against you simply by their existence, just not effectively. You must be actively and purposefully selling against them. One company will win the sale. Why not you?

TIP #18: Ask for the Sale! Just say, *"Buy Now"* . . . *"Here's where to buy"* . . . *"Here's the next step:"* . . . *"Step one, read this. Step two, click here. Step three, pay with PayPal, Visa, or MasterCard."* In other words, lead them step by step. Do not be shy in asking for the sale. Otherwise, you're like a sales-person who never opens her mouth, gives you the full presentation, turns around and walks home, and doesn't understand why she didn't get the sale.

TIP #19: Promote Your Guarantee! Your guarantee is not an afterthought; it's one of your strongest sales points. Make it the strongest possible. If your competition offers thirty days, make yours sixty, ninety days, six months. If theirs is three months, make yours a year. If theirs is a year, make yours three years . . . five years . . . even a lifetime guarantee. Fact is, the longer your guarantee, the fewer returns you're going to get because most people simply forget about it. Play up your guarantee big. Don't put it in a little hidden link. Make it big and bold!

TIP #20: Pack It with Credibility! Load your pitch with stats, reviews, and feedback. With testimonials, include names and faces, cities, states, and countries. Has any testing been done? Do you have official data you can show? Do you have pie charts? *Many people don't buy because they simply don't believe you.* Give them reasons to do so!

TIP #21: Create a Reaction Video! Remember, there are two types of testimonials: those that convey how people feel *after* they use a product, and those that show the process of people overcoming their initial-trial skepticism, moving through skepticism to belief, like the Zungle sun-glasses video. It's very candid, strong, and believable. Your testimonials don't need to be long or highly produced. In fact, they're most effective when they look like an informally produced candid video.

TIP #22: Say What They're Thinking! You're selling a security product to New Yorkers, and you know crime is on the rise, so say it! You're sell-ing low-cost swamp coolers to people living in Indio, California, so say, *"Average temps were over 112 degrees this month. How's your electric bill looking?"* Let them know you feel their pain. Use their words. Talk their language. Let them know that *you* know where they're coming from.

TIP #23: Target with Questions! *"Do you?" "Can you?" "Would you?"* and others. For example: *"Do you love chocolate?" "Do you love cats?" "Do you* *want your dog to live a long life?" "Do you want to bake pizza like a pizzai-ola from Naples?"* Questions such as these instantly cull *your* market from the masses. Only those interested will read or watch further. This lets you jump into your pitch immediately without any warm-up required.

TIP #24: Show Recognizable Symbols! Display the PayPal logo, Visa logo, MasterCard logo. Show symbols that assure safe ordering. Are there symbols in your industry that people immediately recognize? Remember, to prospects, you're a stranger. Everything on that site is foreign to them. You can reduce this foreign feeling by showing familiar symbols. This, in turn, provides a degree of comfort that's otherwise completely absent. It's like going to a foreign country. You don't speak the language, you can't read the signs, and you don't know anybody. All of a sudden you see an old friend walking down the street—*BOOM!*—instant comfort. Make sense?

TIP #25: Load It with Emotions! Load your ads and videos with emotion. *Be a human talking to other humans!* Add fear . . . sentimentality . . . a little sadness . . . worry . . . happiness . . . anger . . . any kind of emotion. That's what people go to the movies for. They want to be moved somehow. And it's especially impactful when it's teamed with logic and emotion. We use our left brain to justify the expenditure, but emotion drives us to make the purchase.

TIP #26: Play Consumer Advocate! Start selling by *teaching*. In your ads and videos, give them info they can use: *"5 Ways to . . ." "7 Secrets for . . ." "How Not to Get Ripped Off When You . . . ,"* and a million variations. Teach them something: how to do something better, live a better life, get a better job, make more money, save more time, and be more effective. In turn, they'll warm up to you because you're helping them to improve their lives. You are, in effect, on their side.

TIP #27: Emphasize Ease and Simplicity! People want to do things quickly and easily. Human inertia is powerful. It's what makes the internet especially interesting when you know you should be going to the gym. So tell them it's quick and easy. *"Installs in just 20 seconds" . . . "Look how easy it is to " . . . "So easy, a child could do it in 4 minutes" . . . "Easy, 3-Step Directions"* and scores of variations.

TIP #28: Study Infomercials! There's no better source of advertising training on TV than infomercials. Within thirty minutes, you're going to get a masterclass in how to write benefit copy, how to structure imagery, how to use testimonials and demonstrations, and how to push for the order. Study them relentlessly. Watch as many as you can. They follow a formula that you can easily copy.

TIP #29: Use Professional Designers! Much of social media ad creation is essentially a matter of filling in the forms that the platform provides, but you still need to provide quality imagery. Your website is where professional design really matters because the entire site is an orchestration of design from layout to typography; to navigation, imagery, and call-to-action elements; to color palette, whitespace, and card design; and more. It's simply not a job for someone who'd rather spend their time strategizing how to bring in more business.

Templates are one option for sure, but they're limiting and many look like what they are—templates. Use professional designers who know direct response. Check the freelancer sites like Fiverr, Upwork, 99designs, DesignCrowd, and others. There are literally thousands of designers ready to make you look good. Be selective, however. Many are profoundly unqualified. Some of these guys show other designers' work and claim it to be their own. In fact, years ago I spotted my own *Cashvertising* website included in the portfolio of an unknown designer who claimed he'd designed it! He almost fainted when I told him it was mine. Talk about a crazy coincidence. Needless to say, he didn't get my job. If this doesn't impress you to be careful who you hire, nothing will.

Browse some of your biggest competitors. Look at the websites of the giants in your industry. Then "cookbook" using their sites as a guiding recipe. The big guys hire the best and most expensive in the business. They test, retest, modify, and test again. If something works better, they keep it. If not, it's dropped. You can be reasonably assured that their current site is the best-performing version of what they've tried to date. Think how much time and money you can potentially save by letting them secretly guide you.

Epilogue

Whew, we've covered a *lot* of ground in a short time. Writing this book over the past six months has truly been a labor of love. My fingers and eyes are now ready for a break. But not for too long. That's because the *illustrated* book version of my *Cashvertising* seminar is on the drawing board . . . literally . . . from this same great publisher, Red Wheel/Weiser. (More about that to be announced at *DrewEricWhitman.com*.)

Digging into the seemingly endless labyrinthine maze of advertising research is a blast, even though some of it requires a decoder ring, Rosetta Stone, and an understanding of some of the most inscrutable mathematics you could imagine. But my goal has always been to take the science behind what makes people buy and translate that raw data into practical, how-to steps and techniques that you can put to immediate use. I hope I achieved that with this book.

My claim and suggestion to you—after reading this book—are no different from those at the end of the original *Cashvertising*:

> **"Whether you realize it or not, you now know more about how to create effective advertising than the majority of your competitors.**
>
> **"Want to prove this? Ask them about any of the ideas we've discussed. In response, you'll likely get wrong answers and blank stares.**
>
> **"That's because most of your competition is too busy running their businesses to stop and learn how to make them more successful. I congratulate you for doing so."**

It's a Fact: While many of your competitors are busily trying one thing after another—guided mostly by personal preference ("I like this font," "This color looks cool," "Clever headlines are best!") or bits and pieces of advice from articles they've Googled—you'll be making decisions based on testing data derived from thousands of study participants and hundreds of thousands of data points from real-world response testing.

Indeed, the suggestions in this book aren't the result of direct-response daydreams. Instead, they were derived from empirical evidence produced by both highly respected academic researchers via tightly controlled experimentation and live-ad testing by many of today's leading internet marketing organizations.

Bottom line: When you're following the advice in this book, you're no longer going it alone. You're being guided by millions of dollars' worth of research and, by doing so, exponentially increasing your chances for success.

There's a great Vietnamese proverb that says, *"When eating fruit, remember the one who planted the tree."* I'm grateful for all those whose hard work before me made my work herein possible. And I'm grateful to you, dear reader, for your interest in my teachings and the generosity of your support. It's my sincerest hope that what I do benefits you in even the smallest way. Doing so makes all my effort worthwhile.

Although I may not yet know you personally—or perhaps we've met in my *Cashvertising* workshops, keynotes, or we've done business together—I want the fact that we've become friends through the printed word to make a difference for you. If I can assist you in any way, please feel free to email me at *Drew@DrewEricWhitman.com* and visit me online at *Drew EricWhitman.com*. I love hearing from my readers and learning how the ideas I've shared have helped you!

Until then, I wish you health, happiness, and prosperity!

DREW ERIC WHITMAN
OCTOBER 2023

Notes

CHAPTER 1

1. "Former Facebook Exec: We Made It as Addictive as Cigarettes on Purpose," *Business Insider*, September 24, 2020, *businessinsider.com*.

2. "The Global State of Digital 2022," *Hootsuite*, 2022, *hootsuite.com*.

3. NBC Sports Pressbox, February 15, 2022, *nbcsportsgrouppressbox.com*.

4. "Super Bowl Ad Slots Selling for Record $6.5 Million, Nearly Sold Out," *USA Today*, January 19, 2022.

5. "How Instagram Is Intentionally Designed to Mimic Addictive Pain-killers," *Business Insider*, August 11, 2021, *businessinsider.com*.

6. J. Rosenstein, "Addictive Features of Social Media/Messenger Platforms and Freemium Games Against the Background of Psychological and Economic Theories," *NCBI*, July 23, 2019, *ncbi.nlm.nih.gov*.

7. "Social Theory at HBS: McGinnis' Two FOs," *The Harbus*, May 10, 2004, *harbus.org*.

8. L. Festinger, "A Theory of Social Comparison Processes," *Human Relations* 7, no. 2 (1954): 117–40.

CHAPTER 2

1. E. Schwartz, *Breakthrough Advertising* (Boardroom Books: 2004).

2. "First Impressions Are Everything: New Study Confirms People with Straight Teeth Are Perceived as More Successful, Smarter and Having More Dates," *PR Newswire*, April 19, 2012, *prnewswire.com*.

3. G. Zaltman, *How Customers Think: Essential Insights into the Mind of the Market* (Harvard Business School Press: 2003).

CHAPTER 4

1. "The New York Times: Insights—The Psychology of Sharing," *Media and Information Literacy Clearinghouse*, August 3, 2011, *milunesco.unaoc.org*.

2. J. Berger and K. L. Milkman, "What Makes Online Content Viral?" *Journal of Marketing Research* 49, no. 2 (April 2012): 192–205.

3. D. Ogilvy, *Confessions of an Advertising Man* (Southbank Publishing: 2011).

CHAPTER 5

1. "Federal Reserve Board—Survey of Consumer Finances (SCF)," Board of Governors of the Federal Reserve System, 2019, *federalreserve.gov.*

2. L. Gillespie and T. Rubloff, "Bankrate's Annual Emergency Fund Report," *Bankrate*, February 23, 2023, *bankrate.com.*

3. C. Dickey, "Average Credit Card Debt in the U.S.," *Bankrate*, February 24, 2023, *bankrate.com.*

4. "Newswire | Consumer Trust in Online, Social and Mobile Advertising Grows," *Nielsen, nielsen.com.*

5. L. Matteucci, "5.3 Billion Cell Phones to Become Waste in 2022: Report," October 13, 2022, *phys.org.*

6. "The Smart Reason We Waste Our Dollars on Coffee," *Forbes,* May 22, 2015, *forbes.com.*

7. M. Armstrong and A. Kiefer, "Budgeting for Baby's First Year: Diapers, Childcare, Gear & More," *Healthline*, July 1, 2021, *healthline.com.*

8. L. Ross, "The Importance of Online Customer Reviews [Infographic]," *Invesp, invespcro.com*; "18 Online Review Statistics Every Marketer Should Know." *Search Engine Journal*, January 13, 2023, *searchengine journal.com*; J. Anthony, "62 Customer Reviews Statistics You Must Learn: 2023 Market Share Analysis & Data," *Financesonline.com*; J. Pitman, "Local Consumer Review Survey 2022: Customer Reviews and Behavior," *BrightLocal*, January 26, 2022, *brightlocal.com.*

9. Pitman, "Local Consumer Review Survey 2022."

10. S. Kurt and K. K. Osueke, "The Effects of Color on the Moods of College Students," *SAGE Open* 4, no. 1 (2014); M. Aves and J. Aves, *Interior Designers' Showcase of Color* (AIA Press, 1994).

11. J. Hallock. "Colour Assignment—By Joe Hallock," 2003. *joehallock.com.*

12. S. Singh, "Impact of Color on Marketing," *University of Winnipeg,* 2006, *ion.uwinnipeg.ca.*

13. P. Bottomley and J. R. Doyle, "The Interactive Effects of Colors and Products on Perceptions of Brand Logo Appropriateness," *Marketing Theory* 6 (2006): 63–83; T. L. Childers and J. Jass, "All Dressed Up with Something to Say: Effects of Typeface Semantic Associations on Brand Perceptions and Consumer Memory," *Journal of Consumer Psychology* 12, no. 2 (2002): 93–106; P. W. Henderson, and J. A. Cote, "Guidelines for Selecting or Modifying Logos," *Journal of Marketing* 62, no. 2 (1998): 14–30; K. L. Keller, S. E. Heckler, and M. J. Houston, "The Effects of Brand Name Suggestiveness on Advertising Recall," *Journal of Marketing* 62, no. 1 (1998): 48–57.

14. R. Oprea, "Color Psychology in Marketing and Its Importance in Driving Sales," *Brand Minds*, June 20, 2018, *brandminds.com*.

15. H. H. Choi, S. A. Lim, and J. HeeKim, "Promotional Video of Editing Techniques Utilizing Color and Brand Balance," *International Journal of Software Engineering & Applications* 8 (2014): 149–58.

16. I. Justesen, "11 CTA Tips That Will Turn Your Blog into a Lead Machine," *Constant Content*, August 28, 2018, *constant-content.com*.

17. M. Aagaard, "CTA Placement: Where to Position Calls-to-Action on Your Website," *Content Verve*, October 14, 2014, *contentverve.com*.

18. "11 Ways to Improve Your Calls to Action," *QuickSprout*, March 14, 2013, *quicksprout.com*.

19. "Big Wins from the Inbox: Email Strategies to Get More Conversions," *Unbounce*, *unbounce.com*.

20. J. Premick, "Buttons vs. Text Links | AWeber Email Marketing," *AWeber Blog*, March 25, 2008, *blog.aweber.com*.

21. "Facebook CTA: How to Add a Call-to-Action Button to Facebook," *HubSpot*, *blog.hubspot.com*.

22. "11 Ways to Improve Your Calls to Action," *QuickSprout*.

23. N. Patel, "Videos Can Boost Sales: The Psychology of Videos," *neilpatel.com*.

24. K. Kurcwald, "Social Sharing Boosts Email CTR by 158% [Report + Infographic]," *GetResponse*, March 27, 2013, *getresponse.com*.

25. M. Buccini, "Where to Place CTAs for an 83% Increase in Blog Revenue," *Brafton*, *brafton.com*.

26. "8 Email Optimization Strategies Used by Well-Known Businesses," *Campaign Monitor*, June 22, 2020, *campaignmonitor.com*.

27. A. J. Beltis, "How the HubSpot Blog Generates Leads [+ How Yours Can, Too]," *HubSpot*, January 8, 2021, *blog.hubspot.com*.

28. M. Aagaard, "How Failed A/B Tests Can Increase Conversion Rates—Case Studies," *Unbounce*, October 16, 2013, *unbounce.com*.

29. J. Wiebe, "6 Proven Ways to Boost the Conversion Rates of Your Call-to-Action Buttons," *Copyblogger*, November 21, 2013, *copyblogger.com*.

30. "11 Ways to Improve Your Calls to Action," *QuickSprout*.

31. "How to Increase Your Landing Page Conversion Rates," *VWO*, February 16, 2023, *vwo.com*.

32. J. Vocell, "Personalized Calls to Action Perform 202% Better Than Basic CTAs [New Data]." *HubSpot*, June 29, 2018, *blog.hubspot.com*.

33. Wiebe, "6 Proven Ways to Boost the Conversion Rates of Your Call-to-Action Buttons."

34. N. Patel, "Why the Fold is a Myth—and Where to Actually Put Your Calls to Action," *neilpatel.com*.

35. "The Global State of Digital 2022," *Hootsuite*, 2022, *hootsuite.com*.

36. M. Kratky, "2022 PageFair AdBlock Report," *Blockthrough*, July 14, 2022, *blockthrough.com*.

37. "P&G: Slashed Digital Ad Spend by $200 Million in 2017," *Marketing Magazine Asia*, March 2, 2018, *marketingmagazine.com*.

38. W. Geyser, "The State of Influencer Marketing 2022: Benchmark Report," *Influencer Marketing Hub*, March 2, 2022, *influencer marketinghub.com*.

39. J. Berger and Keller Fay Group, "New Research Shows Micro-Influencers Drive Consumer Buying Behavior at Much Higher Rates Than Previously Thought," *Business Wire*, March 30, 2016, *businesswire.com*.

40. N. Ellering and N. Ojaokomo, "What 14 Studies Say About the Best Time to Send Email," *CoSchedule*, January 13, 2023, *coschedule.com*.

41. D. Kahneman, J. L. Knetsch, and R. H. Thaler, "Anomalies: The Endowment Effect, Loss Aversion, and Status Quo Bias," *Journal of Economic Perspectives* 5, no. 1 (1991): 193–206; R. Thaler, "Toward

a Positive Theory of Consumer Choice," *Journal of Economic Behavior and Organization* 1 (1980): 39–60.

42. D. Kahneman, J. L. Knetsch, and R. H. Thaler, "Experimental Tests of the Endowment Effect and the Coase Theorem," *Journal of Political Economy* 98, no. 6 (1990): 1325–48; J. List, "Experimental Tests of the Endowment Effect and the Coase Theorem," *Natural Field Experiments* 00687, (2020), *fieldexperiments.com*.

43. "Topic: Digital Coupons and Deals in the United States," *Statista*, June 29, 2022, *statista.com*.

44. S. Hyken, "Businesses Lose $75 Billion Due to Poor Customer Service," *Forbes*, May 17, 2018, *forbes.com*.

45. K. B. Nuckolls, J. Cassel, and B. H. Kaplan, "Psychosocial Assets, Life Crisis and the Prognosis of Pregnancy," *American Journal of Epidemiology* 95, no. 5 (May 1972): 431–41.

46. Hyken, "Businesses Lose $75 Billion Due to Poor Customer Service."

47. "U.S. Companies Losing Customers as Consumers Demand More Human Interaction, Accenture Strategy Study Finds," *Newsroom | Accenture*, March 23, 2016, *newsroom.accenture.com*.

48. B. Barnhart, "Why You Need to Speed Up Your Social Media Response Time (and How)," *Sprout Social*, June 24, 2020, *sproutsocial.com*.

49. "U.S. Companies Losing Customers as Consumers Demand More Human Interaction, Accenture Strategy Study Finds," *Newsroom | Accenture*.

50. N. Cole, "The Power of Live Chat: 5 Surprising Statistics That Show How Consumers Want Their Questions Answered," *Inc. Magazine*, April 25, 2017, *inc.com*.

51. "48 Cart Abandonment Rate Statistics 2023," *Baymard Institute*, August 15, 2022, *baymard.com*.

52. R. L. Frantz, J. M. Ordy, and A. F. Parisi, "Visual Preference for Perceived and Actual Face-to-Face and TV Interaction in 4-Week-Old Infants," *Nature* 190, no. 4772 (1961): 623–24.

53. "Visual Cliff," Wikipedia, *en.wikipedia.org*.

54. S. Bakhshi, D. Shamma, and E. Gilbert, "Faces Engage Us: Photos with Faces Attract More Likes and Comments on Instagram," *Conference on Human Factors in Computing Systems—Proceedings*, 2014.

55. J. Zote, "26 Key Facebook Statistics Marketers Should Know in 2023," *Sprout Social*, February 14, 2023, *sproutsocial.com*.

56. J. Mawhinney, 50 Visual Content Marketing Statistics You Should Know in 2022," *HubSpot*, February 16, 2021, *blog.hubspot.com*.

57. Y. Y. Li and Y. Xie, "Is a Picture Worth a Thousand Words? An Empirical Study of Image Content and Social Media Engagement," *Journal of Marketing Research* 57, no. 1 (2020): 1–19; "What Encourages Facebook Engagement?" *eMarketer*, November 8, 2011, *emarketer.com*; A. Vavrek, "Image SEO: Pictures Can Increase Your Readership [Photo from Research]," Skyword, June 6, 2012, *skyword.com*.

58. Li and Xie, "Is a Picture Worth a Thousand Words?"; C. Szegedy, V. Vanhoucke, S. Ioffe, J. Shlens, and Z. Wojna, "Rethinking the Inception Architecture for Computer Vision," *Proceedings of the IEEE Conference on Computer Vision and Pattern Recognition* (2016): 2818–26.

59. R. Pieters and M. Wedel, "Attention Capture and Transfer in Advertising: Brand, Pictorial, and Text-Size Effects," *Journal of Marketing* 68 (2004): 36–50.

60. M. Wedel and R. Pieters, "The Buffer Effect: The Role of Color When Advertising Exposures Are Brief and Blurred," *Marketing Science* 34 (2015): 134–43; A. Finn, "Print Ad Recognition Readership Scores: An Information Processing Perspective," *Journal of Marketing Research* 25 (May 1988): 168–77.

61. Li and Xie, "Is a Picture Worth a Thousand Words?"; D. Cyr, M. Head, H. Larios, B. Pan, "Exploring Human Images in Website Design: A Multi-Method Approach," *MIS Quarterly* 33, no. 3 (2009): 539–66.; L. Xiao and M. Ding, "Just the Faces: Exploring the Effects of Facial Features in Print Advertising," *Marketing Science* 33, no. 3 (2014): 338–52.

62. Li and Xie, "Is a Picture Worth a Thousand Words?"; H. Hagtvedt, V. M. Patrick, "Air Infusion, the Influence of Visual Art on the Perception and Evaluation of Consumer Products," *Journal of Marketing Research* 45, no. 3 (2008): 379–89; S. Zhang, D. Lee, P. V. Singh, and K. Srinivasan, "How Much Is an Image Worth? Airbnb Property Demand Estimation Leveraging Large Scale Image Analytics," working paper, 2017, *ssrn.com*.

63. Li and Xie, "Is a Picture Worth a Thousand Words?"; S. E. Heckler and T. L. Childers, "The Role of Expectancy and Relevancy in Memory for Verbal and Visual Information: What Is Incongruency?" *Journal of Consumer Research* 18, no. 4 (1992): 475–92; Y. H. Lee and C. Mason, "Responses to Information Incongruency in Advertising: The Role of Expectancy, Relevancy, and Humor," *Journal of Consumer Research* 26, no. 2 (1999): 156–69.

64. N. Bruce, "Effective Display Advertising: Improving Engagement with Suitable Creative Formats," *GfK Marketing Intelligence Review*, (2017): 9; A. Goldfarb and C. Tucker, "Online Display Advertising: Targeting and Obtrusiveness," *Marketing Science* 30 (2011): 389–404.

65. Bruce, "Effective Display Advertising."

66. J. Berger, "Word of Mouth and Interpersonal Communication: A Review and Directions for Future Research," *Journal of Consumer Psychology* 24 (2014): 586–607.

67. C. Tan, L. Lee, and B. Pang, "The Effect of Wording on Message Propagation: Topic- and Author-Controlled Natural Experiments on Twitter," *Proceedings of the ACL 2014. Association for Computational Linguistics* (2014): 185–90.

68. J. Berger and K. L. Milkman, "What Makes Online Content Viral?" 2012, *jonahberger.com*.

69. Berger and Milkman, "What Makes Online Content Viral?"

70. G. Packard, S. Moore, and B. McFerran. "(I'm) Happy to Help (You): The Impact of Personal Pronoun Use in Customer-Firm Interactions," *Journal of Marketing Research* 55, no. 4 (2018).

71. C. Janiszewski, H. Noel, and A, Sawyer, "A Meta-Analysis of the Spacing Effect in Verbal Learning: Implications for Research on Advertising Repetition and Consumer Memory," *Journal of Consumer Research* 30 (2003): 138–49.

72. B. Wansink and M. Ray, "Advertising Strategies to Increase Usage Frequency," *Journal of Marketing*, January 1996, *researchgate.net*.

73. A. Aravindakshan and P. Naik, "Understanding the Memory Effects in Pulsing Advertising," *Operations Research* 61 (2015): 35–47.

74. "What Is Ad Retargeting?" *Mailchimp, mailchimp.com*.

75. P. de Braux, "12 Statistics to Make You Consider Retargeting," *Spiralytics*, September 2, 2021, *spiralytics.com*; K. Saleh, "Ad

Retargeting in Numbers—Statistics and Trends," *Invesp*, May 23, 2022, *invespcro.com*; "Retargeting Statistics to Make You Launch Retargeting Campaign," *MotoCMS*, December 20, 2019, *motocms .com*; C. Costello, ("Retargeting Statistics | Conversion Rates | [Marketing Metrics]," *Kenshoo*, May 13, 2019, *skai.io*; "Display Network: Definition—Google Ads Help," *Google Support, support.google.com*.

76. "Average Facebook Engagement Rate [Updated Dec 2022]," *Oberlo*, *oberlo.com*.

77. D. Lee, K. Hosanagar, and H. Nair, "The Effect of Advertising Content on Consumer Engagement: Evidence from Facebook." *researchgate.net*.

78. Lee, Hosanagar, and Nair, "The Effect of Advertising Content on Consumer Engagement."

79. "New Research Shows Incentivized Brand Advertising Works to Capture the Active Attention of 91 Percent of People Who Interact with a Brand's Message," *Business Wire*, September 19, 2011, *business wire.com*.

80. P. Rauschnabel, S. Praxmarer, and B. Ivens, "Social Media Marketing: How Design Features Influence Interactions with Brand Postings on Facebook," in M. Eisend, T. Langner, and S. Okazaki (eds.) *Advances in Advertising Research* (Vol. III). (European Advertising Academy, Gabler Verlag: 2012).

81. A. Gotter, "The 27 Facebook Statistics That Every Marketer Must Know to Win in 2021," *AdEspresso*, December 16, 2020, *adespresso.com*.

82. *The Web Credibility Project, credibility.stanford.edu*.

83. "The Value of Online Customer Reviews," *Northwestern Scholars*, September 7, 2016, *scholars.northwestern.edu*.

84. "How Does Expert Endorsement Affect Consumer's Perceived Credibility?" *DiVA Portal, diva-portal.org*.

85. Chen, Yubo, et al. "Online Social Interactions: A Natural Experiment on Word of Mouth versus Observational Learning." *Journal of Marketing Research* 48, no. 2 (April 2011): 238–254.

86. E. van Herpen, F. G. M. Pieters, and M. Zeelenberg, "When Less Sells More and When It Does Not: Scarcity Causing Snob versus Bandwagon Effects," Paper presented at 37th EMAC Conference, Marketing Landscapes: A Pause for Thought, (2008): 1–9.

87. N. Gilbert, "45 Interesting FOMO Statistics: 2023 Effects, Demographics & Marketing," *Financesonline.com.*

88. E. van Herpen, F. G. M. Pieters, and M. Zeelenberg, "How Product Scarcity Impacts on Choice: Snob and Bandwagon Effects," *Advances in Consumer Research* 32 (2005): 32.

89. "Dynamic Email Content Leads to 400% Increase in Conversions for Black Friday Email | Adestra," *Upland Software, uplandsoft ware.com.*

90. "What Users Want Most from Mobile Sites Today," *Think with Google, thinkwithgoogle.com.*

91. "What Users Want from Mobile," Web Performance Guru, *webperformanceguru.files.wordpress.com.*

92. T. Fessenden, "Scrolling and Attention," *Nielsen Norman Group,* April 15, 2018, *nngroup.com.*

93. "10 Web Design Statistics." *Ironpaper,* March 6, 2014, *ironpaper.com.*

94. "First Impressions Form Quickly on the Web, Eye-Tracking Study Shows." *ScienceDaily,* February 15, 2012, *sciencedaily.com.*

95. Fessenden, "Scrolling and Attention."

96. A. Dodonova, "An Experimental Test of Anchoring Effect," *Applied Economics Letters* 16, no. 7 (2009): 677–78.

97. P. O'Donovan, A. Agarwala, and A. Hertzmann, "Color Compatibility from Large Datasets," *ACM Transactions on Graphics,* 2011, *dgp .toronto.edu.*

98. R. P. Nelson, *The Design of Advertising* (Brown & Benchmark: 1994).

99. D. Parkhurst, K. Law, and E. Niebur, "Modeling the Role of Salience in the Allocation of Overt Visual Attention," *Vision Research* 42, no. 1 (January 2002): 107–23.

100. A. K. Shah and D. M. Oppenheimer, "Easy Does It: The Role of Fluency in Cue Weighting," *Judgment and Decision Making* 2, no. 6 (December 2007): 371–379.

101. H. Petrie et al., "Tension, What Tension?" Proceedings of the International Cross-Disciplinary Workshop on Web Accessibility— W4A, 2004.

102. S. E. Asch, "Studies of Independence and Conformity: I. A Minority of One Against a Unanimous Majority," *Psychological Monographs: General and Applied* 70, no. 9 (1956): 1–70.

103. A. S. Atalay, H. O. Bodur, and D. Rasolofoarison, "Shining in the Center: Central Gaze Cascade Effect on Product Choice," *Journal of Consumer Research* 39, no. 4 (2012): 848–66.

104. N. J. Emery, "The Eyes Have It: The Neuroethology, Function and Evolution of Social Gaze," *Neuroscience and Biobehavioral Reviews* 24, no. 6 (2000): 581–604.

105. S. Djamasbi, M. Siegel, and T. Tullis, "Designing Noticeable Bricklets by Tracking Users' Eye Movements," *45th Hawaii International Conference on System Sciences*, Maui, Hawaii, 2012: 525–32.

106. "E-Commerce Checkout Usability: An Original Research Study," *Baymard Institute, baymard.com.*

107. P. van Schaik and J. Ling, "The Effectiveness of a 'Reject Option' in Online Decision-Making," *Journal of Interactive Marketing* 30 (2015): 34–45.

108. "A Tale of Two Pizzas: Building Up from a Basic Product Versus Scaling Down from a Fully-Loaded Product—Marketing Letters," *Springer Link, link.springer.com*; I. P. Levin, G. J. Gaeth, J. Schreiber, and M. Lauriola, "A New Look at Framing Effects: Distribution of Effect Sizes, Individual Differences, and Independence of Types of Effects," *Organizational Behavior and Human Decision Processes* 88, no. 1 (2002): 411–29.

109. R. W. Proctor and D. W. Schneider, "Hick's Law for Choice Reaction Time: A Review," *Quarterly Journal of Experimental Psychology* 71, no. 6 (2018): 1281–99; "Hick's Law," *Wikipedia, en.wikipedia.org*; W. E. Hick, "On the Rate of Gain of Information," *Quarterly Journal of Experimental Psychology* 4 (1952): 11–26; R. Hyman, "Stimulus Information as a Determinant of Reaction Time," *Journal of Experimental Psychology* 53 (1953): 188–96.

110. V. van Veen, M. K. Krug, J. W. Schooler, and C. S. Carter, "Neural Activity Predicts Attitude Change in Cognitive Dissonance," *Nature Neuroscience* 12, no. 11 (2009): 1469–74.

111. S. S. Krishnan and R. K. Sitaraman, "Understanding the Effectiveness of Video Ads: A Measurement Study," University of Massachusetts Amherst, IMC '13: Proceedings of the 2013 Conference on Internet Measurement (October 2013): 149–62.

112. "Capture Attention with Updated Features for Video Ads," *Facebook, facebook.com.*

113. T. J. McCue, "Verizon Media Says 69 Percent of Consumers Watching Video with Sound Off," *Forbes*, July 31, 2019, *forbes.com*.

114. B. Friedman, "Adobe's Q1 Social Intelligence Report Is Filled with Useful Data for Marketers," *Social Media Today*, April 28, 2014, *socialmediatoday.com*; "Best Time to Post on Facebook: A Complete Guide," *Buffer*, January 22, 2019, *buffer.com*; N. Ellering, "The Best Times to Post on Social Media in 2022," *CoSchedule, coschedule.com*; P. Cooper and B. Cohen, "The Best Time to Post on Facebook, Instagram, Twitter, and LinkedIn," *Hootsuite, blog.hootsuite.com*.

115. "Inside Twitter: An In-Depth Look Inside the Twitter World," *sysomos.com*; K. Lee, "The Best Time to Tweet & Why," *Buffer Resources*, April 27, 2016, *buffer.com*; Cooper, Paige, and Cohen, "The Best Time to Post on Facebook, Instagram, Twitter, and LinkedIn"; L. K. Cox, "The Best Times to Post on Social Media in 2023 [New Data]," *HubSpot*, January 24, 2023, *blog.hubspot.com*.

116. Cox, "The Best Times to Post on Social Media in 2023 [New Data]"; Cooper, Paige, and Cohen, "The Best Time to Post on Instagram in 2023 [Complete Guide]"; A. Demeku and M. Thomas, "The Best Time to Post on Instagram in 2023," *Later*, November 25, 2022, *later.com*; M. Keutelian, "The Best Times to Post on Social Media in 2022," *Sprout Social, sproutsocial.com*; N. M. Ferreira, "Best Time to Post on Social Media in 2022 [Updated]," *Oberlo*, May 19, 2022, *oberlo.com*.

117. Cox, "The Best Times to Post on Social Media in 2023 [New Data]"; Ferreira, "Best Time to Post on Social Media in 2022 [Updated]"; Keutelian, "The Best Times to Post on Social Media in 2022"; V. Magyar and J. Michalski, "Best Time to Post on LinkedIn," *Quintly*, June 5, 2019, *quintly.com*; C. Newberry, "LinkedIn Marketing Strategy: 17 Tips for 2023," *Hootsuite*, December 1, 2022, *blog.hootsuite.com*.

118. M. Bretous, "Best Times to Post on YouTube in 2022 [Research]," *HubSpot*, May 2, 2022, *blog.hubspot.com*; C. Singh, "What Is the Best Time to Post on YouTube in 2023?" *SocialPilot*, December 29, 2022, *socialpilot.co*.

119. N. Landsberg, "Best Times to Post on TikTok for 2023," *Influencer Marketing Hub*, December 14, 2022, *influencermarketinghub.com*; K. Mikolajczyk, "When Is the Best Time to Post on TikTok in 2023? [Cheat Sheet]," *Hootsuite, blog.hootsuite.com*.

120. Cox, "The Best Times to Post on Social Media in 2023 [New Data]"; "The Best Times to Post on Social Media in 2022," *Public Sector Marketing Institute, publicsectormarketingpros.com*; M. Jeromchek, "Best Times to Post on Pinterest in 2023: An Analysis of 30,000+ Accounts [Original Research]," *CoSchedule*, July 11, 2022, *coschedule.com*.

121. A. Hassan and S. J. Barber, "The Effects of Repetition Frequency on the Illusory Truth Effect," *Cognitive Research* 6 (2021): 38.

122. Hassan and Barber, "The Effects of Repetition Frequency on the Illusory Truth Effect"; G. V. Johar and A. L. Roggeveen, "Changing False Beliefs from Repeated Advertising: The Role of Claim-Refutation Alignment," *Journal of Consumer Psychology* 17 (2007): 118–27; G. Pennycook, T. D. Cannon, and D. G. Rand, "Prior Exposure Increases Perceived Accuracy of Fake News," *Journal of Experimental Psychology: General* 147 (2018): 1865–80; H. R. Arkes, C. Hackett, and L. Boehm, "The Generality of the Relation Between Familiarity and Judged Validity," *Journal of Behavioral Decision Making* 2 (1989): 81–94; N. DiFonzo, J. W. Beckstead, N. Stupak, and K. Walders, "Validity Judgments of Rumors Heard Multiple Times: The Shape of the Truth Effect," *Social Influence* 11 (2016): 22–39; M. S. Zaragoza and K. J. Mitchell, "Repeated Exposure to Suggestion and the Creation of False Memories," *Psychological Science* 7 (1996): 294–300.

123. Hassan and Barber, "The Effects of Repetition Frequency on the Illusory Truth Effect"; Arkes, Hackett, and Boehm, "The Generality of the Relation Between Familiarity and Judged Validity"; L. Hasher, D. Goldstein, and T. Toppino, "Frequency and the Conference of Referential Validity," *Journal of Verbal Learning and Verbal Behavior* 16 (1977): 107–12; A. S. Brown and L. A. Nix, "Turning Lies into Truths: Referential Validation of Falsehoods," *Journal of Experimental Psychology: Learning, Memory, and Cognition* 22 (1996): 1088–1100; L. A. Henkel and M. E. Mattson, "Reading Is Believing: The Truth Effect and Source Credibility," *Consciousness and Cognition* 20 (2011): 1705–21.

124. R. Reber and N. Schwarz, "Effects of Perceptual Fluency on Judgments of Truth," *Consciousness and Cognition* 8, no. 3 (1999): 338–42.

125. S. Lev-Ari and B. Keysar, "Why Don't We Believe Non-Native Speakers? The Influence of Accent on Credibility," *Journal of Experimental Social Psychology* 46, no. 6 (2010): 1093–96.

126. H. Song and N. Schwarz, "If It's Hard to Read, It's Hard to Do: Processing Fluency Affects Effort Prediction and Motivation," *Psychological Science* 19, no. 10 (2008): 986–88.

127. S. Moorthy and S. Hawkins, "Advertising Repetition and Quality Perception," *Journal of Business Research* 58 (2005): 354–60.

128. M. Eisend and S. Schmidt, "Advertising Repetition: A Meta-Analysis on Effective Frequency in Advertising," *Journal of Advertising* 44, no. 4 (2015): 415–28.

129. C. Pechmann and D. Stewart, "Advertising Repetition: A Critical Review of Wearin and Wearout," *Current Issues and Research in Advertising* 11 (1988).

130. Hassan and Barber, "The Effects of Repetition Frequency on the Illusory Truth Effect."

131. M. Dass, C. Kohli, P. Kumar, and S. Thomas, "A Study of the Antecedents of Slogan Liking," *Journal of Business Research* 67, no. 12 (2014): 2504–11.

132. L. Lai and A. Farbrot, "What Makes You Click? The Effect of Question Headlines on Readership in Computer-Mediated Communication," *Social Influence* 9, no. 4 (2013): 288–99.

133. R. Cruz, J. Leonhardt, and T. Pezzuti, "Second Person Pronouns Enhance Consumer Involvement and Brand Attitude," *Journal of Interactive Marketing* 39 (2017).

134. Cruz, Leonhardt, and Pezzuti, "Second Person Pronouns Enhance Consumer Involvement and Brand Attitude."

135. Lai and Farbrot, "What Makes You Click?" 289–99.

136. Lai and Farbrot, "What Makes You Click?" 289–99.

137. The Web Credibility Project, *credibility.stanford.edu*.

138. E M. González, E. Esteva, A. L. Roggeveen, and D. Grewal, "Amount Off Versus Percentage Off—When Does It Matter?" *Journal of Business Research* 69, no. 3 (2016): 1022–27; A. Guha, A. Biswas, D. Grewal, S. Verma, S. Banerjee, and J. Nordfält, "Reframing the Discount as a Comparison Against the Sale Price: Does It

Make the Discount More Attractive?" *Journal of Marketing Research* 55, no. 3 (2018): 339–51.

139. X. Liu et al., "Optimal Pricing of Online Products Based on Customer Anchoring-Adjustment Psychology," *International Transactions in Operational Research*, April 21, 2022.

140. B. J. Fogg, C. Soohoo, and D. Danielson, "How Do People Evaluate a Web Site's Credibility? Results from a Large Study," Persuasive Technology Lab, Stanford University, 2002, *credibility.stanford.edu*.

141. "Social Media Use in 2021," *Pew Research Center*, April 7, 2021, *pewresearch.org*.

142. "Special Report on Aging and Vision Loss," American Foundation for the Blind, January 2013, *afb.org*.

143. M. Bernard et al. "The Effects of Font Type and Size on the Legibility and Reading Time of Online Text by Older Adults," *CHI '01 Extended Abstracts on Human Factors in Computing Systems*, 2001.

144. F. Nah, "A Study on Tolerable Waiting Time: How Long Are Web Users Willing to Wait?" *Behaviour & Information Technology* 23, (2003): 285. See also Zona Research Report, "The Need for Speed," July 1999; P. Selvidge, "How Long Is Too Long for a Website to Load?" *Usability News* 1, no. 2 (1999), *psychology.wichita.edu*; J. A. Hoxmeier and C. DiCesare, "System Response Time and User Satisfaction: An Experimental Study of Browser-Based Applications," Proceedings of the Association of Information Systems Americas Conference, Long Beach, California. August 2000.

145. A. J. Szameitat et al. "Behavioral and Emotional Consequences of Brief Delays in Human-Computer Interaction," *International Journal of Human-Computer Studies* 67, no. 7 (2009): 561–70; J. L. Guynes, "Impact of System Response Time on State Anxiety," *Communication of the ACM* 31 (1988): i3.

146. W. Hong et al., "When Filling the Wait Makes It Feel Longer: A Paradigm Shift Perspective for Managing Online Delay," *MIS Quarterly* 37, no. 2 (2013): 383–406; K. L. Katz, B. M. Larson, and R. C. Larson, "Prescription for the Waiting-in-Line Blues: Entertain, Enlighten, and Engage," *Sloan Management Review* 32, no. 2 (1991): 44–53; S. Taylor, "Waiting for Service: The Relationship Between Delays and Evaluations of Service," *Journal of Marketing* 58 (1994): 56–69; M. K. Hui and A. C. Tse, "What to Tell Consumers in Waits of Differ-

ent Lengths: An Integrative Model of Service Evaluation," *Journal of Marketing* 60 (1996): 81–90; B. G. C. Dellaert and B. E. Kahn, "How Tolerable Is Delay? Consumers' Evaluation of Internet Web Sites After Waiting," *Journal of Interactive Marketing* 13, no. 1 (1999): 41–54.

147. Y. Lee, A. N. K. Chen, and V. Ilie, "Can Online Wait Be Managed? The Effect of Filler Interfaces and Presentation Modes on Perceived Waiting Time Online," *MIS Quarterly* 36, no. 2 (2012): 365.

148. Taylor, "Waiting for Service"; A. R. Gilliland, J. Hofeld, and G. Eckstrand, "Studies in Time Perception," *Psychological Bulletin* 43 (1946): 162–76; K. Katz, B. Larson, and R. Larson, "Prescription for the Waiting-in-Line Blues: Entertain, Enlighten and Engage," *Sloan Management Review* (Winter 1991): 44–53.

149. Hong et al., "When Filling the Wait Makes It Feel Longer"; F. Nah, "A Study on Tolerable Waiting Time"; M. K. Hui and L. Zhou, "How Does Waiting Duration Information Influence Customers' Reactions to Waiting for Services?" *Journal of Applied Social Psychology* 26 (1996): 1702–17; B. D. Weinberg, "Don't Keep Your Internet Customers Waiting Too Long at the (Virtual) Front Door," *Journal of Interactive Marketing* 14, no. 1 (2000), 30–39.

150. F. Nah, "A Study on Tolerable Waiting Time"; B. Shneiderman, "Response Time and Display Rate in Human Performance with Computers," *Computing Surveys* 16 (1984): 265–85; R. B. Miller, "Response Time in Man-Computer Conversational Transaction," *Proceedings of AFIPS Fall Joint Computer Conference* 33 (1968): 267–77.

151. "The Importance of Irrelevant Alternatives," *The Economist*, May 22, 2009, *economist.com*.

152. S. Yang and M. Lynn, "More Evidence Challenging the Robustness and Usefulness of the Attraction Effect," *Journal of Marketing Research* 51, no. 4 (2014): 508–13.

153. S. Malkoc, W. Hedgcock, and S. Hoeffler, "Between a Rock and a Hard Place: The Failure of the Attraction Effect Among Unattractive Alternatives," *Journal of Consumer Psychology* 23 (2013): 317–29; J. Huber, J. W. Payne, and C. P. Puto, "Let's Be Honest About the Attraction Effect," *Journal of Marketing Research* 51, no. 4 (2014).

154. K. Coulter, P. Choi, and K. Monroe, "Comma N' Cents in Pricing: The Effects of Auditory Representation Encoding on Price

Magnitude Perceptions," *Journal of Consumer Psychology* 22 (2012): 395–407.

155. N. Hagemann et al., "When the Referee Sees Red . . . ," *Psychological Science* 19, no. 8 (2008): 769–71; R. A. Hill and R. A. Barton, "Red Enhances Human Performance in Contests," *Nature* 435 (2005): 293.

156. A. J. Elliot and D. Niesta, "Romantic Red: Red Enhances Men's Attraction to Women," *Journal of Personality and Social Psychology* 95, no. 5 (2008): 1150–64.

157. R. Bagchi and A. Cheema, "The Effect of Red Background Color on Willingness-to-Pay: The Moderating Role of Selling Mechanism," *Journal of Consumer Research* 39, no. 5 (2013): 947–60; N. Mandel and E. J. Johnson, "When Web Pages Influence Choice: Effects of Visual Primes on Experts and Novices," *Journal of Consumer Research* 29, no. 2 (2002): 235–45.

158. E. Van Droogenbroeck, L. Van Hove, and S. Cordemans, "Do Red Prices Also Work Online? An Extension of Puccinelli et al. (2013)," *Color Research & Application* 43 (2018): 110–13; N. M. Puccinelli et al., "Are Men Seduced by Red? The Effect of Red Versus Black Prices on Price Perceptions," *Journal of Retailing* 89, no. 2 (2013): 115–25.

159. K. Coulter and R. Coulter, "Size Does Matter: The Effects of Magnitude Representation Congruency on Price Perceptions and Purchase Likelihood," *Journal of Consumer Psychology* 15 (2005): 64–76.

160. M. Shen et al., "Interplay Between the Object and Its Symbol: The Size-Congruency Effect," *Advances in Cognitive Psychology* 12, no. 2 (2016): 115–29; S. Dehaene, "The Psychophysics of Numerical Comparison: A Reexamination of Apparently Incompatible Data," *Perception and Psychophysics* 45, no. 6 (1989): 557–66.

161. Y. Huang and J. Ye, "Numbers Talk Louder When They Are Larger: The Effect of Font Size of Numerical Stimuli on Advertisement Persuasion," in eds. T. W. Bradford, A. Keinan, and M. M. Thomson, *NA—Advances in Consumer Research*, Volume 49 (Association for Consumer Research: 2021): 395–96.

162. S. S. Yang et al., "$ or Dollars: Effects of Menu-Price Formats on Restaurant Checks," *Cornell eCommons*, May 1, 2009, *ecommons .cornell.edu.*

163. "48 Cart Abandonment Rate Statistics 2023," *Baymard Institute*.

164. "Email Subject Lines—Statistics and Trends." *Invesp, invespcro.com*.

165. D. Kirkpatrick and P. Adams, "Study: Personalized Email Subject Lines Increase Open Rates by 50%," *Marketing Dive*, September 12, 2017, *marketingdive.com*.

166. "Email Subject Lines," *Invesp*.

167. "Email Subject Lines," *Invesp*.

168. "Ecommerce Industry Benchmark Report: Abandoned Carts," *Klaviyo, klaviyo.com*.

169. P. Weltman, "Best Practices for Browse Abandonment Email Subject Lines," *Klaviyo*, February 13, 2018, *klaviyo.com*.

170. C. Ouellette, "Email Subject Line Statistics to Help You Maximize Your Open Rates," *OptinMonster*, April 23, 2020, *optinmonster.com*.

171. "Ecommerce Industry Benchmark Report," *Klaviyo*.

172. "Emojis in Email Subject Lines: Do They Affect Open Rates? [Data]." *Search Engine Journal*, September 10, 2020, *searchenginejournal.com*.

173. "Top Sales Follow-Up Statistics & Tips [2021 Data]." *Yesware*, April 21, 2021, *yesware.com*.

174. "Boomerang infographic_OL." *Baydin, baydin.com*.

CHAPTER 7

1. A. Hirose, "24 Twitter Demographics That Matter to Marketers in 2023," *Hootsuite*, September 20, 2022, *blog.hootsuite.com*; C. Newberry, "42 Facebook Statistics Marketers Need to Know in 2023," *Hootsuite*, January 17, 2023, *blog.hootsuite.com*; C. Newberry, "34 Instagram Stats Marketers Need to Know in 2023," *Hootsuite*, January 24, 2023, *blog.hootsuite.com*; H. Macready, "38 Pinterest Stats That Matter to Marketers in 2023," *Hootsuite*, February 2023, *blog.hootsuite.com*; "How to Grow Your Small Business on Social Media," *LinkedIn*, November 18, 2022, *linkedin.com*.

Index

About the Author

Most people determine their career path in high school or college, but Drew Eric Whitman—a.k.a. *"Dr. Direct!"*™—couldn't wait to get started. He began creating advertising at age eleven by writing and designing direct-response catalogs of jokes, gags, and novelties. Complete with product illustrations, order forms, and postage charts, he distributed them to his fifth-grade classmates by the armful and collected cash orders in equal abundance.

Although his teachers did not encourage Drew's entrepreneurial spirit (perhaps because of the live whoopee cushion demonstration he performed on the teacher without her knowledge . . . yes, really), it marked the beginning of an exciting career in the wacky and wonderful world of creative writing and advertising.

Many years later, after extensive experience in face-to-face selling of everything from printing to clothing . . . from jewelry to mortgages and real estate . . . an advertising degree from Philadelphia's Temple University started the ball rolling.

Drew's advertising career began as an independent copywriter before he joined a suburban Philadelphia ad agency. He later became a senior copywriter at the direct-response division of Weightman Advertising, Philadelphia's largest agency, and a senior direct-response copywriter at Union Fidelity, a prominent global direct-to-the-consumer insurance company. Drew also served as assistant copy director at Day-Timers, a leading productivity tools provider. He created powerfully effective advertising for companies, ranging from small retail shops to giant multimillion dollar corporations. His work has been used by many of the most successful companies and organizations in the United States, including the American Automobile Association, the American Legion, Amoco, Faber-Castell, Texaco, Day-Timers, Panasonic, *TV Guide*, Staples, and many others.

Drew is the author of *Cashvertising* (Career Press)—translated into eleven languages worldwide and widely considered *the* leading title of its kind among today's online performance/affiliate marketers—and *Brain-Scripts for Sales Success* (McGraw-Hill). He's a popular keynote speaker and delivers dynamic presentations to intimate audiences of dozens to packed European convention centers of thousands.

When he's not writing, Drew is thinking about what he *should* be writing, delivering seminars, working out in the gym, experimenting with amateur radio, or just enjoying time with his wonderful wife, Lindsay, and their two Energizer-bunny-like boys, Chase and Reid.

Today—with nearly four decades of in-the-trenches ad-industry experience—Drew is an outspoken, humorous, and philosophical advertising speaker, trainer, writer, and consultant who receives tremendous positive feedback and reviews from businesspeople around the world who attend his live seminars and read his books and articles.